Oliver Ruepp

Structure and Motion Recovery under Difficult Imaging Conditions

Oliver Ruepp

Structure and Motion Recovery under Difficult Imaging Conditions

Südwestdeutscher Verlag für Hochschulschriften

Impressum / Imprint

Bibliografische Information der Deutschen Nationalbibliothek: Die Deutsche Nationalbibliothek verzeichnet diese Publikation in der Deutschen Nationalbibliografie; detaillierte bibliografische Daten sind im Internet über http://dnb.d-nb.de abrufbar.

Alle in diesem Buch genannten Marken und Produktnamen unterliegen warenzeichen-, marken- oder patentrechtlichem Schutz bzw. sind Warenzeichen oder eingetragene Warenzeichen der jeweiligen Inhaber. Die Wiedergabe von Marken, Produktnamen, Gebrauchsnamen, Handelsnamen, Warenbezeichnungen u.s.w. in diesem Werk berechtigt auch ohne besondere Kennzeichnung nicht zu der Annahme, dass solche Namen im Sinne der Warenzeichen- und Markenschutzgesetzgebung als frei zu betrachten wären und daher von jedermann benutzt werden dürften.

Bibliographic information published by the Deutsche Nationalbibliothek: The Deutsche Nationalbibliothek lists this publication in the Deutsche Nationalbibliografie; detailed bibliographic data are available in the Internet at http://dnb.d-nb.de.

Any brand names and product names mentioned in this book are subject to trademark, brand or patent protection and are trademarks or registered trademarks of their respective holders. The use of brand names, product names, common names, trade names, product descriptions etc. even without a particular marking in this works is in no way to be construed to mean that such names may be regarded as unrestricted in respect of trademark and brand protection legislation and could thus be used by anyone.

Coverbild / Cover image: www.ingimage.com

Verlag / Publisher:
Südwestdeutscher Verlag für Hochschulschriften
ist ein Imprint der / is a trademark of
OmniScriptum GmbH & Co. KG
Heinrich-Böcking-Str. 6-8, 66121 Saarbrücken, Deutschland / Germany
Email: info@svh-verlag.de

Herstellung: siehe letzte Seite /
Printed at: see last page
ISBN: 978-3-8381-3804-6

Zugl. / Approved by: München, TU, Diss., 2012

Copyright © 2014 OmniScriptum GmbH & Co. KG
Alle Rechte vorbehalten. / All rights reserved. Saarbrücken 2014

Contents

List of Figures   v

List of Tables   xi

1 Motivation   **1**
    1.1 Contribution 5

2 Bundle Adjustment Basics   **7**
    2.1 Feature-Based Bundle Adjustment 8
    2.2 Intensity-Based Bundle Adjustment 16

3 Approach   **23**
    3.1 The Constant Light Case 29
    3.2 Light Source Modelling 29
    3.3 The Case of a Point Light at the Optical Center 33
    3.4 The Case of Fully Calibrated Light 34

4 Efficient and Flexible Nonlinear Optimization   **39**
    4.1 Sequential Quadratic Programming 42
    4.2 On Computation of Hessian Matrices 44
        4.2.1 Full Computation 45
        4.2.2 Gauß-Newton-Approximation 47
        4.2.3 Non-Least-Squares Hessian Approximation . . 48
    4.3 Established Algorithms for Derivative Computation . . 49
        4.3.1 Finite Difference Approximation 49

CONTENTS

      4.3.2 Symbolic Derivatives via Computer Algebra Systems 50
      4.3.3 Automatic Differentiation 51
      4.3.4 Hand-Coded Derivatives 53
  4.4 A Modular Approach to Computing Derivatives 54
      4.4.1 An Example: Feature-Based Bundle Adjustment 58
  4.5 Basic Modules of our Framework 64
      4.5.1 Vector-Valued Functions 64
            4.5.1.1 Compositional Function Module . . . 65
            4.5.1.2 Input Map 70
            4.5.1.3 Function Stack 70
      4.5.2 Cost Functions 72
            4.5.2.1 Squared Differences 76
            4.5.2.2 Blake-Zisserman 76
            4.5.2.3 Huber and Pseudo-Huber 78
            4.5.2.4 Comparison of Robust Cost Functions 79
            4.5.2.5 Cost Functions for Batch Matching . . 81
            4.5.2.6 Another Alternative: Mutual Information 84
      4.5.3 The Lagrangian Term Module 87

5 Modules for Implementing Bundle Adjustment   **89**
  5.1 Rigid Transformations 95
      5.1.1 Interpretation of Quaternions as Rotations . . . 96
      5.1.2 Quaternions in Multiple View Geometry 99
  5.2 The Depth Map Model 101
      5.2.1 On B-Spline Curves and Surfaces 103
            5.2.1.1 B-Spline Linearity in Parameters . . . 106
            5.2.1.2 B-Spline Derivatives w.r.t. Curve Coordinates 110

CONTENTS

    5.2.1.3 B-Spline Derivatives w.r.t. Surface Coordinates 113
  5.2.2 Surfaces Induced by Depth Maps 116
    5.2.2.1 Derivatives w.r.t. Surface Parameters 119
    5.2.2.2 Tangents 120
    5.2.2.3 Normals 122
  5.2.3 Surfaces Induced by Inverse Depth Maps . . . 127
    5.2.3.1 Derivatives w.r.t. Surface Parameters 128
    5.2.3.2 Tangents 129
    5.2.3.3 Normals 130
  5.2.4 Inverse Depth Maps using B-Splines 131
 5.3 Perspective Projection 134
 5.4 Image Interpolation 136
 5.5 Brightness Warping 139
 5.6 Unit Quaternion Constraints 144
 5.7 A Scale Uniqueness Constraint 145
 5.8 Regularization 146
 5.9 Efficient Sparse-Sparse Matrix Products 153

6 Light Source Calibration   159
 6.1 Estimation of the Projection Center 162
 6.2 Optimization of the Objective 167
 6.3 Modelling Constant Intensity Disturbances 168
 6.4 Determining the Intensity Profile 170

7 Experimental Results   173
 7.1 Ground Truth Comparison Method 173
  7.1.1 Depth Map Registration Approach 177
  7.1.2 Rotation and Translation Similarity Measures . 181
 7.2 Synthetic Datasets Used for our Evaluation 182
 7.3 Static Lighting Conditions 189

CONTENTS

      7.3.1   Importance of Adequate Initialization 189
      7.3.2   Sensitivity of the Initialization to Motion 191
             7.3.2.1   Ambiguous Configurations 202
      7.3.3   Importance of Window Size 204
      7.3.4   Influence of Regularization 205
      7.3.5   Effect of Spline Resolution 210
      7.3.6   Behaviour for Medium and Weak Textures . . . 216
      7.3.7   The Tube Scenario 217
      7.3.8   Results on Independent Benchmarks 221
      7.3.9   Non-Verified Reconstruction Results 222
  7.4   Camera-Centered Light Source 224
      7.4.1   Non-Verified Reconstruction Results 238
      7.4.2   A Short Evaluation of Mutual Information . . . 240
      7.4.3   Effect of Camera-Light Source Displacement . 243
  7.5   Light Source Calibration Results 249
  7.6   Tracking with a Calibrated Light Source 251
  7.7   Performance Considerations 252

8 Conclusion   **255**
  8.1   Future Work 256

A Mathematical Notation   **259**

B Diagram Conventions   **263**

Complete List of Author's Publications   **265**

References   **267**

List of Figures

1.1	Video-Endoscopy example image.	2
1.2	Difficult face reconstruction example.	3
1.3	Detected SIFT features for difficult face reconstruction.	3
2.1	Bundle adjustment toy problem.	9
2.2	Relation between pixel coordinates and 3D coordinates.	11
2.3	Illustration of rigid transformations.	12
2.4	Reprojection Error.	14
2.5	Comparison of direct depths and inverse depths.	18
2.6	Intensity reprojection error.	19
3.1	Basic algorithm flowchart.	25
3.2	A simple 2D depth profile.	27
3.3	Face reconstruction example.	30
3.4	Direct BA with Light Shading Correction.	32
3.5	Treating the light source as inverse camera.	35
3.6	Schematic of the image warping process under calibrated light.	37
4.1	Overview of the Optimization System.	44
4.2	Example for computational graph.	51
4.3	Schematic of QP System Assembly.	56
4.4	Computational Graph of Bundle Adjustment.	61
4.5	Parameter and function stacking.	73

LIST OF FIGURES

4.6 Several cost functions. 75
4.7 Fitting results when using robust cost functions. . . . 75
4.8 Gradient direction and magnitude for line fitting with Pseudo-Huber cost. 81
4.9 Gradient direction and magnitude for line fitting with Blake-Zisserman cost. 82
4.10 Gradient direction and magnitude for a hypothetical optimal cost function. 82

5.1 First part of computational Graph for Reconstruction under Constant Light. 91
5.2 Second part of computational Graph for Reconstruction under Constant Light. 92
5.3 First part of computational Graph for Reconstruction with Light Model. 93
5.4 Second part of computational Graph for Reconstruction with Light Model. 94
5.5 Overview of surface representations. 103
5.6 A B-spline curve. 105
5.7 Interaction of brightness warping modules. 142
5.8 Inverse Depth Regularization. 148

6.1 The light source as an inverse camera. 160
6.2 Example calibration images for light calibration. . . . 161
6.3 Lambertian reflectance on two calibration planes. . . 163
6.4 Basic idea of light calibration objective. 164
6.5 Bounding box used for calibration. 168
6.6 Effect of ambient light term. 170

7.1 Sample images from cone sequence. 175
7.2 Example images for a corrupted depth map estimate. 176
7.3 Example similarity values for cone result. 177

LIST OF FIGURES

7.4 Normalization-based similarity measure vs. registration-based similarity measure. 178

7.5 Overview of scenes used for validation. 184

7.6 Motion paths used for evaluation scenarios. 186

7.7 Textures used in synthetic scenes. 187

7.8 Motion path used for initialization test. 190

7.9 Importance of adequate initialization. 192

7.10 Evaluation of movement paths a and b at different speeds for plane scenario. 193

7.11 Evaluation of movement paths c and d at different speeds for plane scenario. 194

7.12 Evaluation of movement paths a and b at different speeds for sphere scenario. 195

7.13 Evaluation of movement paths c and d at different speeds for sphere scenario. 196

7.14 Evaluation of movement paths a and b at different speeds for cone scenario. 197

7.15 Evaluation of movement paths c and d at different speeds for cone scenario. 198

7.16 Evaluation of movement paths a and b at different speeds for plane-with-bumps scenario. 199

7.17 Evaluation of movement paths c and d at different speeds for plane-with-bumps scenario. 200

7.18 Inverted reconstruction on synthetic data. 203

7.19 Inverted reconstruction phenomenon for real data. . . 204

7.20 Evaluation results for sliding window size 1. 206

7.21 Evaluation results for sliding window size 2. 207

7.22 Evaluation results for sliding window size 3. 208

7.23 Evaluation results for sliding window size 4. 209

7.24 Evaluation results for different regularization strengths 211

LIST OF FIGURES

7.25 Evaluation results for different spline resolutions . . . 213
7.26 Evaluation results for different spline resolutions . . . 214
7.27 Evaluation results for different spline resolutions . . . 215
7.28 Tube reconstruction results for different spline resolutions. 216
7.29 Plane with bumps reconstruction results for different spline resolutions. 217
7.30 Evaluation results for different texture types 218
7.31 Tube scenario reconstruction results. 220
7.32 Planar tracking benchmark results. 223
7.33 Reconstruction of a white piece of cloth. 225
7.34 Face reconstruction example. 226
7.35 Another face reconstruction example. 227
7.36 Static lighting vs. camera-centred lighting 229
7.37 Evaluation of movement paths a and b at different speeds for plane scenario. 230
7.38 Evaluation of movement paths c and d at different speeds for plane scenario. 231
7.39 Evaluation of movement paths a and b at different speeds for sphere scenario. 232
7.40 Evaluation of movement paths c and d at different speeds for sphere scenario. 233
7.41 Evaluation of movement paths a and b at different speeds for cone scenario. 234
7.42 Evaluation of movement paths c and d at different speeds for cone scenario. 235
7.43 Evaluation of movement paths a and b at different speeds for plane-with-bumps scenario. 236
7.44 Evaluation of movement paths c and d at different speeds for plane-with-bumps scenario. 237

LIST OF FIGURES

7.45 Reconstruction results on real images. 239
7.46 Mutual information results for dynamic lighting. 242
7.47 Evaluation results for light displacement 245
7.48 More evaluation results for light displacement 246
7.49 Light displacement cone reconstruction results. . . . 247
7.50 Light displacement cone reconstruction results. . . . 248
7.51 Light calibration results on synthetic data. 250
7.52 Evaluation results for tracking and reconstruction under calibrated light 253
B.1 HSV color scale. 264

LIST OF FIGURES

List of Tables

A.1　Mathematical notation 262

1. Motivation

The recovery of scene geometry and camera motion from monocular image sequences is a long-standing, highly relevant research problem within the area of Computer Vision. The applications of such techniques include localization for navigation of mobile robots, augmented reality applications as well as navigation in videoendoscopy, to name just a few. Many different approaches for solving this problem have been pursued, leading to a multitude of methods that work well for the settings that they have been conceived for. The main contribution of this work is the development of a number of methods that aim at recovering scene structure and camera motion under "difficult" conditions: Changing lighting and poor scene texture.

Typical methods for scene and motion recovery can be split up into two categories: feature-based methods and direct methods. Feature-based methods rely on feature extraction mechanisms, such as SIFT [10], SURF [11], BRISK [12] etc., using only the 2D position of landmarks. Direct methods, on the other hand, work directly on image intensities, and are naturally better suited for cases where the scene does not provide much texture.

Early examples for feature-based systems are MONOSLAM by Davison [13] and V-GPS by Burschka and Hager [14]. FRAMESLAM by Agrawal and Konolidge [15] and PTAM by Klein and Murray [16] are more recent developments. There has been a strong trend in recent feature-based approaches towards sliding-window methods

1. MOTIVATION

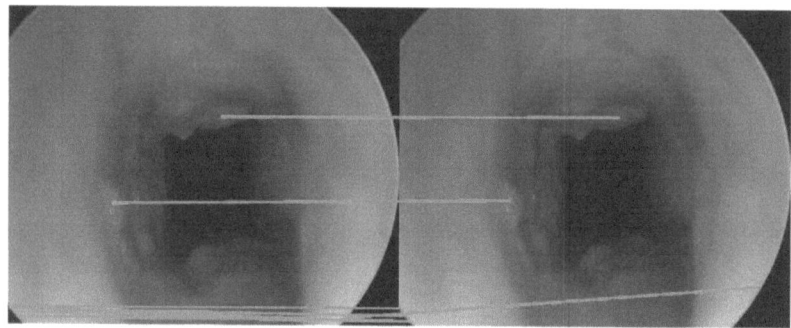

Figure 1.1: Example images from video-endoscopy, showing SIFT matches.

that do not update their estimates based on only one image at a time, but instead perform an update over a small set of key-frame images via bundle adjustment. Strasdat et al. [17] have investigated this approach and found it to perform favourably compared to traditional methods, both in terms of performance and accuracy, except for very small feature sets.

Feature-based methods work fine as long as enough features can be detected and matched in images. However, this is by far not always the case. Consider Figure 1.1, which shows an example image from a video-endoscopy sequence. Note that the image quality is rather bad, and that there is not much texture in the scene. Not surprisingly, feature detection and matching turns out to be quite difficult on such images. We have run SIFT on two images of the sequence, which yielded 9 matches. However, only 2 of these 9 were actual good matches, and 2 matches are definitely not enough for recovering pose or any scene structure.

Performing structure and motion recovery from such low-quality images remains challenging for intensity-based methods as well. But, as we will see in Chapter 7, we are at least able to perform an approximate reconstruction.

Another example for a difficult reconstruction scenario is shown

 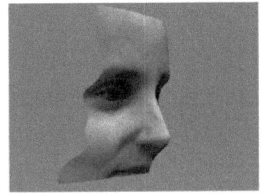 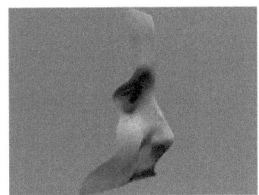

(a) Template image.   (b) Reconstruction at ~ 45° angle.   (c) Profile view of reconstruction.

Figure 1.2: Face reconstruction example. Note that the forehead region exhibits almost no texture at all, except for a slight gradient due to shadowing.

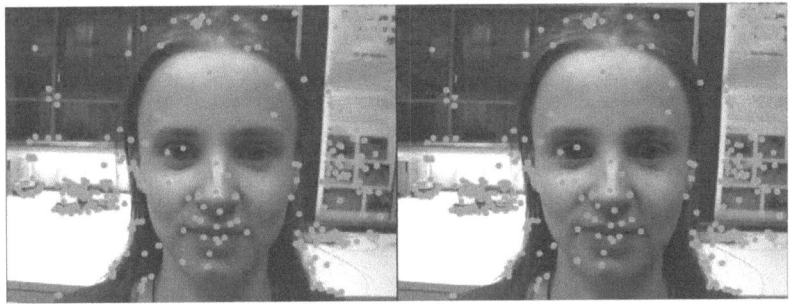

Figure 1.3: Detected SIFT features in two images of the face reconstruction sequence.

in Figure 1.2, along with reconstruction results produced by one of our algorithms. Note that the reconstruction works quite well despite large, homogeneous regions that are present in the image. We have also run the SIFT feature detection and matching algorithm on some images, and found only a very small number of features. Especially on the forehead, features are very sparse, and definitely insufficient to reconstruct the associated surface. The detected features are shown in Figure 1.3. We do not show the feature matching lines for the sake of clarity.

Direct methods are better suited for such difficult cases, since they can make better use of the information that is present in the images [18]. Consider again the video-endoscopy example of Fig-

1. MOTIVATION

ure 1.1: while there are no strong edges, corners, or other features, the shading of the environment does provide information in brightness variation that can be used for matching. The methods developed in this thesis make use of this idea, and combine it with the sliding-window approach that has been used with great success in feature-based approaches.

Earlier direct methods are typically restricted to planar surfaces, such as the method proposed by Benhimane and Malis [19]. These methods have subsequently been extended by Malis [20] to account for more general surface types. One of the contributions of this thesis is the combination of the sliding-window paradigm with such direct methods.

Silveira and Malis have also proposed a method that accounts for changing lighting conditions [21]. Their idea is quite general and allows for significant variation in lighting, modelling the lighting variation as a parametrized image that is multiplied with the intensities of the image to be tracked. In this thesis, we will also present an approach for dealing with lighting variations, but our approach will be more specialized than that of Silveira and Malis. More specifically, we will explicitly model the light source and compute its influence on image formation as is done in shape-from-shading.

Shape from shading methods [22, 23] are single-view methods that also use the entire image to assign a 3D position to each pixel, but are typically a lot less accurate than multi-view methods. They assume either a point light at the camera center or distant light, Lambertian surface reflectance, and a uniform albedo of the surface under consideration. Especially the assumption of an uniform albedo is problematic, because it is rarely fulfilled in real scenarios. Nevertheless, these methods have been applied with some success in video-endoscopic settings [24, 25]. However, they will typically run into problems whenever some of their premises are not fulfilled.

In this thesis, we pick up the idea of modelling a point light source as well, thus combining the approach of shape-from-shading with direct, multi-view structure and motion recovery. Thus, we combine the advantages of both methods and are able to perform reconstruction also under difficult lighting conditions, by which we mean that there is only one source of light in the scene which is linked rigidly to the camera. A very relevant real-world example for such a scenario is video-endoscopy.

1.1 Contribution

The contribution of this work is threefold:

1. An optimization engine is provided to solve intensity-based bundle adjustment problems. We have developed a specialized, modular engine that is flexible yet efficient at the same time. This optimization engine will be described in Chapter 4.

2. Three different variants of intensity-based bundle adjustment algorithms have been implemented. The modules needed to implement them within our optimization framework will be described in detail in Chapter 5.

3. Furthermore, we have developed a method that is capable of calibrating the position and the spatial intensity distribution of a small light source from camera images showing a calibration pattern. The light source should be small compared to the distance at which objects are observed, such that it can be approximated as a point light source. This method will be discussed in Chapter 6.

1. MOTIVATION

The main focus of this work, however, is on the three mentioned variants of direct bundle adjustment algorithms that are useful for surface and motion recovery in different, special settings. We will introduce our notation and recapitulate some basics of bundle adjustment in Chapter 2. Chapter 3 will provide detailed problem specifications, while Chapter 7 contains experimental results obtained with each of our methods, and discusses the applicability of these methods in different situations. Finally, Chapter 8 concludes the thesis with a summary and outlook on future work.

2. Bundle Adjustment Basics

Bundle-adjustment (BA) is a well-known technique that allows simultaneous retrieval of scene geometry and extrinsic camera parameters from a set of images. All of the algorithms developed in this work have been inspired by intensity-based bundle adjustment methods. While these methods have been known for a long time (see e.g. [26, 27, 28]), computer hardware development only recently reached a point where such algorithms run in real-time [21] or at least close to real-time [29, 30].

A different interpretation of such techniques is that of image registration algorithms. To this end, intensity-based bundle adjustment methods can be seen as instances of optical flow algorithms [31, 32] equipped with a special parameterization that encodes the structure of the scene and extrinsic camera parameters.

Bundle adjustment was originally conceived as a method that retrieves scene structure and camera parameters accurately from large sets of images. However, in recent years, sliding-window approaches have become increasingly popular [33, 15, 16]. These methods are suitable for real-time navigation with high accuracy. The basic idea is to apply bundle adjustment only to a small subset of images, including the most recent image. Until now, such methods have been limited to the case of feature-based bundle adjustment. One of the contributions of this work is the development of sliding-window intensity-based bundle adjustment algorithms.

A good introduction to bundle adjustment is contained in Hart-

2. BUNDLE ADJUSTMENT BASICS

ley's book [34]. The paper by Triggs et al. [35] provides a detailed overview. For the reader's convenience, and also to introduce our notation, we are going to give a brief overview of bundle adjustment methods and intensity-based approaches in this chapter.

Since we are now going to explain the mathematics underlying our algorithms in detail, we want to point the reader to the appendix Chapters A and B, where we introduce the most important parts of our mathematical notation and explain our convention of using color-coded images to display depth images, error images, etc.

2.1 Feature-Based Bundle Adjustment

Intensity-based bundle adjustment methods are very closely related to more common case of feature-based bundle adjustment. Actually, as Triggs et al. [35] point out, the only difference to the feature-based case is that the objective function is composed with a smooth approximation of the image function itself, such that residuals are computed in image intensity space instead of pixel coordinate space. For this reason, we are going to quickly recapitulate the basics of feature-based methods, before we explain intensity-based methods in more detail.

The problem addressed by classic bundle adjustment is as follows: given n images of the same scene, taken from different camera positions, and some features in these images that were detected and matched, determine the camera positions associated with the n images and the 3D coordinates of the detected feature points. The feature matching step is typically performed by using SIFT [10], SURF [11], or similar feature detection methods. Figure 2.1 shows a schematic overview.

In what follows, we are going to focus on the case of a finite projective camera whose intrinsic parameters are known [34, pp.

2.1 Feature-Based Bundle Adjustment

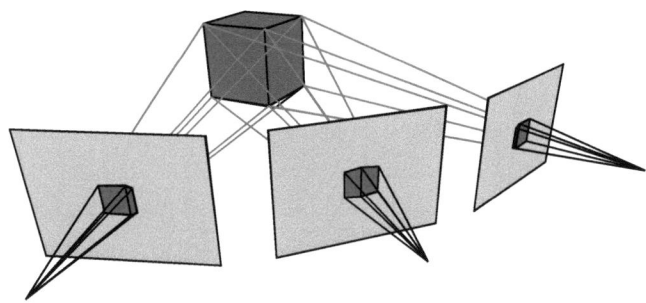

Figure 2.1: Toy problem illustrating bundle adjustment: A cube is observed from several different locations. Feature points project to different coordinates in those different views. The task is to reconstruct the camera position as well as the 3D coordinates associated with the feature points.

153-157]. We will describe the projective properties of cameras using 3×3 camera matrices $\mathbf{K}$ that contain the intrinsic calibration parameters. The most practically relevant case is that of a pinhole camera, where the camera matrix has the structure

$$\mathbf{K} = \begin{pmatrix} \alpha_x & 0 & p_x \\ 0 & \alpha_y & p_y \\ 0 & 0 & 1 \end{pmatrix}, \tag{2.1}$$

where α_x and α_y are the focal lengths and p_x, p_y are the coordinates of the principal point of the camera. Throughout this thesis, we assume that cameras have been calibrated (using, e.g., the method by Zhang [36]), and that any significant radial distortions have been rectified.

The matrix $\mathbf{K}$ maps inhomogeneous 3D coordinates $\mathbf{b} \in \mathbb{R}^3$ to homogeneous 2D pixel coordinates $\mathbf{K} \cdot \mathbf{b}$. To get the inhomogeneous pixel coordinates from $\mathbf{K} \cdot \mathbf{b}$, we would then need to divide

2. BUNDLE ADJUSTMENT BASICS

through the homogeneous component, a process that is known in computer graphics as *projective divide*. It will be convenient for us to define a function $\pi : \mathbb{R}^3 \to \mathbb{R}^2$ that performs the perspective divide:

$$\pi(\mathbf{x}) = \left(\frac{x_1}{x_3}, \frac{x_2}{x_3}\right)^T. \tag{2.2}$$

Conversely, feature detection and localization yields feature coordinates $\pi(\mathbf{K} \cdot \mathbf{b}) \in \mathbb{R}^2$ that are usually related to homogeneous 2D coordinates by extending the 2D vector $\pi(\mathbf{K} \cdot \mathbf{b})$ with an entry of 1. The resulting homogeneous coordinates represent the same point as $\mathbf{K} \cdot \mathbf{b}$, since homogeneous coordinates are equivalent up to scale (indicated by the symbol $\propto$):

$$\begin{pmatrix} \pi(\mathbf{K} \cdot \mathbf{b}) \\ 1 \end{pmatrix} = \begin{pmatrix} \frac{(\mathbf{K} \cdot \mathbf{b})_1}{(\mathbf{K} \cdot \mathbf{b})_3} \\ \frac{(\mathbf{K} \cdot \mathbf{b})_2}{(\mathbf{K} \cdot \mathbf{b})_3} \\ 1 \end{pmatrix} \propto \begin{pmatrix} (\mathbf{K} \cdot \mathbf{b})_1 \\ (\mathbf{K} \cdot \mathbf{b})_2 \\ (\mathbf{K} \cdot \mathbf{b})_3 \end{pmatrix} = \mathbf{K} \cdot \mathbf{b}. \tag{2.3}$$

We can then use the inverse camera matrix $\mathbf{K}^{-1}$ to determine a 3D direction vector that points from the camera's principal point towards b, such that

$$\mathbf{b} \propto \mathbf{K}^{-1} \cdot \begin{pmatrix} \pi(\mathbf{K} \cdot \mathbf{b}) \\ 1 \end{pmatrix}, \text{ or } \mathbf{b} = b_3 \cdot \mathbf{K}^{-1} \cdot \begin{pmatrix} \pi(\mathbf{K} \cdot \mathbf{b}) \\ 1 \end{pmatrix} \tag{2.4}$$

Note that the parameter b_3 represents the z-coordinate of the point b, measured in the camera's frame of reference. A vector from the principle point of the camera to the 2D projection of the point b onto an xy plane at distance 1 computes as $\mathbf{K}^{-1} \cdot (\pi(\mathbf{K} \cdot \mathbf{b})^T, 1)^T$, as illustrated in Figure 2.2.

In the mathematical framework of projective cameras described above, images taken from different viewpoints correspond to images

2.1 Feature-Based Bundle Adjustment

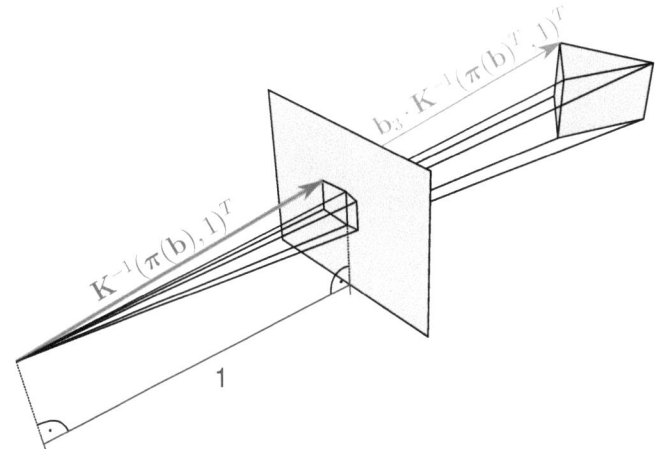

Figure 2.2: Relation between pixel coordinates and 3D coordinates.

of the same point cloud as seen from different camera frames. Discussing the intrinsic parameters of cameras, we have shown now how 3D coordinates that are relative to a camera's frame can be mapped to 2D coordinates. However, we also need to introduce the extrinsic camera parameters, which are used to describe transformations of 3D coordinates from one camera frame to another.

Transforming coordinates is done via so-called rigid transformations, and these transformations consist of a rotation and translation in 3D space. It is well-known that the minimal number of parameters needed to describe such a rigid transformation is 6, encompassing 3 parameters for translation and 3 parameters for rotation. Rotations can be represented using many different schemes, such as, e.g., Euler angles, quaternions, rotation matrices, each of which uses at least 3 parameters. The topic of rotation representation is indeed quite complex and will be discussed in more detail later on. For our algorithms, we have decided to use quaternions for our rotation representation, such that extrinsic parameters can be represented by 7-dimensional vectors $\mathbf{a} = (\mathbf{a}_t^T, \mathbf{a}_q^T)^T$, where $\mathbf{a}_t \in \mathbb{R}^3$ is a vector

2. BUNDLE ADJUSTMENT BASICS

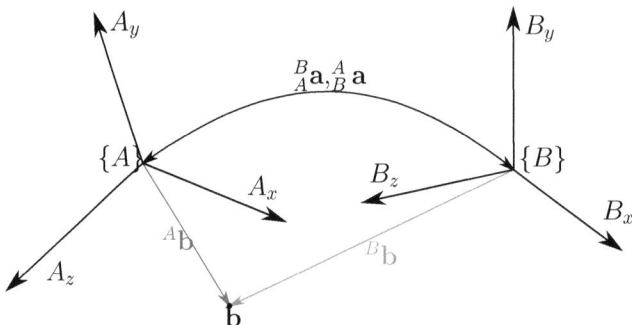

Figure 2.3: Illustration of rigid transformations.

of translation between our coordinate frames, and $a_q \in \mathbb{R}^4$ is the rotation quaternion representing the rotation between frames.

Using this scheme, our definition of rigid transformations becomes

$$\mathbf{T}(\mathbf{a}, \mathbf{b}) = \mathbf{R}(\mathbf{a}_q)^\mathrm{T}(\mathbf{b} - \mathbf{a}_t), \qquad (2.5)$$

where $\mathbf{R}(\mathbf{a}_q)$ denotes the 3×3 rotation matrix corresponding to the rotation quaternion $\mathbf{a}_q \in \mathbb{R}^4$, and $\mathbf{b} \in \mathbb{R}^3$ are the 3D coordinates of a point to be transformed. Thus, in our case rigid transformations are functions of type $\mathbb{R}^3 \times \mathbb{R}^7 \to \mathbb{R}^3$ that take point coordinates in one frame together with transformation parameters to point coordinates in another frame.

Sometimes, it will be convenient to refer to the specific coordinate frames involved in a certain rigid transformation. This requires us to introduce some new notation, which is shown in Figure 2.3. There, a rigid transformation relates point coordinates relative to coordinate frame $\{A\}$ to point coordinates relative to frame $\{B\}$ and vice versa. In the following, whenever we want to be be more specific about the coordinate frames involved, we will use leading sub- and superscripts to refer to the source and destination coordinate frames of a rigid transformation, such that the transforma-

2.1 Feature-Based Bundle Adjustment

tion parameters for moving from coordinate frame $\{A\}$ to coordinate frame $\{B\}$ would be denoted as $^B_A\mathbf{a}$. Similarily, we may denote the frame of reference of the coordinates of some point with a leading superscript, such that the coordinates of point b relative to frame A would be $^A\mathbf{b}$. Mathematically, the following Equations hold: $\mathbf{T}(^B_A\mathbf{a}, {}^A\mathbf{b}) = {}^B\mathbf{b}$ and $\mathbf{T}(^A_B\mathbf{a}, {}^B\mathbf{b}) = {}^A\mathbf{b}$.

Now we are ready to formulate the basic idea underlying bundle adjustment: Assume we have applied a feature detection and matching algorithm to a set of N images $\mathfrak{I}_n$, where $1 \leq n \leq N$. The algorithm has produced, for each image $\mathfrak{I}_n$, a set of M 2D image feature coordinates $\mathbf{p}_{n,m}$. Not all features are neccessarily visible in all frames, so the algorithm also produces values $v_{n,m}$ indicating whether feature m has been found in image n. The numbering is such that $\mathbf{p}_{i,k}, \mathbf{p}_{j,k}$ denote the image coordinates of some feature k that has been detected and matched in the two images $\mathfrak{I}_i, \mathfrak{I}_j$. Neglecting for now the possibility of false matches and assuming the feature localization to be 100% accurate, this means that $\mathbf{p}_{i,k}, \mathbf{p}_{j,k}$ are 2D projections of the same 3D point $\mathbf{b}_k$, seen from two different positions. Let $\mathbf{a}_i$ denote the extrinsic camera parameters (rotation and translation) and $\mathbf{b}_j$ the 3D coordinates of a point j. Furthermore, define a and b to be the vectors resulting from stacking all $\mathbf{a}_i$ respectively $\mathbf{b}_j$ on top of each other.

The *image reprojection error* associated with a point $\mathbf{b}_j$ seen in view $\mathbf{a}_i$ is defined as

$$|\pi(\mathbf{K} \cdot \mathbf{T}(\mathbf{a}_i, \mathbf{b}_j)) - \mathbf{p}_{i,j}|, \qquad (2.6)$$

which is simply the length of the displacement vector between the predicted position of a point and its actually measured position. The goal of bundle adjustment algorithms is to find solutions $\mathbf{b}_j, \mathbf{a}_i$ that minimize these reprojection errors.

2. BUNDLE ADJUSTMENT BASICS

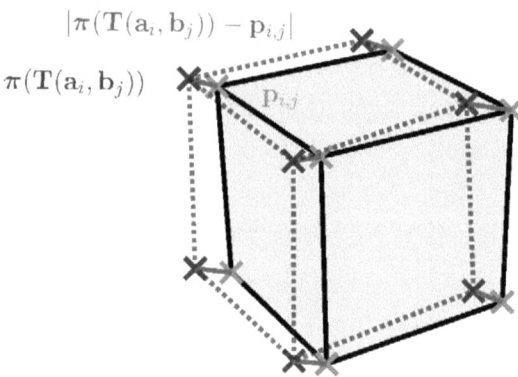

Figure 2.4: Illustration of reprojection errors: Blue crosses indicate current projection estimates, green crosses are measured projection coordinates, red line segments show the reprojection error.

This is typically achieved by minimizing the following sum of squared image reprojection error vectors:

$$^F E(\mathbf{a},\mathbf{b}) = \sum_{i=1}^{N} \sum_{j=1}^{M} v_{i,j} \left(\pi(\mathbf{K} \cdot \mathbf{T}(\mathbf{a}_i, \mathbf{b}_j)) - \mathbf{p}_{i,j} \right)^2 \qquad (2.7)$$

Note that the pre-superscript F is used to distinguish this error term from the intensity-based one that will be introduced later on.

The minimization of above objective function is typically performed using a non-linear optimization method. Such optimization involves repeated solution of sparse linear systems, and the exploitation of this sparsity of these systems is essential. Solving the involved linear problems would be infeasible if the linear system was treated as a dense system.

In the hypothetic case of perfectly accurate values $\mathbf{a}_i, \mathbf{b}_i$, the image reprojection error would be 0. More realistically, the values will never be completely accurate, but still, the reprojection error will be minimal if the parameters $\mathbf{a}_i, \mathbf{b}_j$ reflect the real values of point coordinates and extrinsic camera parameters as closely as possi-

2.1 Feature-Based Bundle Adjustment

ble. This is our basic formulation of the bundle adjustment problem: Given measurements $\mathbf{p}_{i,j}$, determine parameters $\mathbf{a}_i, \mathbf{b}_j$ such that the sum of squared reprojection error (2.7) is minimized.

In practice, this problem is typically solved as a two-step process:

1. Initial estimates for all $\mathbf{a}_i, \mathbf{b}_j$ are generated via algorithms for fundamental matrix estimation and successive triangulation [37]. Another option to perform this initialization is the use of an L_∞-norm (maximum norm) formulation of above problem together with second-order cone programming methods [38].

2. The initial fit is subsequently refined using a nonlinear optimization technique that minimizes the reprojection error. This is usually done using the Levenberg-Marquardt non-linear optimization method [39].

It is quite common that feature coordinates determined by feature detection algorithms are unreliable, and affected by noise, gross outliers, and false matches. This has a drastically deteriorating effect on the quality of the solution found by solving the BA equation (2.7), at least if the equation is used in its original formulation. A typical approach for reducing the influence of such corrupted measurements is the usage of robust cost functions [34, pp. 616-622].

Such a cost function basically takes as input a displacement vector, and assigns to it a specific cost. Robust cost functions are typically designed such that they assign less cost to outliers. We reformulate Equation (2.7) for the case of using some cost function $\mathcal{C}$ as follows:

$$^\text{F}E_\mathcal{C}(\mathbf{a},\mathbf{b}) = \sum_{i=1}^{N}\sum_{j=1}^{M} v_{i,j} \cdot \mathcal{C}\left(\pi(\mathbf{K}\cdot\mathbf{T}(\mathbf{a}_i,\mathbf{b}_j)), \mathbf{p}_{i,j}\right) \qquad (2.8)$$

2. BUNDLE ADJUSTMENT BASICS

We see that the original formulation (2.7) is coincident with this slightly generalized version for the case of $\mathcal{C}(\mathbf{x},\mathbf{y})$ being the well-known sum of squared differences $(\mathbf{x}-\mathbf{y})^\mathrm{T} \cdot (\mathbf{x}-\mathbf{y})$.

Sliding-window based approaches also solve the bundle adjustment problem, but typically, this is only done for a relatively small set of images taken from a camera stream. Thus, their main purpose is the computation of an incremental motion and structure update. Georg Klein's widely known PTAM system [16] can probably be considered the gold standard when it comes to implementing this idea. One of our contributions is the transfer of sliding-window methods to the case of intensity-based bundle adjustment.

This concludes our discussion of classical feature-based bundle adjustment, and we will now turn to the intensity-based variant of bundle adjustment, which is the main idea underlying all algorithms presented in this thesis.

2.2 Intensity-Based Bundle Adjustment

As we have mentioned before, the intensity-based bundle adjustment formulation is very similar to the feature-based one, but some small changes have to be made. First of all, we will no longer rely on a feature detection mechanism, but instead match a reference image $\mathcal{I}_0$ to the other images $\mathcal{I}_1, \mathcal{I}_2, \ldots, \mathcal{I}_N$. Furthermore, we will associate some camera parameters a_0 with the reference image, and all other images should be localized relative to that image. If we still model the scene as consisting of single points, the image

2.2 Intensity-Based Bundle Adjustment

re-projection error would be rewritten as

$$E_{\mathcal{C}}(\mathbf{a}, \mathbf{b}) = \sum_{i=1}^{N} \sum_{j=1}^{M} v_{i,j} \cdot \mathcal{C}\left(\, \mathcal{I}_i(\pi(\mathbf{K} \cdot \mathbf{T}(\mathbf{a}_i, \mathbf{b}_j))),\right.$$
$$\left. \mathcal{I}_0(\pi(\mathbf{K} \cdot \mathbf{T}(\mathbf{a}_0, \mathbf{b}_j)))\,\right). \quad (2.9)$$

This formulation, however, is slightly problematic, since it indirectly assumes that pixels can be identified solely based on their intensity. However, images usually contain many pixels of the same intensity value, which makes finding a correct match very unlikely. On the other hand, pixels that are close to each other in an image have a high probability that their depth values are also close together. This observation leads to the idea of restricting the points to lie on some kind of surface.

The natural choice for such a surface model is that of a depth map z that assigns a depth value $z(\mathbf{p}, u, v)$ or an inverse depth value $\frac{1}{z(\mathbf{p},u,v)}$ to pixels (u, v) of the template image. We will call the former approach a direct depth parametrization, and the latter approach an inverse depth parametrization. It has been shown that for several reasons, inverse depth parametrizations are superior to direct depth parametrizations in the context of SLAM methods [40], which is why we will employ an inverse depth parametrization in our algorithm.

The concept of depth maps has been applied with considerable success in many reconstruction methods. One quite recent example is the on-line dense reconstruction algorithm by Newcombe [41], where a per-pixel depth map is determined directly from image data, and a total variation regularizer to enforce a certain degree of smoothness on the depth map. Figure 2.5 shows an example of a direct depth map and an inverse depth map for an artificially rendered

2. BUNDLE ADJUSTMENT BASICS

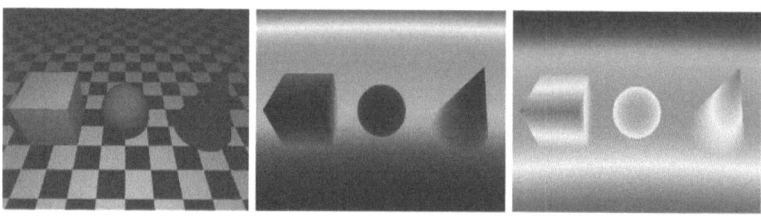

Figure 2.5: Left: Synthetic scene, Middle: Direct depth map, Right: Inverse depth map.

scene.

These considerations finally lead to a formulation of intensity-based bundle adjustment where all images are involved. Thus, we will call this the complete intensity-based objective, as opposed to the pair-wise and sliding-window variants that we will define later. The complete objective is defined as

$$^{\text{CI}}E_{\mathcal{C}}(\mathbf{a},\mathbf{p}) = \sum_{i=1}^{N} \sum_{j=1}^{M} \mathcal{C}\left(\, \mathfrak{I}_i(\pi(\mathbf{K} \cdot \mathbf{T}(\mathbf{a}_i, \mathbf{d}_z(\mathbf{p}, u_j, v_j)))), \mathfrak{I}_0(u_j, v_j) \,\right),$$
(2.10)

where $\mathbf{d}_z$ denotes the surface induced by the depth map function z. The reference pixel coordinates (u_j, v_j) are typically chosen before the optimization process, and remain constant. Due to the computational expense of intensity-based bundle adjustment, it is quite common not to include all image pixels in the set of reference pixels. In our case, the reference pixels will be distributed uniformly across a user-chosen rectangular region of interest. Figure 2.6 shows the concept for the simple case of alignment between two frames.

This formulation of intensity-based bundle adjustment makes use of the well-known color constancy assumption, which is intuitively understood as the assumption that the same scene point has the same color when seen from different points of view. For nearly Lambertian surfaces, constant illumination and negligible camera

2.2 Intensity-Based Bundle Adjustment

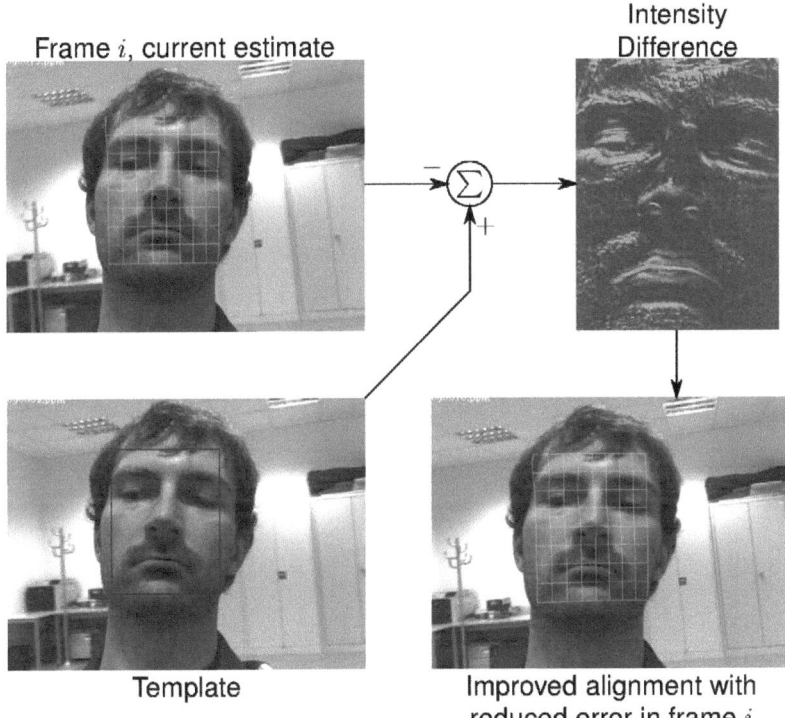

Figure 2.6: The intensity matching process: The current estimate yields a prediction of intensity values, which are compared to the template image values. This yields the image intensity error. Intensity-based bundle adjustment minimizes the intensity re-projection error, yielding an improved surface and camera position estimate.

2. BUNDLE ADJUSTMENT BASICS

vignetting, the color constancy assumption is a reasonable approximation.

The objective term formulated above is a bit complicated, thus we will define a helper function to keep our presentation concise. Exploiting the fact that the reference pixel coordinates (u_j, v_j) remain constant, we can define a warping function $\mathbf{w}_j$ for each reference pixel (u_j, v_j) as

$$\mathbf{w}_j(\mathbf{p}, \mathbf{a}_i) = \pi(\mathbf{K} \cdot \mathbf{T}(\mathbf{a}_i, \mathbf{d}_z(\mathbf{p}, u_j, v_j))). \qquad (2.11)$$

This function represents a warp of 2D coordinates, since it describes, for any surface point (u_j, v_j), its 2D position in a different frame. The warping function can thus be interpreted as the optical flow of the reference points (u_j, v_j). Using this warping function, we can shorten above objective term to

$$^{\text{CI}}E_\mathcal{C}(\mathbf{a}, \mathbf{p}) = \sum_{i=1}^{N} \sum_{j=1}^{M} \mathcal{C}\left(\mathfrak{I}_i(\mathbf{w}_j(\mathbf{p}, \mathbf{a}_i)), \quad \mathfrak{I}_0(u_j, v_j) \right). \qquad (2.12)$$

In the case of changing illumination, the situation gets more difficult, since the color of one point might change from one image to the next. It is, in general, quite difficult to incorporate lighting changes into intensity-based reconstruction methods. One way to deal with the problem is the approach suggested by Silveira and Malis [21], where the lighting variation is parametrized in a similar way as the surface model, and the lighting parameters are then simply estimated along with the surface and camera parameters. This approach, however, can only work if the surface to be reconstructed and tracked provides enough texture, since the lighting change model provides quite a lot of degrees of freedom. In case of a weakly textured surface, it seems likely that such an algorithm

2.2 Intensity-Based Bundle Adjustment

would not be able to discern whether a color change is due to a change in lighting or due to movement of the surface.

2. BUNDLE ADJUSTMENT BASICS

3. Approach

We are now going to provide exact problem descriptions for each of the three algorithms that we have mentioned earlier, and sketch the solutions we have developed. Since the problem of motion and scene recovery from monocular images is an ill-posed problem, we need to rely on a couple of assumptions to make it feasible. The assumptions that are made for all three cases are the following:

- The surface to be reconstructed is a smooth Lambertian surface.

- The surface is not occluded and fully visible.

- Intrinsic camera parameters and camera distortion coefficients are known, and do not change during an image sequence. The images we are working with have been rectified, such that distortion effects are removed.

- The photometric properties of the camera (inverse response function and vignetting profile) have been calibrated, and the images we are working with show no significant photometric distortions or have been rectified accordingly.

For each of the three algorithm variants, there are some specific additional assumptions as follows:

1. Lighting conditions are arbitrary, but do not change during the reconstruction.

3. APPROACH

2. There is a point-shaped light source that is located at the camera's principle point. Except for that light, there is no other source of light in the scene. Light inter-reflections from surfaces are neglected.

3. There is a small light source that is linked rigidly to the camera itself. The light is very small, but not a perfect point source. Thus, we treat the light source as having a non-uniform spatial intensity profile. A calibration method is used to determine both the light's position and the intensity profile. Again, we ignore inter-reflections between illuminated surfaces.

All of our algorithms are formulated as optimization problems, and their problem structure is very similar, and closely related to the intensity-based bundle adjustment methods as described in Chapter 2.

Basically, the algorithms work by finding parameters that warp the image intensity values in the current frame back to the reference image, minimizing the intensity differences. Figure 3.1 shows a coarse overview in form of a flow chart. We apply a coarse-to-fine pyramidal optimization scheme as is done frequently in optical flow algorithms [42], with a downscaling factor of 0.5 and three pyramid levels.

For solving the optimization problem, we employ the well-known SQP method [43]. This is basically a Newton-type optimization method that supports enforcing some constraints on the problem parameters. It has also been suggested by Triggs et al. [35] as the method of choice when solving constrained bundle-adjustment problems. The need for constrained optimization arises because of our choice of unit quaternions as rotation representation, and because of the need to constrain the scale of there reconstruction, which is non-observable. We have developed an efficient and flexi-

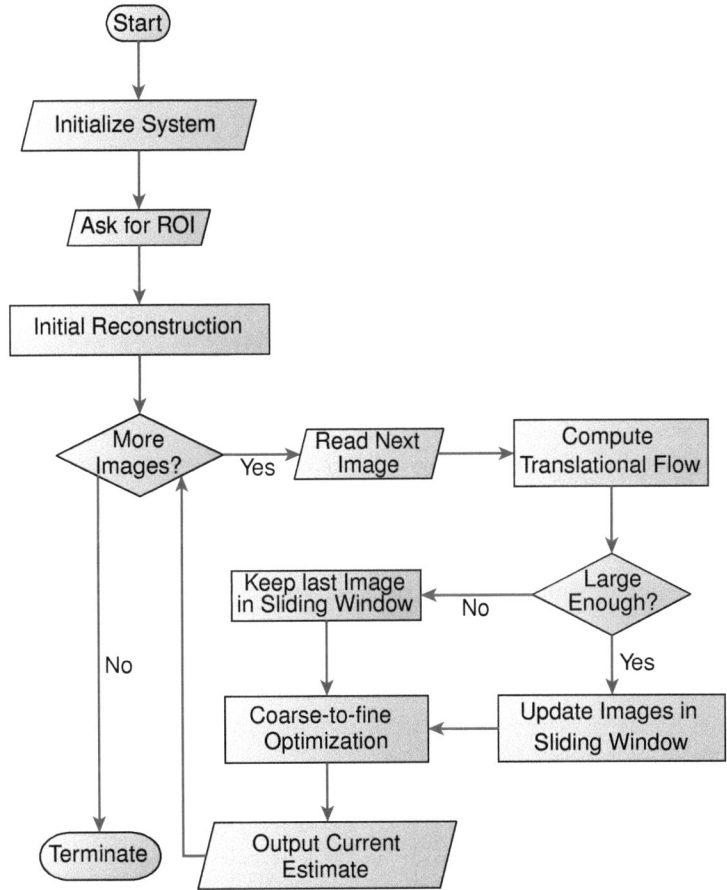

Figure 3.1: Coarse flowchart overview showing the overall structure of our surface and motion recovery algorithms.

3. APPROACH

ble optimization framework that will be described in detail in Chapter 4.

The optimization is performed over a sliding window of images. To assure that the baseline between images in the sliding window is large enough, we check the average translational flow magnitude of every new image before adding it to the sliding window. A new image is accepted into the sliding window buffer if its average translational flow magnitude against the reference image and all other images in the buffer is larger than some threshold value. We are using a threshold value of 10 pixels that has been determined empirically.

As we have mentioned in Chapter 2, it is typically very difficult to match points through their image intensities alone, so usually they are constrained to lie on some kind of parametric surface. A very common scene representation for dense scene recovery methods is that of a direct or inverse depth map. Figure 3.2 shows an example of curves induced by a cosine depth profile for the 2D case, which is analogous to the 3D case.

Our surface model is that of an inverse B-spline depth map, where different spline orders and different amounts of control points can be chosen. These parameters influence the smoothness and the the level of detail that the surface model can represent. Typically, we use 8 control points for the spline surface in each direction, and a spline order of 2 in both directions, corresponding to a biquadratic spline surface.

Because the optimization is computationally very expensive, we do not perform an exhaustive minimization of the objective for every pixel of the ROI. Instead, we only sample a certain number of pixels for each control point. Typically, the sampling resolution is 8×8 pixels per control point, and the sampling points are spread evenly over

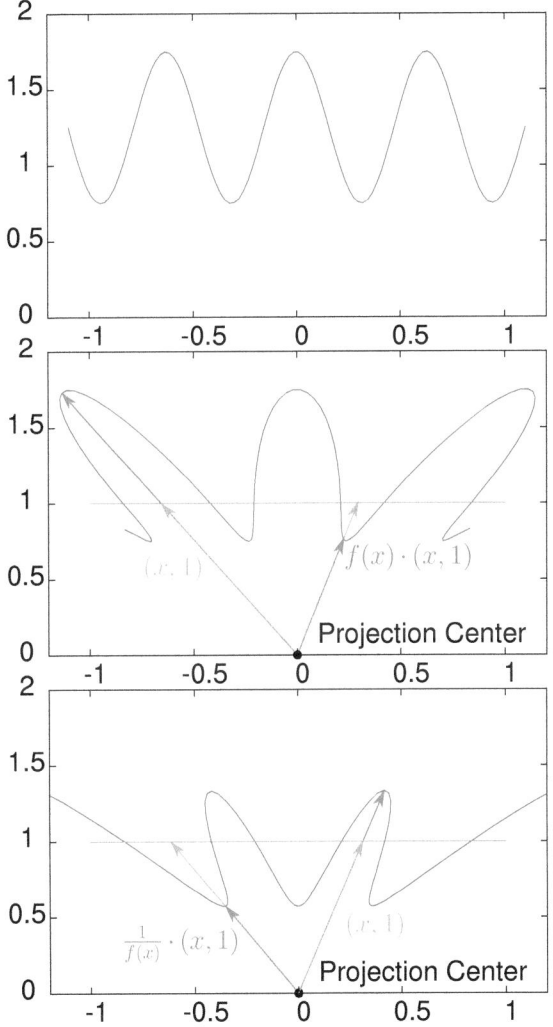

Figure 3.2: A very simple, synthetic example for a 2D depth profile. The function shown in the topmost plot is defined as $f(x) = \frac{1}{2} \cdot (\cos(10 \cdot x) + 2.5)$. The middle and bottom plots show the corresponding direct and inverse depth maps in the 2D case, respectively.

3. APPROACH

the ROI. More sophisticated methods for determining effective pixel sampling sets have been proposed by Brooks et al. [44]. Essentially, such a method allows for higher computational performance without losing much accuracy. We have not yet integrated their scheme into our algorithms, but would like to do this in the future.

In the case of constant lighting conditions, the resulting algorithm is basically an optical flow method, trying to find the 2D position of reference points in another image. In the other two cases, we do not only warp the 2D positions of pixels, but also their brightness values according to the illumination model. In our implementation, the difference between these methods is merely the usage of different modules within our optimization framework, thus optimizing different objectives.

This concludes our introduction of the common concepts that are shared by all of our algorithms. The only remaining difference between the algorithms is then the optimization objective used, and the rest of this chapter will be devoted to introducing the different objective functions.

In the next Section, we will discuss the first of these three cases, which is the sliding-window method for constant lighting. It is basically a small modification of the original intensity-based bundle adjustment Equation (2.10). Before going into detail about the other two methods that use an explicit illumination model, we introduce the reader to the theory of image formation for Lambertian surfaces for point light sources in Section 3.2. Using this knowledge, we can provide mathematical specifications for the second and third algorithm variants in Sections 3.3 and 3.4.

3.1 The Constant Light Case

The first algorithm uses a cost function similar to the one in Equation (2.10), and makes use of the color constancy assumption. Our main contribution is the development of a sliding-window approach, which improves the robustness and accuracy of the approach. The sliding-window paradigm has been applied with great success in feature-based bundle adjustment [45, 16].

Typical direct methods compare only two images, minimizing the pair-wise objective

$$^{PI}E_{\mathcal{C}}(\mathbf{a}_i, \mathbf{p}) = \sum_{j=1}^{M} \mathcal{C}\left(\mathfrak{I}_i(\mathbf{w}_j(\mathbf{p}, \mathbf{a}_i)),\ \mathfrak{I}_0(u_j, v_j)\right), \quad (3.1)$$

where i is the index of the newest image. Our method, however, will use the objective function

$$^{SI}E_{\mathcal{C}}(\mathbf{a}_\mathcal{V}, \mathbf{p}) = \sum_{i \in \mathcal{V}} \sum_{j=1}^{M} \mathcal{C}\left(\mathfrak{I}_i(\mathbf{w}_j(\mathbf{p}, \mathbf{a}_i)),\ \mathfrak{I}_0(u_j, v_j)\right), \quad (3.2)$$

where $\mathcal{V}$ is a set of image indices containing the newest image, and $\mathbf{a}_\mathcal{V}$ is a vector containing the corresponding extrinsic parameters. An example reconstruction obtained using this method is shown in Figure 3.3.

3.2 Light Source Modelling

Furthermore, we developed two variants of the aforementioned algorithm that are able to cope with two special cases of changing illumination. The second variant of our algorithm assumes that the only source of light in a scene is a point light source located at the camera's optical center. A typical, very relevant example

3. APPROACH

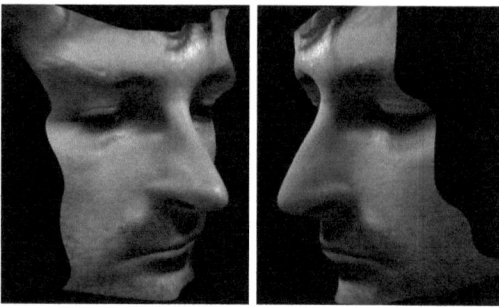

Figure 3.3: Face reconstruction example. The input data was the same as used in Figure 2.6.

for real-world applications of this idea is medical video-endoscopy. The idea has been previously exploited in the case of shape-from-shading [46, 23].

To our knowledge, nobody has applied this idea yet to bundle-adjustment algorithms, so our main contribution is transferral of the explicit light model to direct bundle adjustment. Besides assuming that the light source is located at the camera center, the mentioned shape-from-shading approaches also assume that the surface reflectance is Lambertian with uniform albedo, and that there are no inter-reflections. In comparison, our method has the substantial advantage that it does not require an uniform albedo, but is able to deal with varying albedo as well.

The third variant of our algorithm is a further generalization which allows the point light source to be located at an arbitrary fixed position relative to the camera, and it furthermore allows the light source to have a non-uniform, direction-dependent intensity distribution.

The objective functions for these variants of intensity-based bundle adjustment combine the original objective (2.10) with a correction factor that couples the image intensity differences with the camera motion. We will now discuss the mathematical theory behind modelling of point light sources, which is illustrated in Figure 3.4.

3.2 Light Source Modelling

Following the approach presented by Prados et al. [23], we can compute the intensity values as

$$\mathcal{I}_i(\mathbf{w}_j(\mathbf{p}, \mathbf{a}_i)) = \mathbf{C} \cdot \frac{\cos \alpha(\mathbf{p}, \mathbf{a}_i, u_j, v_j)}{|\mathbf{d}_{l_t}(\mathbf{p}, \mathbf{a}_i, u_j, v_j)|^2}, \quad (3.3)$$

$$\mathcal{I}_0(u_j, v_j) = \mathbf{C} \cdot \frac{\cos \alpha(\mathbf{p}, \mathbf{a}_0, u_j, v_j)}{|\mathbf{d}_{l_t}(\mathbf{p}, \mathbf{a}_0, u_j, v_j)|^2}, \quad (3.4)$$

where $\mathbf{C}$ is a constant depending on light intensity and surface albedo at the scene point with surface coordinates (u_j, v_j), the vector $\mathbf{d}_{l_t}(\mathbf{p}, \mathbf{a}_i, u_j, v_j)$ points from the surface point (u_j, v_j) to the light source in frame i, and $\alpha(\mathbf{p}, \mathbf{a}_i, u_j, v_j)$ is the angle between the surface normal $\mathbf{n}_z(\mathbf{p}, u_j, v_j)$ and the incident light at the surface point in frame i. In our algorithms, the light source is linked rigidly to the camera, so we have

$$\mathbf{d}_{l_t}(\mathbf{p}, \mathbf{a}_i, u_j, v_j) = \mathbf{T}(\widetilde{\mathbf{a}}_i, \mathbf{l}_t) - \mathbf{d}_z(\mathbf{p}, u_j, v_j), \quad (3.5)$$

where $\mathbf{l}_t$ is the constant position of the light source relative to the camera, expressed in the camera's frame of reference, and $\widetilde{\mathbf{a}}_i$ are the inverse extrinsic parameters such that

$$\mathbf{T}(\widetilde{\mathbf{a}}_i, \mathbf{T}(\mathbf{a}_i, \mathbf{b})) = \mathbf{b}. \quad (3.6)$$

Thus, $\mathbf{T}(\widetilde{\mathbf{a}}_i, \mathbf{l}_t)$ computes the position of the light source in frame i with respect to the reference frame's coordinate system $\mathbf{a}_0$.

Above equations can be rearranged into

$$\mathcal{I}_i(\mathbf{w}_j(\mathbf{p}, \mathbf{a}_i)) \cdot \frac{|\mathbf{d}_{l_t}(\mathbf{p}, \mathbf{a}_i, u_j, v_j)|^2}{\cos \alpha(\mathbf{p}, \mathbf{a}_i, u_j, v_j)} = \mathbf{C}, \quad (3.7)$$

$$\mathcal{I}_0(u_j, v_j) \cdot \frac{|\mathbf{d}_{l_t}(\mathbf{p}, \mathbf{a}_0, u_j, v_j)|^2}{\cos \alpha(\mathbf{p}, \mathbf{a}_0, u_j, v_j)} = \mathbf{C}, \quad (3.8)$$

3. APPROACH

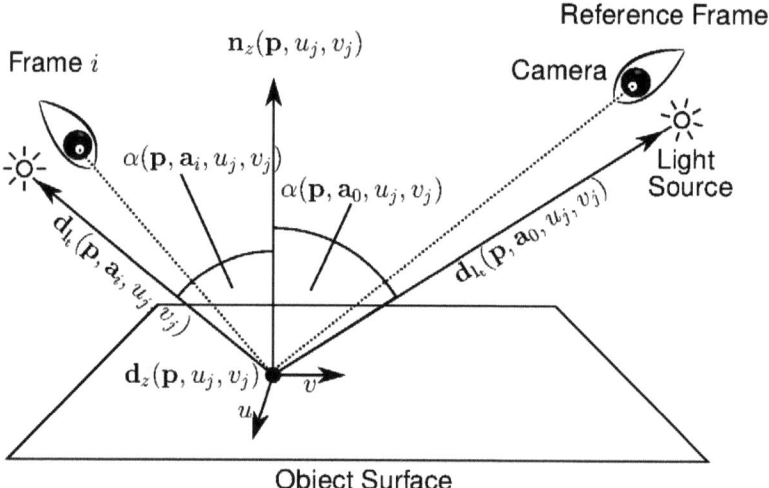

Figure 3.4: Lighting situation in case of a point light source moving with the camera.

which in turn leads to

$$\mathfrak{I}_0(u_j, v_j) - \mathfrak{I}_i(\mathbf{w}_j(\mathbf{p}, \mathbf{a}_i)) \cdot \frac{|\mathbf{d}_{l_t}(\mathbf{p}, \mathbf{a}_i, u_j, v_j)|^2}{\cos \alpha(\mathbf{p}, \mathbf{a}_i, u_j, v_j)} \cdot \frac{\cos \alpha(\mathbf{p}, \mathbf{a}_0, u_j, v_j)}{|\mathbf{d}_{l_t}(\mathbf{p}, \mathbf{a}_0, u_j, v_j)|^2} = 0, \quad (3.9)$$

the left hand side of which constitutes the new intensity reprojection error to be minimized. The term multiplied to the right of $\mathfrak{I}_i$ is a correction factor that maps the intensities as measured in frame i to intensities as measured in frame 0, compensating intensity changes due to the moving light source.

To simplify the notation, we will now define an abbreviation of the correction term formula by means of a brightness warping function ${}^{l_t}_{B}w_j(\mathbf{p}, \mathbf{a}_i)$ as

$${}^{l_t}_{B}w_j(\mathbf{p}, \mathbf{a}_i) = \frac{|\mathbf{d}_{l_t}(\mathbf{p}, \mathbf{a}_i, u_j, v_j)|^2}{\cos \alpha(\mathbf{p}, \mathbf{a}_i, u_j, v_j)} \cdot \frac{\cos \alpha(\mathbf{p}, \mathbf{a}_0, u_j, v_j)}{|\mathbf{d}_{l_t}(\mathbf{p}, \mathbf{a}_0, u_j, v_j)|^2}. \quad (3.10)$$

3.3 The Case of a Point Light at the Optical Center

This brightness warping function will be useful for both variants of our algorithms that perform light source modelling.

3.3 The Case of a Point Light at the Optical Center

Having explored the properties of light modelling, we are now ready to formulate the objective function underlying the second variant of our algorithm, where it is assumed that the scene is lit merely by a point light source at the optical center of the camera. Making use of the intensity warping function defined above, the objective function is

$$^L E_\mathcal{C}(\mathbf{a}_\mathcal{V}, \mathbf{p}) = \sum_{i \in \mathcal{V}} \sum_{j=1}^{M} \mathcal{C}\left(\mathfrak{I}_i(\mathbf{w}_j(\mathbf{p}, \mathbf{a}_i)) \cdot {}^0_B w_j(\mathbf{p}, \mathbf{a}_i),\quad \mathfrak{I}_0(u_j, v_j) \right). \tag{3.11}$$

Note that the light source position relative to the camera is 0.

During our experiments, we have found that the initialization of this system is significantly more difficult than in the case of static lighting. This can be explained as follows: The objective function in the case of static lighting is already a non-convex function, which is inherently difficult to optimize. Using our assumption that the camera is moving smoothly, and thus image displacements are not too big, we are, however, still able to find a good initial optimum and thus a good initial surface approximation in most cases. This is mostly due to the fact that the objective does not exhibit very strong non-linearity: The pseudo-Huber cost function that we are using looks like a square function for inliers and like a linear function for outliers. This means that the objective can be approximated well through a Taylor approximation, which can be seen as basis for our optimization method.

The objective function (3.11) for this illumination-modelling ap-

3. APPROACH

proach now introduces additional non-linearity through the intensity warping function, which basically computes as a fraction of some terms that even include third-order powers. This is our explanation for the increased difficulty of optimization this objective.

To aid with this initialization, we provided a crude initialization to the system by estimating a pixel's depth from its intensity. The underlying assumption is that the surface albedo is constant, and that the angle between light source and surface is constant. Starting from Equation (3.3), and denoting our initial depth estimates as $z_{i,j}$ and the constant surface-light-angle as α', these assumptions lead to the following formula:

$$|\mathcal{I}_i(\mathbf{w}_j(\mathbf{p},\mathbf{a}_i))| \approx \left|\frac{\mathbf{C}\cdot\cos(\alpha')}{z_{i,j}}\right| \Leftrightarrow |z_{i,j}| \approx \sqrt{\frac{|\mathbf{C}|\cdot|\cos(\alpha')|}{|\mathcal{I}_i(\mathbf{w}_j(\mathbf{p},\mathbf{a}_i))|}} \quad (3.12)$$

Note that $|\mathbf{d}_{\mathbf{l}_t}(\mathbf{p},\mathbf{a}_i,u_j,v_j)|^2 = z_{i,j}^2$, since $\mathbf{l}_t = 0$. The reconstruction is in any case only up to scale, so the constant values $|\mathbf{C}|$ and $|\cos(\alpha')|$ can be chosen arbitrarily and are set to 1 in our case. After the per-pixel initial values have been determined using this formula, we compute an initial interpolation using the depth map surface. The depth surface is subsequently normalized such that our scale constraint is fulfilled.

3.4 The Case of Fully Calibrated Light

The third variant of direct bundle adjustment considered in this work goes one step further by using a light source whose position is not coincident with the camera, but has an arbitrary fixed position relative to the camera. In addition to that, the light source is assumed to have a non-uniform intensity profile. Both the position of the light and its intensity profile are calibrated using a novel calibration algo-

3.4 The Case of Fully Calibrated Light

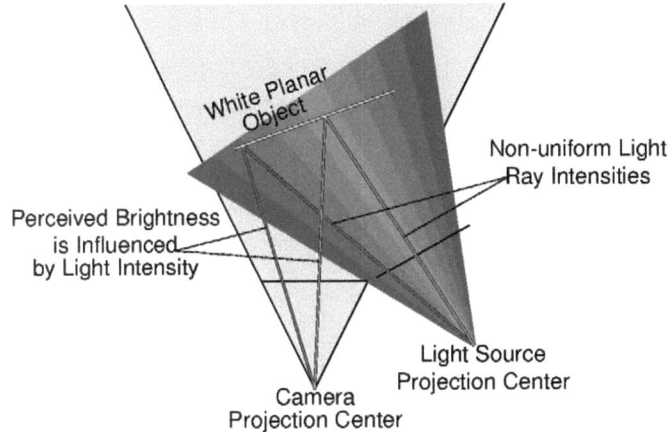

Figure 3.5: When using a calibrated light source, we treat the source as an inverse camera: Instead of measuring incoming light, it projects light into the scene. Since common light sources are hardly perfect point-shaped sources, the projected light usually exhibits a non-uniform intensity in different directions.

rithm that will be described in Chapter 6.

Figure 3.5 shows a 2D schematic view of the situation when a light source is used that is not located at the optical center. A point light source can be modelled as an inverse camera which projects light into the scene instead of measuring it. Actual light sources are, however, not perfect point-shaped sources, and exhibit a non-uniform light intensity in different directions. Our calibration method determines both the position of the light source relative to the camera as well as the intensity profile in terms of a light intensity image $_L\mathcal{J}$.

The basic idea underlying this algorithm is the same as in the previous two cases: Using our mathematical model for image formation, we are able to remap the intensities found in some image i to the reference frame. In the case of the uniform point light source, it was enough to take into account the intensity warping factor $^0_B w_j$.

35

3. APPROACH

In the more complex case of calibrated light, it is not enough to merely take that intensity warping into account, but we also need to remove the non-uniform light pattern from the intensities of frame i, and finally re-project the pattern again to the reference frame's intensities. Figure 3.6 illustrates the concept. After the intensities have been re-projected into the reference frame, they can be compared to each other.

When treating the light source as an inverse camera, determining the brightness of a light ray hitting a surface point becomes an easy task: We merely have to transform the point in question to the light source's frame of reference, and perform the 3D-2D projection according to the light source's projection matrix. We shall define a new coordinate warping function $_L^1\mathbf{w}_j$ for this case as follows:

$$_L^1\mathbf{w}_j(\mathbf{p}, \mathbf{a}_i) = \pi(\mathbf{K}_L \cdot \mathbf{T}(\mathbf{l}, \mathbf{T}(\mathbf{a}_i, \mathbf{d}_z(\mathbf{p}, u_j, v_j)))), \qquad (3.13)$$

where $\mathbf{K}_L$ denotes the light source's projection matrix, and l denotes the constant extrinsic parameters of the light source with respect to the camera frame. Note that the only two differences to the original warping function $\mathbf{w}_j$ is the additional rigid transformation according to the light's extrinsic parameters l and usage of a different projection matrix $\mathbf{K}_L$. The vector of extrinsic light parameters consists of a translation portion and a rotation portion, just like the extrinsic camera parameters: $\mathbf{l} = (\mathbf{l}_t, \mathbf{l}_r)$.

Together with the intensity warping function from the previously discussed algorithm, this allows us to re-project the image intensities of some frame i to the reference frame with reference lighting. The idea is then as follows:

1. Multiply each image intensity $\mathfrak{I}(\mathbf{w}_j(\mathbf{p}, \mathbf{a}_i))$ with the inverse light intensity $_L\widehat{\mathfrak{I}}(_L^1\mathbf{w}_j(\mathbf{p}, \mathbf{a}_i))$. This will neutralize the light's intensity profile.

3.4 The Case of Fully Calibrated Light

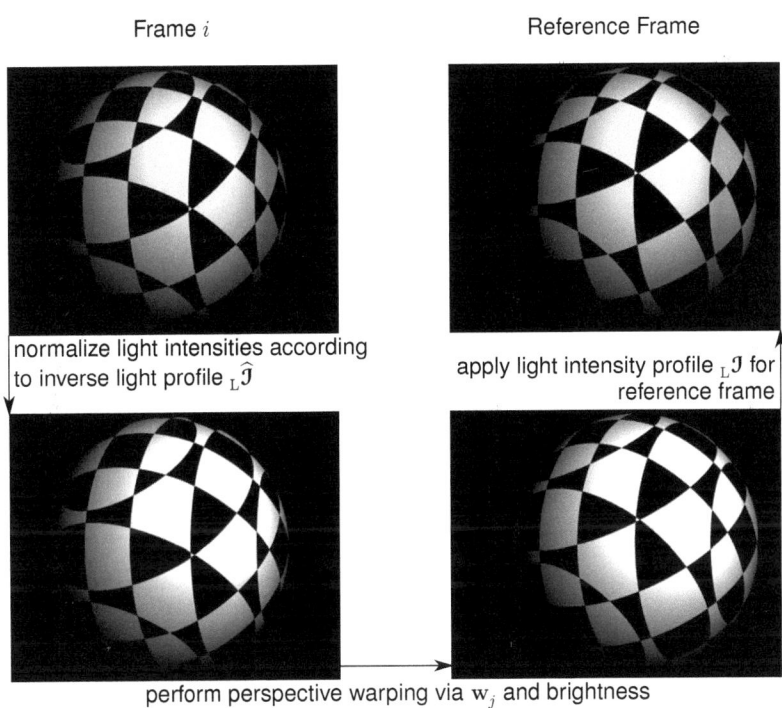

Figure 3.6: Images of a synthetic scene, illustrating the overall warping process from image i back to the reference frame.

3. APPROACH

2. Multiply the resulting intensities with the brightness warping values $^0_\text{B}w_j(\mathbf{p}, \mathbf{a}_i)$, to account for the brightness changes due to the translation of the point source.

3. Finally, multiply the intensity values with the directional light intensities $_\text{L}\mathfrak{I}(^1_\text{L}\mathbf{w}_j(\mathbf{p}, \mathbf{a}_0))$, in order to fully reproduce the lighting conditions in the reference image.

After these steps have been performed, the computed intensity values can then be matched against the template intensity values. Formulated as an objective function, this would look as follows:

$$^\text{CL}E_\text{e}(\mathbf{a}_\mathcal{V}, \mathbf{p}) = \sum_{i \in \mathcal{V}} \sum_{j=1}^{M} e\bigg(\mathfrak{I}_i(\mathbf{w}_j(\mathbf{p}, \mathbf{a}_i)) \cdot {}_\text{L}\widehat{\mathfrak{I}}(^1_\text{L}\mathbf{w}_j(\mathbf{p}, \mathbf{a}_i)) \cdot \\ {}^0_\text{B}w_j(\mathbf{p}, \mathbf{a}_i) \cdot {}_\text{L}\mathfrak{I}(^1_\text{L}\mathbf{w}_j(\mathbf{p}, \mathbf{a}_0)), \quad \mathfrak{I}_0(u_j, v_j) \bigg). \quad (3.14)$$

Note that the intensity warping now depends on the baseline between the camera and the light source, which means that this method is no longer an up-to-scale reconstruction, but provides a metric reconstruction instead. This also means that the surface scale constraint is not applied in this variant.

4. Efficient and Flexible Nonlinear Optimization

While we have already introduced the mathematical formulation of both feature- and intensity-based bundle adjustment methods in the previous chapter, this chapter is dedicated to the theory and practice of nonlinear optimization, which is the core technology applied for solving bundle adjustment.

The mathematical discipline of non-linear optimization or non-linear programming is a well-studied field that has produced a multitude of methods for solving the following type of problem: Given an objective function $o : \mathbb{R}^n \to \mathbb{R}$, and functions $\mathbf{g} : \mathbb{R}^n \to \mathbb{R}^m$, $\mathbf{h} : \mathbb{R}^n \to \mathbb{R}^k$, solve the minimization problem

$$\min_{\mathbf{x} \in \mathbb{R}^n} o(\mathbf{x}) \quad \text{subject to the constraints} \quad \mathbf{g}(\mathbf{x}) \leq 0, \quad \mathbf{h}(\mathbf{x}) = 0$$

where the $\leq$ operator is interpreted in an element-wise fashion. The functions $\mathbf{g}$ and $\mathbf{h}$ thus allow specification of inequality and/or equality constraints on the solution. Many methods for solving this type of problem are known, and each specific method has benefits and drawbacks. For more information about general non-linear optimization methods, see the well-known book by Nocedal and Wright [43].

The bundle adjustment problem that we have introduced earlier is also a problem of this type, but so far, without any constraints. However, when using quaternions for representing rotations, it is necessary to constrain the quaternions to be of unit length, and this is something that can easily be achieved by integrating appropriate

4. EFFICIENT AND FLEXIBLE NONLINEAR OPTIMIZATION

constraints in an optimization formulation.

The implementation of bundle adjustment by Lourakis [47] employs the Levenberg-Marquardt (LM) method [39, 48] to solve the non-linear optimization problem. In its original form, the LM method does not take into account any types of constraints. While there are variants, such as the well-known LEVMAR [49] package, that implement at least linear constraints, we require at least quadratic constraints for our specific problem. Thus, we use the slightly more general method of sequential quadratic programming (SQP). Both methods are actually very similar and belong to the class of Newton-type optimization problems.

We have developed our own optimization framework implementing a sparse SQP method for optimization problems that exhibit a modular structure, in the sense that their objective functions are actually compositions of sub-functions, and each of these sub-functions performs a specific, well-identifiable task. In the case of bundle adjustment problems, such sub-functions would be, e.g., the cost function, the rigid transformation, the perspective projection, and so on.

Most optimization problems are of this structure, so it is usually possible to decompose such a problem, represented by the objective function $o(\mathbf{x})$, into several smaller parts as follows:

$$o(\mathbf{x}) = \mathcal{C} \circ \mathbf{f}_n \circ \mathbf{f}_{n-1} \circ \ldots \circ \mathbf{f}_1(\mathbf{x}). \tag{4.1}$$

We have designed an optimization framework that implements the SQP algorithm and takes advantage of the modular structure of optimization problems. Our main goals were the following:

- Flexibility: Our objective functions are seen as compositions of modular functions, and treated as such within our framework. This means that we are always able to exchange modules, e.g., cost functions, at will, which makes the process of evaluating different alternative algorithms especially simple, and allows for great re-usability of modules.

- Performance: We have taken great care to make sure that the computations are optimized to a very high degree. The main expense during optimization of complex compositional functions is the evaluation of a chain product of sparse Jacobian matrices of the involved functions. Since computing sparse-sparse matrix products is usually an operation with poor performance, we have developed a specialized solution to alleviate this performance problem.

However, our solution is also somewhat specialized to the problems considered in this work, and thus it is also restricted in some ways. More specifically:

- The framework is laid out for sparse matrices, and nothing else. Thus, it will perform suboptimal in the case that dense matrices (Jacobians and/or Hessians) appear in the optimization problem.

- Furthermore, it is required that the sparsity structure of the various derivative matrices is static and *not* dependant on the parameters.

- The modules represent functions with at least multidimensional domain and often also multidimensional range. Implementation of those modules requires implementing derivative computation routines, which can be a quite complex, error-prone and cumbersome task in some cases.

While the framework works very well for the intensity-based bundle adjustment problems we are interested in, its restrictions might also limit its usability for some other applications.

4. EFFICIENT AND FLEXIBLE NONLINEAR OPTIMIZATION

The rest of this chapter is structured as follows: In the next Section, we will review the basics of SQP optimization. The topic of Section 4.2 is a discussion of the mathematical theory of Hessian approximation schemes. The core problem for solving any optimization problem is the computation of the derivatives of the objective function, and we will devote Section 4.3 to a discussion of several available techniques for their computation. Our conclusion will be that none of the available methods is completely satisfying for our purposes, so we will introduce our own approach in Section 4.4. We will explain our approach of partitioning the objective function and the equality constraints into a number of sub-modules, and we will show an example for our approach. Section 4.5, then concludes the chapter with a presentation of some basic building blocks that are available within our framework.

4.1 Sequential Quadratic Programming

We will now give a short, basic overview of the theory behind the SQP method for equality-constrained problems. It is well-known that for optimization problems such as the one described above, the so-called Karush-Kuhn-Tucker (KKT) conditions must hold for any value x^* that is a minimum. In the equality-constrained case, these conditions can be formulated in equation form as:

$$\begin{pmatrix} \nabla_\mathbf{x}(o(\mathbf{x}) + \boldsymbol{\lambda}^T \cdot \mathbf{h}(\mathbf{x})) \\ \mathbf{h}(\mathbf{x}) \end{pmatrix} = \begin{pmatrix} \mathbf{0}_n \\ \mathbf{0}_k \end{pmatrix}. \tag{4.2}$$

For the equality-constrained case, the KKT conditions are coincident with the linear dependence condition of the Lagrange multiplier. Thus, the term $\boldsymbol{\lambda} \in \mathbb{R}^k$ is the Lagrange multiplier associated with the minimum. This is, in general, a nonlinear system of equations. The

4.1 Sequential Quadratic Programming

Lagrange-Newton Method can be applied to these equations, and we can compute an update $\Delta \mathbf{x}$ to $\mathbf{x}$ and a new Lagrange multiplier $\boldsymbol{\lambda}^+$ by solving the symmetric system of equations

$$\begin{pmatrix} \nabla^2_{\mathbf{xx}}(o(\mathbf{x}) + \boldsymbol{\lambda}^T \cdot \mathbf{h}(\mathbf{x})) & \nabla_{\mathbf{x}}\mathbf{h}(\mathbf{x}) \\ \nabla_{\mathbf{x}}\mathbf{h}(\mathbf{x})^T & 0_{k,k} \end{pmatrix} \begin{pmatrix} \Delta \mathbf{x} \\ \boldsymbol{\lambda}^+ \end{pmatrix} = - \begin{pmatrix} \nabla_x o(\mathbf{x}) \\ \mathbf{h}(\mathbf{x}) \end{pmatrix}. \quad (4.3)$$

It is apparent that any implementation of this algorithm must be able to evaluate the Hessian matrices $\nabla^2_{xx}(o(\mathbf{x}))$ and $\nabla^2_{xx}(\boldsymbol{\lambda} \cdot \mathbf{h}(\mathbf{x}))$ as well as the transposed Jacobian $\nabla_{\mathbf{x}} \mathbf{h}$ of $\mathbf{h}$. Since o is, in our case, a quite complex composition of multi-dimensional functions, it is not feasible to compute the exact Hessian. Instead, it is common practice to use one of several well-known approximation schemes to the Hessian. The next section is dedicated to the discussion of several possibilities to compute function derivatives, and the theory behind second-order derivative approximation will be discussed in Section 4.2.

After evaluation of the required derivatives, the QP system (4.3) is solved repeatedly until convergence. For increased robustness of this process, we add a damping term $\mu \mathbf{I}$ to the Hessian of the system. This method is well-known in the context of Levenberg-Marquardt optimization and can be applied to the SQP method as well. The equation system itself is then solved by employing a sparse Cholesky transformation on the whole system. The efficient Eigen library for Linear Algebra[1] is used to handle this. Finally, when a solution to the system has been found, a simple step size search according to the Armijo rule is performed.

We have mentioned in the introduction that we are exploiting a certain modular structure of optimization problems. After our introduction of the basic theory of equality-constrained SQP, we are now

---

[1] http://eigen.tuxfamily.org/

4. EFFICIENT AND FLEXIBLE NONLINEAR OPTIMIZATION

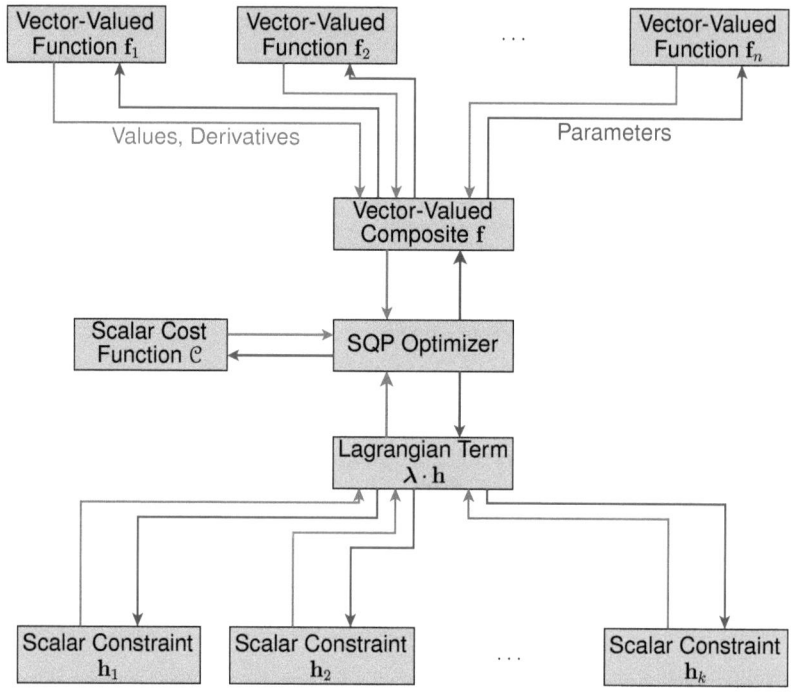

Figure 4.1: Overview of the Optimization System: The SQP optimization module interacts directly with three modules: The cost function module, a composite function module, and a Lagrangian term module. The composite function module and the Lagrangian term module themselves interact with other modules.

ready to present an overview of the structure of our framework in Figure 4.1.

4.2 On Computation of Hessian Matrices

Usually, the computation of the full Hessian of the objective function is a quite complex problem, and is avoided for this reason. Instead of performing the full computation, the Hessian is then approximated using an approximation scheme, such as the Gauß-Newton approximation. More accurate approximation schemes are also available,

4.2 On Computation of Hessian Matrices

such as the ESM method proposed by Malis [50].

In this section, we will discuss some basics concerning the full computation of Hessian matrices, as well as the Gauß-Newton approximation scheme. Finally, we are going to explain the approximation scheme used in our implementation, which uses the full Hessian of the cost function $\mathcal{C}$, but only first-order derivatives of the function $\mathbf{f}$.

4.2.1 Full Computation

While computation of the full Hessian is commonly avoided in practice, we will discuss some basic aspects of full Hessian computation here in preparation for discussing the approximation methods. More specifically, we will consider compositional functions, and there are two cases we are going to investigate:

1. The composition of a scalar function $\mathcal{C} : \mathbb{R}^m \to \mathbb{R}^1$ (which is, in our applications, the cost function) with a general multi-dimensional function $\mathbf{f} : \mathbb{R}^n \to \mathbb{R}^m$.

2. The composition of two multi-dimensional functions $\mathbf{g} : \mathbb{R}^m \to \mathbb{R}^l, \mathbf{f} : \mathbb{R}^n \to \mathbb{R}^m$. In that case, we are interested in the Hessian matrices of the components $g_i(\mathbf{f}(\mathbf{x}))$ of the composite.

The first-order derivatives are easily determined for both cases. The gradient of the composite function in the first case is computed according to the chain rule as

$$\nabla_{\mathbf{x}} \mathcal{C}(\mathbf{f}(\mathbf{x})) = \mathbf{J}_{\mathbf{f}}^T(\mathbf{x}) \cdot \nabla_{\mathbf{f}(\mathbf{x})} \mathcal{C}(\mathbf{f}(\mathbf{x})). \quad (4.4)$$

For the second case, the gradient of the i-th component of $\mathbf{g} \circ \mathbf{f}$ can be computed as:

$$\nabla_{\mathbf{x}}(g_i(\mathbf{f}(\mathbf{x}))) = \mathbf{J}_{\mathbf{f}}^T(\mathbf{x}) \cdot \nabla_{\mathbf{x}} g_i(\mathbf{x}). \quad (4.5)$$

4. EFFICIENT AND FLEXIBLE NONLINEAR OPTIMIZATION

Note that we consider the gradient to be a column vector, thus it is technically the transpose of the first order derivative. Computation of the Hessian for the composite $\mathcal{C}(\mathbf{f}(\mathbf{x}))$ can be performed as follows: Consider a function $\mathbf{d}(\mathbf{x}, \mathbf{y})$, defined as

$$\mathbf{d}(\mathbf{x}, \mathbf{y}) = \mathbf{J}_\mathbf{f}^T(\mathbf{x}) \cdot \nabla_{\mathbf{f}(\mathbf{x})} \mathcal{C}(\mathbf{f}(\mathbf{y})). \tag{4.6}$$

It is clear that $\mathbf{d}(\mathbf{x}, \mathbf{x})$ is equal to the function for gradient computation specified in (4.4), thus $\frac{d}{d\mathbf{x}}\mathbf{d}(\mathbf{x}, \mathbf{x})$ is equal to the Hessian of the composite. We can rewrite $\mathbf{d}(\mathbf{x}, \mathbf{y})$ as

$$\mathbf{d}(\mathbf{x}, \mathbf{y}) = \sum_{i=1}^{m} \left[\nabla_{\mathbf{f}(\mathbf{x})} \mathcal{C}(\mathbf{f}(\mathbf{y})) \right]_i \cdot \left[\mathbf{J}_\mathbf{f}^T(\mathbf{x}) \right]_{*,i} \tag{4.7}$$

where the bracket operator is used as follows: In case of a vector, $[\,\cdot\,]_i$ denotes the i-th component, and in case of a matrix, $[\,\cdot\,]_{i,j}$ denotes the element at row i and column j. The asterisk $*$ in place of a row or column index is used to refer to whole columns or rows, respectively. This means that, e.g., $[\,\cdot\,]_{*,i}$ corresponds to the i-th column. Above formula makes it easy to determine the derivatives of $\mathbf{d}$ with respect to $\mathbf{x}$ and $\mathbf{y}$ based on formulas (4.7) and (4.6), respectively:

$$\frac{d}{d\mathbf{x}}\mathbf{d}(\mathbf{x}, \mathbf{y}) = \sum_{i=1}^{m} \left[\nabla_{\mathbf{f}(\mathbf{x})} \mathcal{C}(\mathbf{f}(\mathbf{y})) \right]_i \cdot \mathbf{H}_{\mathbf{f}_i}(\mathbf{x}), \tag{4.8}$$

$$\frac{d}{d\mathbf{y}}\mathbf{d}(\mathbf{x}, \mathbf{y}) = \mathbf{J}_\mathbf{f}^T(\mathbf{x}) \cdot \mathbf{H}_\mathcal{C}(\mathbf{f}(\mathbf{y})) \cdot \mathbf{J}_\mathbf{f}(\mathbf{y}). \tag{4.9}$$

Using the fact that $\mathbf{d}(\mathbf{x}, \mathbf{x}) = \mathbf{d}(\mathbf{x}, \mathbf{x})$, and applying the chain rule, we see that the derivative $\frac{d}{d\mathbf{x}}\mathbf{d}(\mathbf{x}, \mathbf{x})$, and therefore the Hessian of the

4.2 On Computation of Hessian Matrices

composite, is equal to

$$\frac{\mathrm{d}}{\mathrm{d}\mathbf{x}}\mathrm{d}(\mathbf{x},\mathbf{x}) = \mathbf{H}_{\mathcal{C}\circ\mathbf{f}}(\mathbf{x}) = \mathbf{J}_{\mathbf{f}}^{\mathrm{T}}(\mathbf{x})\cdot\mathbf{H}_{\mathcal{C}}(\mathbf{f}(\mathbf{x}))\cdot\mathbf{J}_{\mathbf{f}}(\mathbf{x}) + \sum_{i=1}^{m}\left[\nabla_{\mathbf{f}(\mathbf{x})}\mathcal{C}(\mathbf{f}(\mathbf{x}))\right]_{i}\cdot\mathbf{H}_{\mathbf{f}_{i}}(\mathbf{x}). \quad (4.10)$$

The second case is seen to be analogous to the first case, we merely have to replace $\mathcal{C}$ with g_i. The resulting formula is:

$$\mathbf{H}_{g_i\circ\mathbf{f}}(\mathbf{x}) = \mathbf{J}_{\mathbf{f}}^{\mathrm{T}}(\mathbf{x})\cdot\mathbf{H}_{g_i}(\mathbf{f}(\mathbf{x}))\cdot\mathbf{J}_{\mathbf{f}}(\mathbf{x}) + \sum_{i=1}^{m}\left[\nabla_{\mathbf{f}(\mathbf{x})}g_i(\mathbf{f}(\mathbf{x}))\right]_{i}\cdot\mathbf{H}_{\mathbf{f}_{i}}(\mathbf{x}). \quad (4.11)$$

4.2.2 Gauß-Newton-Approximation

There are several ways to derive the Gauß-Newton optimization scheme from a regular Newton one. Our derivation is based on the preceding considerations regarding computation of the full Hessian of composite functions. The Gauß-Newton method is restricted to optimizing a sum of squared differences, such that the objective function $o(\mathbf{x})$ can be written as

$$o(\mathbf{x}) = \mathbf{f}^{\mathrm{T}}(\mathbf{x})\cdot\mathbf{f}(\mathbf{x}). \quad (4.12)$$

With respect to our elaboration on Hessian computation in Subsection 4.2.1, the objective is equivalent to a composite of a squared norm function $c(\mathbf{x}) = \mathbf{x}^2$ with the multidimensional function $\mathbf{f}(\mathbf{x})$. We can specialize formula (4.10) to this case as follows:

$$\mathbf{H}_{c\circ\mathbf{f}}(\mathbf{x}) = 2\cdot\mathbf{J}_{\mathbf{f}}^{\mathrm{T}}(\mathbf{x})\cdot\mathbf{J}_{\mathbf{f}}(\mathbf{x}) + \sum_{i=1}^{m}2\cdot f_i(\mathbf{x})\cdot\mathbf{H}_{\mathbf{f}_{i}}(\mathbf{x}). \quad (4.13)$$

4. EFFICIENT AND FLEXIBLE NONLINEAR OPTIMIZATION

The approximation consists then in leaving away the right term in above formula, which is seen to contain the higher-order derivatives. This is equivalent to approximating the objective function via a first-order Taylor approximation, and using the approximation as in the Newton method. The step computation of the Newton method looks as follows:

$$\Delta x = [\mathbf{J_f^T}(\mathbf{x}) \cdot \mathbf{J_f}(\mathbf{x})]^{-1} \nabla_\mathbf{x} o(\mathbf{x}_n). \quad (4.14)$$

Note that the factors of 2 have been omitted, since they cancel out. The approximation

$$\mathbf{H}_{c(\mathbf{f}(\mathbf{x}))} \approx \mathbf{J_f^T}(\mathbf{x}) \cdot \mathbf{J_f}(\mathbf{x}) \quad (4.15)$$

is thus called the Gauß-Newton approximation of the Hessian. The approximation scheme is frequently applied in optimization methods. Nevertheless, better approximation schemes are also available, such as the ESM method proposed by Malis [50]. Such higher-accuracy approximations provide higher convergence rates and at the same time increase the convergence basin, so they should be preferred over the Gauß-Newton type approximation whenever applicable.

4.2.3 Non-Least-Squares Hessian Approximation

When using a cost function different from least squares, the Gauß-Newton approximation scheme, as developed in the preceding subsection, can be adapted to the new cost function. In that case, we stick with the following approximation derived from equation (4.10):

$$\mathbf{H}_{c \circ \mathbf{f}}(\mathbf{x}) \approx \mathbf{J_f^T}(\mathbf{x}) \cdot \mathbf{H}_c(\mathbf{f}(\mathbf{x})) \cdot \mathbf{J_f}(\mathbf{x}) \quad (4.16)$$

Again, this is equivalent to leaving away the higher-order derivatives associated with f, but at least the second-order derivatives due to c are taken into account. This is the Hessian approximation method that we are going to use within our framework.

4.3 Established Algorithms for Derivative Computation

A central problem in the nonlinear optimization methods we are using is the efficient and accurate computation of derivatives (gradient and Hessian) of objective functions. Several methods already exist:

1. Approximation via finite differences.

2. Symbolic Differentiation.

3. Automatic Differentiation.

4. Hand-coded derivatives.

Each of these methods has its benefits and drawbacks, and we shall quickly highlight them here, and argue why we developed our own solution.

4.3.1 Finite Difference Approximation

The most straightforward method is the approximation via finite differences, which is equivalent to evaluating the divided difference term

$$\frac{(x+h) - f(x)}{h} \qquad (4.17)$$

for a $\mathbb{R} \to \mathbb{R}$ function f and small values of h. Some variants exist (using forward, backward, and centralized difference computation schemes), however all of them share very similar properties, with the centralized differences method yielding the most accurate results.

4. EFFICIENT AND FLEXIBLE NONLINEAR OPTIMIZATION

A big advantage of using finite difference approximations is that they are very easy to implement: As long as a routine for evaluating the original function f is available, the derivative approximation can be trivially computed by evaluating formula (4.17).

However, the drawbacks of this method strongly outweigh this advantage. Any of the other methods discussed in this section is more efficient and more accurate than the finite difference approximation, which immediately disqualifies the method for our purposes.

4.3.2 Symbolic Derivatives via Computer Algebra Systems

Another way to compute derivatives is by establishing the symbolic equations corresponding to the objective function in a computer algebra system (such as Maple or Mathematica), and subsequently using symbolic differentiation capabilities of these packages to generate formulas for gradient and Hessian computation.

Another interesting alternative to using these established computer algebra systems would be usage of the D^*-package [51], which is an algorithm that specializes purely in derivative code generation, and produces quite efficient code.

While symbolic differentiation, when applied carefully, is able to produce moderately fast and very accurate derivative computation codes, it suffers from several other problems. First of all, generating the symbolic formulas can take extremely long. We have experienced this problem when generating code using Maple, where in one case the generation of derivative code of a moderately complex functions already took days, where other techniques (namely Automatic Differentiation) were able to compute derivatives within seconds. Furthermore, the produced code is usually not flexible, which often times means that all of the code has to be regenerated

4.3 Established Algorithms for Derivative Computation

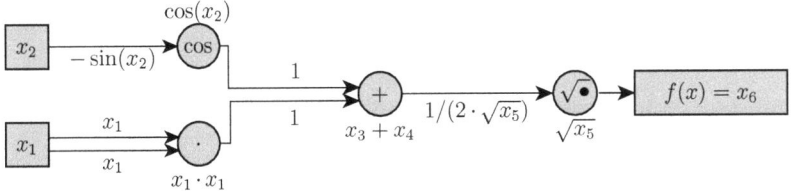

Figure 4.2: Computational graph, complete with derivative annotations on the edges, for the example function $f(x) = \sqrt{x_1^2 + \cos(x_2)}$.

from scratch if some parameters (number of measurements, etc.) of the problem change.

These two problems constitute enough of an obstacle for us to decide against using the method of symbolic differentiation for our algorithms. Even if the code generation performance problem can be tackled, the problem of inflexibility remains.

4.3.3 Automatic Differentiation

The technique of Automatic Differentiation (AD) [52] is known to compute derivatives with both high accuracy and good performance, without requiring any additional implementation effort besides implementing the function f itself. Thus, it is as convenient and easy to apply as the finite differences derivative computation scheme. The basic idea behind AD is that of "recording" every basic operation of a more complex computation in a computational graph. Each of the basic operations (e.g., $\sin, \cos, \log, +, -, \cdot$, etc.) available on standard computers are trivially differentiable, and with extensive use of the chain rule, it is a simple matter to compute the overall derivative of a composite function given the derivatives of these most elemental functions.

As an example, consider Figure 4.2, showing the computational graph of the function $f : \mathbb{R}^2 \to \mathbb{R}, \mathbf{x} \mapsto \sqrt{x_1^2 + \cos(x_2)}$. Every edge represents the flow of one of the values $x_1, x_2, \ldots, x_6$, and nodes

4. EFFICIENT AND FLEXIBLE NONLINEAR OPTIMIZATION

represent elementary functions that perform computations on the incoming values. Temporary results x_4, x_5, x_6 have been introduced. The edges have been annotated with the derivatives of the function nodes with respect to the variable that the edge represents. According to the function graph, the computation would be carried out through the following sequence of assignments:

$$x_3 \leftarrow x_1 \cdot x_1, \quad x_4 \leftarrow \cos(x_2), \quad x_5 \leftarrow x_3 + x_4, \quad x_6 \leftarrow \sqrt{x_5} \quad (4.18)$$

According to the chain rule, the derivative of $f(x)$ with respect to the variable x_i can now be determined by computing the products along all paths from the input node x_i to the output value $f(x)$, and adding those products. In the case of our example, the results would be:

$$\frac{d}{dx_1} f(\mathbf{x}) = \mathbf{x}_1 \cdot 1 \cdot \frac{1}{2 \cdot \sqrt{\mathbf{x}_5}} + \mathbf{x}_1 \cdot 1 \cdot \frac{1}{2 \cdot \sqrt{\mathbf{x}_5}} \quad (4.19)$$

$$\frac{d}{dx_2} f(\mathbf{x}) = -\sin(\mathbf{x}_2) \cdot 1 \cdot \frac{1}{2 \cdot \sqrt{\mathbf{x}_5}}, \quad (4.20)$$

and it is easily verified that these results are correct. Note however that evaluation of the function itself, and thus evaluation of the temporary results x_4, x_5, x_6 is required for this scheme to work.

For scalar-valued functions, the performance of AD is rather good, since the evaluation of a function's derivatives requires time proportional to the time required to evaluate the original function. In the case of computing sparse Jacobian matrices for multidimensional functions, the performance question turns out to be a little more complicated to answer. For these cases, the computational graph typically contains a lot of redundancies, because edges and/or nodes might be used in many of the paths from input to output nodes. Naturally, the computation can be accelerated by identifying re-usable results and computing those results only once.

4.3 Established Algorithms for Derivative Computation

However, this problem is NP-complete in general [53], and a lot of research has been devoted to finding good heuristics [54] for accumulating the values of the Jacobian.

We have tried out the technique of AD for our algorithms, but unfortunately, it turned out that it is not so well suited to our problems. One minor problem is the performance of AD, which is good, but by far not as good as the performance of our own solution. Empirically, we have tested the performance of AD for computing the derivatives of the rigid transformation function, and we have found our own implementation to be about 3 times as fast as the solution using AD.

A more serious problem is that the complexity of the computation graph grows rapidly when large, piecewise defined functions are used. This is the case for our image interpolation function, for which we use a typical bi-cubic interpolation scheme. This leads to very high memory usage, and it also requires a lot of computation time whenever a new image is loaded. For these reasons, we also discard AD as a potential solution to solve our problem of derivative computation.

4.3.4 Hand-Coded Derivatives

Computing derivatives by hand is also a viable alternatives as long as the involved functions do not become too complex. Hand-coding functions is tedious and error-prone, but it is as accurate as automatic or symbolic differentiation, and when done carefully, very likely the most efficient variant. Computer algebra systems typically produce derivative computation formulas that compute derivatives on a per-element basis for vector-valued functions. A human, on the other hand, is capable of computing derivatives at a higher level, recognizing certain algebraic characteristics that result in more ele-

4. EFFICIENT AND FLEXIBLE NONLINEAR OPTIMIZATION

gant and efficient formulae.

As an example, consider computing the Hessian of the following function of type $\mathbb{R}^n \to \mathbb{R}$:

$$f(\mathbf{x}) = \sqrt{\mathbf{x}^T \cdot \mathbf{x}} = |\mathbf{x}|. \qquad (4.21)$$

The gradient and Hessian of that function are:

$$\nabla f(x) = \frac{\mathbf{x}}{\sqrt{\mathbf{x}^T \cdot \mathbf{x}}}, \quad \mathbf{H}_f(x) = \mathbf{I}_n \cdot \sqrt{\mathbf{x}^T \cdot \mathbf{x}} - \frac{\mathbf{x} \cdot \mathbf{x}^T}{\sqrt{\mathbf{x}^T \cdot \mathbf{x}}^3}. \qquad (4.22)$$

These formulas are short and can be implemented very efficiently using optimized computer algebra libraries. The computation of the outer product $\mathbf{x} \; \mathbf{x}^T$ is likely to be much faster than the element-wise computation of the Hessian, which would be the typical solution generated by computer algebra systems. Furthermore, our formula is flexible with respect to the dimensionality n of the domain of f, while formulae implemented using symbolic computation are typically restricted to some fixed size n.

However, for really complex functions, the amount of work involved for manually computing derivatives can be tremendous. Furthermore, the formulas are not very flexible: If one of the functions in the function composition is changed, one would have to recompute all the derivatives from scratch.

4.4 A Modular Approach to Computing Derivatives

Instead of applying any of the methods above directly to the objective function o, we propose a new method that takes advantage of the modular structure that many optimization problems exhibit. The resulting algorithms make heavy use of the chain rule, as is done in automatic differentiation. However, the chain rule is applied on the

4.4 A Modular Approach to Computing Derivatives

higher level of vector-valued functions instead of elementary scalar operations. In our case, such functions would be, e.g., a rigid transformation of a point cloud, a 3D-2D projection, image interpolation etc. Our method combines the flexibility of AD with the speed of hand-coded derivatives. Another advantage of hand-coded derivatives is that they can handle some special function types that are difficult to handle using AD, e.g., piecewise defined functions. This means that we will also be able to deal with the image interpolation function.

In general, the functions we will be optimizing will be functions $o(\mathbf{x})$ that are composed of a number of multi-dimensional functions $\mathbf{f}_i$ and a cost function $\mathcal{C}$:

$$o(\mathbf{x}) = \mathcal{C} \circ \mathbf{f}_n \circ \mathbf{f}_{n-1} \circ \ldots \circ \mathbf{f}_1(\mathbf{x}). \tag{4.23}$$

We will be interested in computing an approximation to the Hessian of o as well as the gradient of o. For notational convenience, we will now define a function $\mathbf{f} := \mathbf{f}_n \circ \mathbf{f}_{n-1} \circ \ldots \circ \mathbf{f}_1$ that represents the overall function composed of all functions $\mathbf{f}_j$. Thus, we can also think of the objective function as being made up of two "modules" $\mathcal{C}$ and $\mathbf{f}$, such that $o(\mathbf{x}) = \mathcal{C} \circ \mathbf{f}(\mathbf{x})$. The function $\mathbf{f}$ is then itself composed of the modules $\mathbf{f}_1, \mathbf{f}_2, \ldots, \mathbf{f}_n$.

The theory behind approximation of Hessian matrices has been discussed in Section 4.2, and we have derived the following approximation scheme:

$$\mathbf{H}_o(\mathbf{x}) = \mathbf{J}_\mathbf{f}^\top(\mathbf{x}) \cdot \mathbf{H}_\mathcal{C}(\mathbf{f}(\mathbf{x})) \cdot \mathbf{J}_\mathbf{f}(\mathbf{x}) \tag{4.24}$$

Note that this computation scheme also naturally suggests the partition of the objective function into parts c and $\mathbf{f}$: If we are able to compute the Hessian $\mathbf{H}_\mathcal{C}$ of $\mathcal{C}$ and the Jacobian $\mathbf{J}_\mathbf{f}$ of $\mathcal{C}$ and $\mathbf{f}$, com-

4. EFFICIENT AND FLEXIBLE NONLINEAR OPTIMIZATION

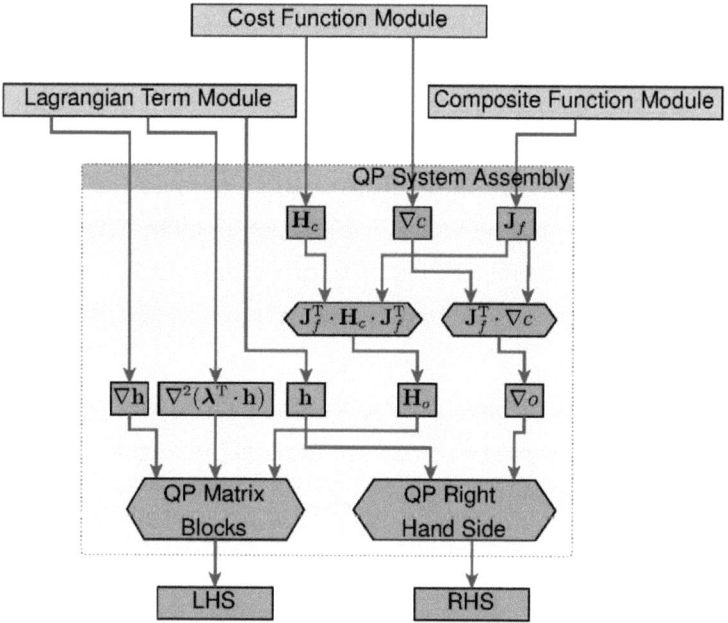

Figure 4.3: Schematic overview of the information flow and steps involved in assembling the QP system. Yellow blocks represent modules, blue blocks symbolize computation results or sub-results. Actual computational steps are represented by green blocks.

puting the approximation to H_o is a simple matter.

Now that we have given a hint at our approach of partitioning the optimization problem into modules, let us consider the problem of assembling the QP system from Equation (4.3). The left hand side matrix is put together by combining various derivatives into a block matrix, and the right hand side vector contains the gradient of the objective function and the value of the constraints function h. A schematic overview of the process is shown in Figure 4.3.

This schematic overview shows how the partitioning approach fits in with the problem of preparing the QP system: A Lagrangian term module provides functionality to compute the values of h and its derivatives, a cost function implements computation of value, gra-

4.4 A Modular Approach to Computing Derivatives

dient and Hessian of C, and the composite function module is in charge of computing the value and Jacobian of f.

Note that the composite function module and the Lagrangian term module are themselves containers for other modules. While the composite function module contains the sub-functions f_i and embodies the function f, the Lagrangian term module contains the components of h, which are $h_1, h_2, \ldots, h_k$, where k is the number of constraints.

This partitioning scheme is applicable only to optimization problems that are of the structure described in Equation (4.23), and for which the Hessian approximation scheme (4.24) is applicable and yields good results. This is certainly a restriction of the proposed method, however, it is still very useful for solving many problems, and it is especially well suited for implementing the BA algorithms discussed in this work.

Now that we have explained the most basic ideas of our modular approach, we can describe the architecture of our framework in more detail. The SQP optimizer module interacts directly with the following three types of modules:

1. Modules representing vector-valued functions with multidimensional domain and range. The functionality provided by this type of module are the evaluation of the function value and computation of its Jacobian.

2. Modules implementing scalar functions with multi-dimensional domain and one-dimensional range. Such modules can evaluate their function value, compute their function gradient, and compute their sparse Hessian.

3. The Lagrangian term module: It represents an equality constraint h as a collection of scalar functions. When looking

4. EFFICIENT AND FLEXIBLE NONLINEAR OPTIMIZATION

at the QP problem (4.3), it is evident that the following functionality is required: Evaluation of $\mathbf{h}$, computation of the constraint Jacobian $(\nabla \mathbf{h})^T = \mathbf{J_h}$, and calculation of the Hessian $\nabla^2(\boldsymbol{\lambda}^T \cdot \mathbf{h})$.

In our C++-implementation, the first two module types exist as abstract base classes, while the actual implementation of any mathematical function would be derived from one of these base classes. The base classes thereby force the user to implement the required functionality of function evaluation and derivative computation.

The Lagrangian term module is not an abstract class, but a separate module that is derived from the scalar function base class. It is a container for scalar functions. Since it adds some very specific functionality to the scalar function base class and plays a specific role in our framework, it is listed separately here.

4.4.1 An Example: Feature-Based Bundle Adjustment

Let us demonstrate the partitioning approach on the simple example of feature-based bundle adjustment. Applying our scheme to this problem is straightforward, since the objective function ^{F}E is very simple. While there are several possibilities, we decide to use the decomposition

$$^{F}E_{\mathcal{C}} = \mathcal{C} \circ \mathbf{f}_2 \circ \mathbf{f}_1, \qquad (4.25)$$

where $\mathcal{C}$ is the cost function, $\mathbf{f}_2$ would be the function performing the projective transformation of a point cloud, and $\mathbf{f}_1$ would be the function performing the rigid transformation of a point cloud of M

4.4 A Modular Approach to Computing Derivatives

points to N camera views. The function f_1 could be defined as

$$f_1(a, b) = \text{vec} \begin{pmatrix} T(a_1, b_1) & T(a_2, b_1) & \cdots & T(a_N, b_1) \\ T(a_1, b_2) & T(a_2, b_2) & \cdots & T(a_N, b_2) \\ \vdots & \vdots & \ddots & \vdots \\ T(a_1, b_M) & T(a_2, b_M) & \cdots & T(a_N, b_M) \end{pmatrix}, \quad (4.26)$$

where $\text{vec}(\bullet)$ denotes the vectorization of matrices, which is a stacking of the columns of a matrix into one vector. The function f_2 then performs the 3D-2D projection, taking a vector x of $N \cdot M$ 3D points as input. Letting x_i denote the i-th point contained in that vector, the function is defined as

$$f_2(x) = \begin{pmatrix} \pi(K \cdot x_1) \\ \pi(K \cdot x_2) \\ \cdots \\ \pi(K \cdot x_{N \cdot M}) \end{pmatrix}. \quad (4.27)$$

The cost function $\mathcal{C}$ takes as input a vector y of $N \cdot M$ 2D points, which consists of a stack of $N \cdot M$ 2D vectors. Using a regular least-squares cost, as in (2.7), it would then be defined as

$$\mathcal{C}(y) = \sum_{i=1}^{N} \sum_{j=1}^{M} v_{i,j} \left(y_{i,j} - p_{i,j} \right)^2, \quad (4.28)$$

where $y_{i,j}$ is the transformed, projected version of point b_j under camera parameter a_i.

We are, however, not finished yet, because we also need an equality constraint to fix the length of the quaternions a_q to 1. For each quaternion, there will be a component in h enforcing its length. Thus, $h(a, b)$ is a N-dimensional vector, where N is the number of

4. EFFICIENT AND FLEXIBLE NONLINEAR OPTIMIZATION

views. We can define $\mathbf{h}$ by defining its components $\mathbf{h}_i$ as

$$\mathbf{h}_i(\mathbf{a}, \mathbf{b}) = 1 - \mathbf{a}_q^2. \tag{4.29}$$

It is easily verified that $\mathbf{h} = 0$ holds if and only if all quaternions have unit size.

Overall, the structure of a compositional systems describing an objective function can be visualized well using a graph, similar to the computation graph shown in Figure 4.2. We will, however, be using graphs whose function nodes contain only informal descriptions of the contained functions, and we will also introduce additional nodes for parameters and intermediate results in order to make the structure easier to understand. An example for such a graph is shown in Figure 4.4.

As for actual optimization algorithms realized using our framework, Algorithm 4.1 shows pseudo-code for implementation of the feature-based BA explained above. While this example is extremely simple, it already shows the typical steps necessary for setting up the framework:

1. Create vector-valued function objects.

2. Create composite function object from vector-valued objects.

3. Create a cost function object.

4. Create equality constraint function objects.

5. Create a Lagrange term object from the equality constraints.

6. Create the SQP optimizer.

After these steps have been performed, the SQP optimizer can be run as often as needed. In the case of new sensor data arriving,

4.4 A Modular Approach to Computing Derivatives

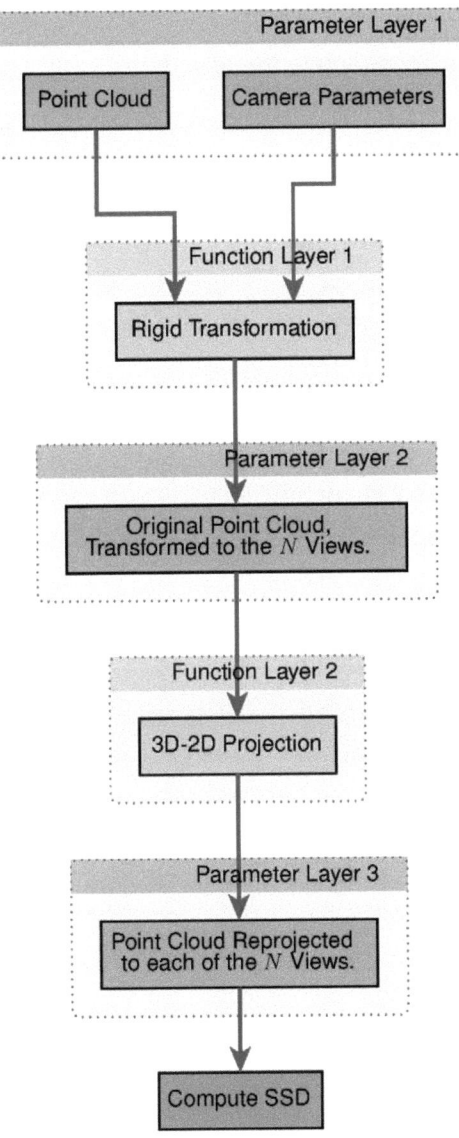

Figure 4.4: Computational graph of classic bundle adjustment. Yellow nodes are function nodes, and blue nodes correspond to intermediate results.

4. EFFICIENT AND FLEXIBLE NONLINEAR OPTIMIZATION

e.g., the data can be sent to the object it concerns via a custom method call, and the SQP optimizer can be run again to update the current estimate according to the new data.

Analysis of the Example: The Composite Function as Essential Building Block
The functions defined for the feature-based BA example would be classified in our framework as follows: f_1 and f_2 clearly are vector-valued functions, while $\mathcal{C}$ is a scalar function, and h would be implemented using a Lagrangian term module. Looking again at Figure 4.3, we see however that we actually need to compute the Jacobian of the function $\mathbf{f} = \mathbf{f}_2 \circ \mathbf{f}_1$. Within our framework, there is a special kind of vector-valued function module that implements such compositional functions. It internally contains arbitrary collections of vector-valued functions, and acts externally as the composition of those functions would.

This compositional function module is a very essential part of the framework. It allows the user to partition complex multi-dimensional functions into smaller parts that are managed more easily. Without the compositional function module, our framework would be restricted to using hand-coded derivatives only, and nothing would have been gained.

Implementation-wise, it is very convenient if the composite function module behaves exactly like a regular vector-valued function module. That way, a composite will be able to contain other composite functions. Furthermore, it can be exchanged for a non-composite function module if necessary, so using the composite function module is not mandatory. In our C++-based implementation, we have used the composite design pattern [55] to implement this behaviour.

4.4 A Modular Approach to Computing Derivatives

Algorithm 4.1: Feature-based bundle adjustment, as it could look like when implemented in our framework. Our pseudo-code notation is similar to C++.

Input: Number of views N, number of cameras M, visibility information v, measured feature positions p, initial parameters a, b.

Output: Optimized parameters a, b

```
// Create array containing two vector-valued
    function modules.
```
NonScalarFunction non_scalar_funcs [2];
non_scalar_funcs [1] = **new RigidTransform**(N, M);
non_scalar_funcs [2] = **new PerspectiveProjection**($N \cdot M$);
```
// Create composite function.
```
CompositeFunction comp_function = **new CompositeFunction**(non_scalar_funcs);
```
// Create cost function object
```
ScalarFunction cost_func = **new LSQCost**($N \cdot M, \mathbf{p}, \mathbf{v}$);
```
// Declare array of scalar function modules,
    used to store constraints.
// There will be one unit quaternion
    constraint for each view.
```
ScalarFunction quat_constraint [N];
for $i = 1$ **to** N **do**
$\quad$ quat_constraint [i] = **new UnitQuaternionConstraint**(N, M, i);
```
// Create Lagrangian term module containing
    all quaternion constraints.
```
LagrangianTerm lagrangian_term = **new LagrangianTerm**(quat_constraint);
```
// Create SQP optimizer and provide the three
    relevant modules.
```
SQPOptimizer sqp_opt =
$\quad$ **new SQPOptimizer**(comp_function, lagrangian_term, cost_func);
```
// Perform optimization.
```
sqp_opt.optimize((a, b));

4. EFFICIENT AND FLEXIBLE NONLINEAR OPTIMIZATION

4.5 Basic Modules of our Framework

There are some functions that are not only useful for optimizing BA-related problems, but can be used for optimization problems in general. One example for this is the composite function module, which we have already outlined in the previous section, and are going to explain in more detail here. We will also discuss some other universally useful vector-valued function modules.

There are also some generally useful scalar function modules that we have implemented within our framework, namely various robust cost functions. We will discuss the implementation and the respective benefits and drawbacks of least squares, Blake-Zisserman, pseudo-Huber, and Mutual Information cost functions.

Finally, we will give a specification of the Lagrangian term module, which is essentially a scalar function module, but with some specialized functionality.

4.5.1 Vector-Valued Functions

We have already mentioned the composite function module, which is a very important building block within our framework. But there are other useful functions belonging to the class of vector-valued functions:

- The function stack module, which allows stacking of an arbitrary number of functions on top of each other, such that the resulting function accepts a stack of parameters and returns a stack of function values. It is another function module that implements the composite pattern.

- An identity function module: Sometimes, it is convenient to simply pass through a certain set of parameters, while oth-

4.5 Basic Modules of our Framework

ers are evaluated by some function. This is made possible by combining the functionality of the function stack module with the identity module.

- A module for mapping input values: It allows the user to specify a function that simply copies its input values to specified locations in the output vector. Thereby, it can be used to permute/replicate function values.

4.5.1.1 Compositional Function Module

The compositional function module represents a vector-valued function

$$\mathbf{f} = \mathbf{f}_n \circ \mathbf{f}_{n-1} \circ \ldots \circ \mathbf{f}_1, \qquad (4.30)$$

and it is implemented in such a way that it internally contains objects that represent the vector-valued functions $\mathbf{f}_1, \mathbf{f}_2, \ldots, \mathbf{f}_n$, and behaves like the composition $\mathbf{f}$ of those functions. The functionality that the module needs to implement is, according to our specification, the computation of the function value $\mathbf{f}(\mathbf{x})$ and the computation of the Jacobian $\mathbf{J}_\mathbf{f}(\mathbf{x})$ of the function.

Evaluation of the function value $\mathbf{f}$ is straightforward. We start by evaluating $\mathbf{f}_1(\mathbf{x})$, then we use that result to compute $\mathbf{f}_2(\mathbf{f}_1(\mathbf{x}))$, and so on. In our framework, this is implemented as a simple loop over all function modules $\mathbf{f}_i$ in ascending order, feeding the parameters $\mathbf{x}$ into the first function $\mathbf{f}_1$ and passing the output of function $\mathbf{f}_{i-1}$ as parameter to function $\mathbf{f}_i$ for all other functions.

For computing the Jacobian, we can make use of the chain rule for vector-valued functions. To put this in a concise mathematical

4. EFFICIENT AND FLEXIBLE NONLINEAR OPTIMIZATION

form, it will be convenient to make use of the definition

$$\mathbf{f}_{\circ(i)} := \begin{cases} \mathbf{f}_i \circ \mathbf{f}_{i-1} \circ \ldots \circ \mathbf{f}_1 & \text{if } i > 0, \\ \text{id} & \text{if } i = 0 \end{cases} \quad (4.31)$$

to refer to the composition of functions $\mathbf{f}_1$ up to $\mathbf{f}_i$, and to the special case of an empty composition $\mathbf{f}_{\circ(0)}$, where id denotes the identity function. We can now specify the computation scheme for the composite Jacobian f as

$$\begin{aligned}\mathbf{J_f}(\mathbf{x}) =& \mathbf{J}_{\mathbf{f}_{\circ(n)}}(\mathbf{f}_{\circ(n-1)}(\mathbf{x})) \cdot \mathbf{J}_{\mathbf{f}_{\circ(n-1)}}(\mathbf{f}_{\circ(n-2)}(\mathbf{x})) \cdot \ldots \cdot \\ & \mathbf{J}_{\mathbf{f}_{\circ(2)}}(\mathbf{f}_{\circ(1)}(\mathbf{x})) \cdot \mathbf{J}_{\mathbf{f}_{\circ(1)}}(\mathbf{x}). \\ =& \prod_{i=n}^{1} \mathbf{J}_{\mathbf{f}_{\circ(n)}}(\mathbf{f}_{\circ(n-1)}(\mathbf{x})). \end{aligned} \quad (4.32)$$

Thus, the Jacobian of f can be computed by evaluating a chain product of Jacobian matrices of the functions $\mathbf{f}_i$. Since all the Jacobian matrices are sparse matrices, this is, at first sight, bad news performance-wise, because computation of sparse-sparse matrix products is known to be a quite inefficient operation. However, we have made an effort to remedy the situation by applying the following techniques:

- The order of evaluating the matrix products can make a tremendous difference in evaluation performance: It is well possible that the evaluation of $(\mathbf{A} \cdot \mathbf{B}) \cdot \mathbf{C}$ has a dramatically different count of multiplication operations than computation of $\mathbf{A} \cdot (\mathbf{B} \cdot \mathbf{C})$. This observation leads to the problem of optimal matrix chain product bracketing [56]. In the context of automatic differentiation, it has been shown that the approach of computing Jacobians as sparse, optimally bracketed chained products is very effective [57].

4.5 Basic Modules of our Framework

- Since the sparsity structure of the Jacobians is static, we can pre-compute the sparsity structures of the result matrices, and we can also pre-compute lists of indices of elements to be multiplied and added. Performing a sparse-sparse matrix product is then reduced to executing a prepared list of multiplications and additions, which is a lot faster than carrying out a general sparse-sparse product.

The problem of computing an optimal bracketing of a matrix chain product can be solved by applying a well-known dynamic programming algorithm [56, p. 331-338]. To give the reader an idea of the computational savings that are possible consider the following example: Suppose A is a 10×30 matrix, B is a 30×5 matrix, and C is a 5×60 matrix, and all of these matrices are dense. Then:

- $(A \cdot B) \cdot C$ takes $(10 \cdot 30 \cdot 5) + (10 \cdot 5 \cdot 60) = 1500 + 3000 = 4500$ multiplications.

- $A \cdot (B \cdot C)$ takes $(30 \cdot 5 \cdot 60) + (10 \cdot 30 \cdot 60) = 9000 + 18000 = 27000$ multiplications.

This observation generalizes to sparse chain products, and the adaptation of the dynamic programming algorithm to the case of sparse matrices is straightforward: The dynamic programming algorithm uses a certain formula to evaluate the cost of matrix-matrix products, and this is the only thing that needs to be changed. Generally, the cost of performing a matrix-matrix product can be evaluated by determining the number of multiplications that need to be carried out in the evaluation. In the case of dense matrix-matrix products, the cost of multiplying a $n \times m$ matrix with a $m \times k$ matrix would thus be $n \cdot m \cdot k$.

For sparse matrices however, the number of multiplications required for evaluating a matrix-matrix product depends on the spar-

4. EFFICIENT AND FLEXIBLE NONLINEAR OPTIMIZATION

sity structure of those matrices. Let $\mathcal{S}$ denote an operator that maps a sparse matrix to its sparsity structure, which is represented as a 0-1 matrix. Consider matrices $\mathbf{A}$, $\mathbf{B}$ with sparsity structures

$$\mathcal{S}(\mathbf{A}) = \begin{pmatrix} 1 & 1 & 0 \\ 1 & 1 & 1 \\ 0 & 1 & 1 \end{pmatrix}, \quad \mathcal{S}(\mathbf{B}) = \begin{pmatrix} 1 & 1 & 0 \\ 0 & 0 & 1 \\ 1 & 0 & 1 \end{pmatrix}. \qquad (4.33)$$

The cost of multiplying $\mathbf{A}$ and $\mathbf{B}$ can be determined by calculating the product $\mathcal{S}(\mathbf{A}) \cdot \mathcal{S}(\mathbf{B})$, and summing up all entries of the resulting matrix. This can be explained as follows: First of all, we note that the product of both sparsity matrices would be

$$\mathcal{S}(\mathbf{A}) \cdot \mathcal{S}(\mathbf{B}) = \begin{pmatrix} 1 & 1 & 1 \\ 2 & 1 & 2 \\ 1 & 0 & 2 \end{pmatrix}, \qquad (4.34)$$

and it is easily verified that each entry of the product matrix contains the number of multiplications that is needed to compute that entry. It is clear then that, by summing up all entries, we compute the total number of multiplications that are needed to evaluate the matrix product. In general, this can be expressed in a concise mathematical form as

$$\mathbf{1}_n^T \cdot \mathcal{S}(\mathbf{A}) \cdot \mathcal{S}(\mathbf{B}) \cdot \mathbf{1}_k, \qquad (4.35)$$

if the matrix dimensions are again $n \times m$ for $\mathbf{A}$ and $m \times k$ for $\mathbf{B}$. By replacing the cost evaluation formula in the original dynamic programming algorithm with this scheme, we obtain an algorithm that computes an optimal bracketing for sparse matrices.

The algorithm for fast computation of sparse matrix-matrix products is quite straightforward, and is best explained using an example, using the matrices $\mathbf{A}, \mathbf{B}$ that have been defined above. The

4.5 Basic Modules of our Framework

sparsity structure of the result matrix C is easily determined as

$$\mathcal{S}(\mathbf{C}) = \begin{pmatrix} 1 & 1 & 1 \\ 1 & 1 & 1 \\ 1 & 0 & 1 \end{pmatrix} \tag{4.36}$$

Whatever the actual values of the non-zero entries of A and B are, the multiplications and additions needed to compute the values of the result matrix C are always the same. They can be stored in list form as follows:

$\mathbf{C}_{0,0}\mathrel{+}=\mathbf{B}_{0,0}\cdot\mathbf{A}_{0,0}, \quad \mathbf{C}_{1,0}\mathrel{+}=\mathbf{B}_{0,0}\cdot\mathbf{A}_{1,0},$

$\mathbf{C}_{1,0}\mathrel{+}=\mathbf{B}_{2,1}\cdot\mathbf{A}_{0,2}, \quad \mathbf{C}_{2,0}\mathrel{+}=\mathbf{B}_{2,1}\cdot\mathbf{A}_{1,2},$

$\mathbf{C}_{0,1}\mathrel{+}=\mathbf{B}_{0,1}\cdot\mathbf{A}_{0,0}, \quad \mathbf{C}_{1,1}\mathrel{+}=\mathbf{B}_{0,1}\cdot\mathbf{A}_{1,0},$

$\mathbf{C}_{0,2}\mathrel{+}=\mathbf{B}_{1,2}\cdot\mathbf{A}_{0,1}, \quad \mathbf{C}_{1,2}\mathrel{+}=\mathbf{B}_{1,2}\cdot\mathbf{A}_{1,1},$

$\mathbf{C}_{2,2}\mathrel{+}=\mathbf{B}_{1,2}\cdot\mathbf{A}_{2,1}, \quad \mathbf{C}_{1,2}\mathrel{+}=\mathbf{B}_{2,2}\cdot\mathbf{A}_{1,2},$

$\mathbf{C}_{2,2}\mathrel{+}=\mathbf{B}_{2,2}\cdot\mathbf{A}_{2,2}$

Obviously, this list can also be determined and stored by a computer program, using simply an array that stores the matrix indices. Performing the matrix-matrix multiplication is then simply a matter of fetching the indices from the list, fetching the values from the matrices, and performing the multiply-add operation.

The performance of this approach is substantially better than that of a generic sparse-sparse matrix multiplication. We have compared the time taken by the Eigen library to compute a general sparse-sparse matrix product to that taken by our algorithm using a prepared multiply-add list, with the result that our algorithm was more than 4 times faster than the general algorithm on a large matrix with random sparsity structure. We have also tried out different degrees of sparsity and different sparsity patterns, but our algorithm

4. EFFICIENT AND FLEXIBLE NONLINEAR OPTIMIZATION

was consistently faster in all cases.

4.5.1.2 Input Map

For some applications, it is necessary to replicate some input data or re-order it. We will call the corresponding function an input map. Such an input map can conveniently be described using a 0-1-matrix. An input map that simply duplicates an input vector of dimension $\mathbb{R}^n$ would, e.g., be described by a matrix stack of two identity matrices of size n, since

$$\begin{pmatrix} \mathbf{I}_n \\ \mathbf{I}_n \end{pmatrix} \cdot \mathbf{x} = \begin{pmatrix} \mathbf{x} \\ \mathbf{x} \end{pmatrix}. \tag{4.37}$$

Another simple example is an input map that reverts a vector. It is described by a mirrored identity matrix, because

$$\begin{pmatrix} 0 & \cdots & 0 & 1 \\ \vdots & \cdot^{\cdot^\cdot} & \cdot^{\cdot^\cdot} & 0 \\ 0 & \cdot^{\cdot^\cdot} & \cdot^{\cdot^\cdot} & \vdots \\ 1 & 0 & \cdots & 0 \end{pmatrix} \cdot \begin{pmatrix} \mathbf{x}_1 \\ \mathbf{x}_2 \\ \vdots \\ \mathbf{x}_n \end{pmatrix} = \begin{pmatrix} \mathbf{x}_n \\ \mathbf{x}_{n-1} \\ \vdots \\ \mathbf{x}_1 \end{pmatrix}. \tag{4.38}$$

Generally, an input mapping function $\mathbf{f}$ is described by some sparse matrix $\mathbf{M}$, and the function evaluation is done simply by evaluating a sparse-dense matrix-vector product:

$$\mathbf{f}(\mathbf{x}) = \mathbf{M} \cdot \mathbf{x}. \tag{4.39}$$

The Jacobian of that function is obviously the matrix $\mathbf{M}$ itself.

4.5.1.3 Function Stack

The function stack module is another module that is a container for vector-valued functions. Let those functions be denoted as $\mathbf{f}_i$, and

4.5 Basic Modules of our Framework

let the domain and range dimensions be N_i and M_i, such that $\mathbf{f}_i$ is of type $\mathbb{R}^{N_i} \to \mathbb{R}^{M_i}$. Mathematically, the stacked function $\mathbf{f}$ is then defined as follows:

$$\mathbf{f}(\mathbf{x}_1, \mathbf{x}_2, \ldots, \mathbf{x}_n) = \begin{pmatrix} \mathbf{f}_1(\mathbf{x}_1) \\ \mathbf{f}_2(\mathbf{x}_2) \\ \vdots \\ \mathbf{f}_n(\mathbf{x}_n) \end{pmatrix}. \qquad (4.40)$$

The stacked function $\mathbf{f}$ accepts a parameter vector of overall dimension $\sum_{i=1}^{n} N_i$, and evaluates to an output vector of dimension $\sum_{i=1}^{n} M_i$. Evaluation of such a function stack is quite simple: Iterate over all $\mathbf{f}_i$, and pass the input value $\mathbf{x}_i$, evaluate its function value. Finally, stack all function value vectors into one vector, which will be the function value of $\mathbf{f}$.

The Jacobian of $\mathbf{f}$ is easily seen to be of the following shape:

$$\mathbf{J_f}(\mathbf{x}_1, \mathbf{x}_2, \ldots, \mathbf{x}_n) = \begin{pmatrix} \mathbf{J_{f_1}}(\mathbf{x}_1) & \mathbf{0}_{N_1, M_2} & \cdots & \mathbf{0}_{N_1, M_n} \\ \mathbf{0}_{N_2, M_1} & \mathbf{J_{f_2}}(\mathbf{x}_2) & \ddots & \vdots \\ \vdots & \ddots & \ddots & \mathbf{0}_{N_{n-1}, M_n} \\ \mathbf{0}_{N_n, M_1} & \cdots & \mathbf{0}_{N_n, M_{n-1}} & \mathbf{J_{f_n}}(\mathbf{x}_n) \end{pmatrix}. \qquad (4.41)$$

Despite its simplicity, the function stacking module is also a very important building block within our framework. For this reason, we are going to use a special scheme to done stacks of parameters and stacks of functions in our computational graphs. An example for this is shown in Figure 4.5, and we have already used it in Figure 4.4. Our concept to visualize stacking of parameters is by showing the blue parameter boxes to be part of larger, surrounding boxes (referred to as "Parameter Layer i"), and for visualizing stacked functions, we analogously use light yellow boxes (referred to as "Func-

4. EFFICIENT AND FLEXIBLE NONLINEAR OPTIMIZATION

tion Layer i") that contain the actual functions.

4.5.2 Cost Functions

Real data obtained from feature detection algorithms is subject to a multitude of disturbances: Camera images are noisy and have only limited resolution, and as a consequence, the pixel coordinates returned from any feature detection mechanism will also be noisy. In addition to that, false matches might be generated, producing outliers. In Chapter 1, we have already mentioned that the robustness of bundle adjustment methods strongly depends on the cost function employed. In this section, we are going to discuss several useful cost functions in detail.

First of all, we will give an intuitive explanation as to why the least squares cost function reacts very strongly to errors in the data. The basis for this discussion will be Equation (2.7), which is the least-squares objective function for feature-based bundle adjustment. The results can, however, easily be transferred to the intensity-based cases. Consider a situation where there is one gross outlier in the data set. The quadratic error term

$$(\pi(\mathbf{K} \cdot \mathbf{T}(\mathbf{a}_i, \mathbf{b}_j)) - \mathbf{p}_{i,j})^2$$

grows rapidly, and will take on very large values for that outlier. A solution minimizing the sum (2.7) is likely to neglect the error associated with the inliers in order to reduce the error for that one outlier, causing a significant shift of the optimization result towards the false match.

A mathematically sound explanation for the outlier sensitivity is found via a probabilistic characterization of least-squares minimization. From this viewpoint, the minimization of the objective (2.7) cor-

4.5 Basic Modules of our Framework

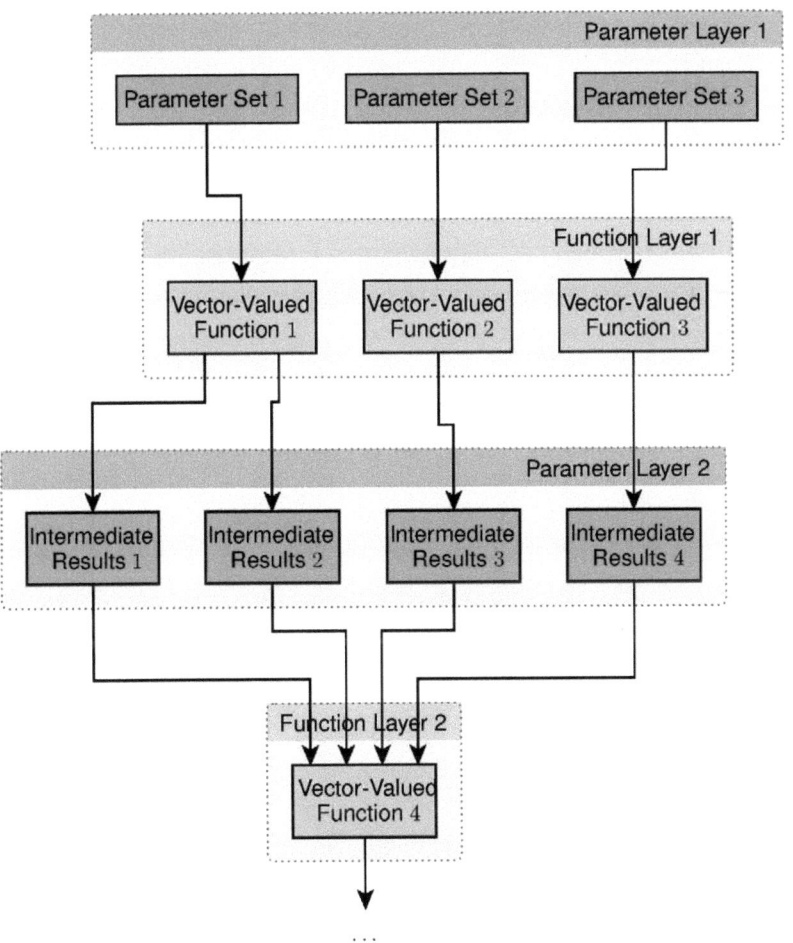

Figure 4.5: Our way to visualize parameter and function stacking: Light blue resp. light yellow surrounding boxes represent parameter resp. function stacking.

4. EFFICIENT AND FLEXIBLE NONLINEAR OPTIMIZATION

responds to computing the maximum likelihood solution for the parameters given measurements that are uniformly affected by Gaussian noise. The assumption of Gaussian noise on measurements is the root cause for the lack of robustness of least-squares estimation: While inliers can be modelled well using a normal distribution, the stochastic behaviour of outliers will not be Gaussian at all.

A number of robust cost functions that are suitable for bundle adjustment problems are described by Hartley and Zisserman [34, pp. 616-622]. Such cost functions aim to address the problem described above by assigning a lower penalty value to outlier terms.

In the following, we consider cost functions $\mathcal{C}(\mathbf{z}, \mathbf{y})$ that assign a scalar cost value to a prediction $\mathbf{z} \subset \mathbb{R}^d$ and a measurement $\mathbf{y} \in \mathbb{R}^d$, as introduced in (2.8). Intuitively, the cost should be small if $\mathbf{z}$ and $\mathbf{y}$ agree, and high otherwise. With $\mathbf{x}$, we denote the parameters of our optimization problem, and $\mathbf{f}$ is the measurement function, such that

$$\mathbf{f}(\mathbf{x}) = \mathbf{z}.$$

Any robust cost function typically depends on an additional parameter, which is the outlier threshold b. The outlier threshold is a value that can be interpreted as the border between inliers and outliers with respect to the error norm $|\mathbf{z} - \mathbf{y}|$. Thus, if the error norm $|\mathbf{z} - \mathbf{y}|$ is bigger than b, the associated value is treated as an outlier, and it is treated as an inlier otherwise.

Note that while these cost functions are discussed here within the framework of feature-based bundle adjustment, they are also applicable to the case of intensity-based bundle adjustment that we will turn to later. Figure 4.6 shows an overview of the cost functions that will be discussed, and Figure 4.7 shows some results of line fitting using different cost functions.

4.5 Basic Modules of our Framework

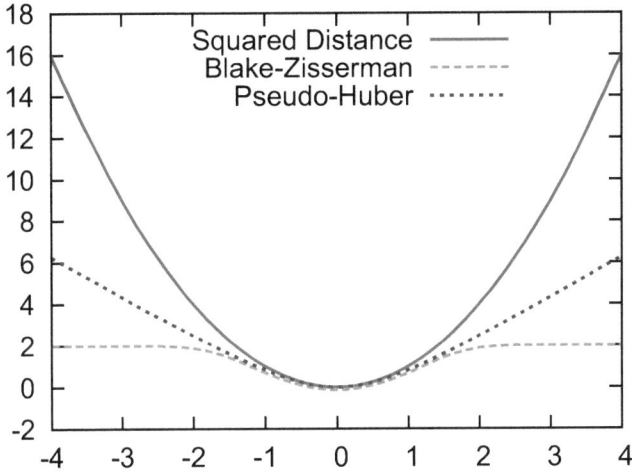

Figure 4.6: Several cost functions.

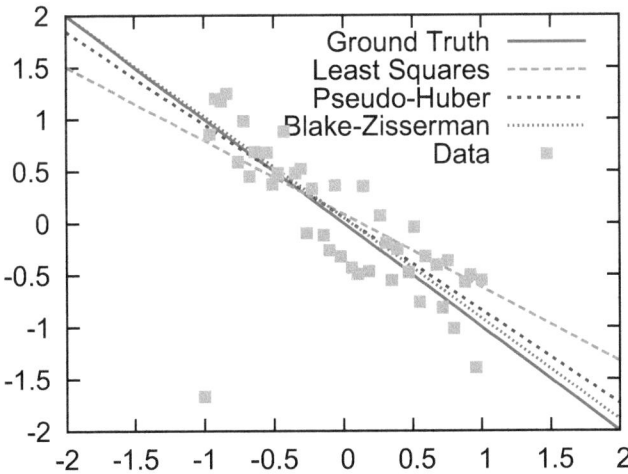

Figure 4.7: Fitting results when using robust cost functions.

4. EFFICIENT AND FLEXIBLE NONLINEAR OPTIMIZATION

4.5.2.1 Squared Differences

The most straightforward cost function is the squared difference measure, which is the one used in the original definition (2.7). It is defined as

$$\mathcal{C}_{\text{LSQ}}(\mathbf{z}, \mathbf{y}) = (\mathbf{z} - \mathbf{y})^{\text{T}} \cdot (\mathbf{z} - \mathbf{y}) = (\mathbf{z} - \mathbf{y})^2.$$

In our experiments, we have found that the least squares cost function is almost unusable for intensity-based bundle adjustment. This is not very surprising, given that the distribution of image intensities differs greatly from a Gaussian distribution.

On the other hand, the property of the squared differences function leading to a maximum likelihood estimate is something that is actually desireable, since the noise distribution of inliers is quite close to a Gaussian distribution. So all of the alternative cost functions seek to preserve this characteristic to a certain degree. This means that the alternative robust cost functions will behave like a squared difference function for inliers, while outliers will be treated differently.

4.5.2.2 Blake-Zisserman

As we have outlined above, the main problem of using the least-squares cost function is its tendency to assign very high penalty values to outliers, thus neglecting the values of inliers that we are actually interested in. For inliers, however, it is usually reasonable to assume a Gaussian noise distribution, for which the least-squares estimation is the best estimator in a maximum-likelihood sense.

The Blake-Zisserman cost function [34, p. 618], [58] is maybe the most straightforward approach to tackle this problem of least squares estimation. The basic idea is to assign a quadratic cost to

4.5 Basic Modules of our Framework

inliers, while a constant cost is used for outliers. Blake and Zisserman [58] have originally defined in a piecewise fashion, such that it would be defined as

$$\mathcal{C}_{\overline{BZ}}(\mathbf{z}, \mathbf{y}) = \min(-(\mathbf{z}-\mathbf{y})^2, b^2) \quad (4.42)$$

when adapted to our notation. However, this function is obviously not continuously differentiable, which is undesirable for continuous optimization problems. It is possible to find a function that is very close to the piecewise function, yet it has continuous derivatives of all orders [34]:

$$\mathcal{C}_{BZ}(\mathbf{z}, \mathbf{y}) = -\log(e^{-(\mathbf{z}-\mathbf{y})^2} + \varepsilon). \quad (4.43)$$

The parameter ε should be chosen as $\varepsilon = e^{-b^2}$. Figure 4.6 shows the resulting function. This is the formulation that we have actually used in our implementation.

Figure 4.7 shows that the Blake-Zisserman cost function actually performs best when trying to fit a line to noisy data. However, it also has one big drawback: It is not convex, which greatly impedes its usefulness when being used in conjunction with non-linear optimization problems. The non-convexity means that the function is likely to introduce local minima, which typically prevent convergence of optimization algorithms to the true minimum.

The gradient and Hessian of this cost function are easily determined as

$$\nabla_{\mathbf{z}} \mathcal{C}_{BZ}(\mathbf{z}, \mathbf{y}) = 2 \cdot (\mathbf{z}-\mathbf{y}) \cdot \frac{e^{-(\mathbf{z}-\mathbf{y})^2}}{e^{-(\mathbf{z}-\mathbf{y})^2} + \varepsilon}, \quad (4.44)$$

$$\nabla^2_{\mathbf{z},\mathbf{z}} \mathcal{C}_{BZ}(\mathbf{z}, \mathbf{y}) = 4 \cdot \frac{e^{-(\mathbf{z}-\mathbf{y})^2}}{e^{-(\mathbf{z}-\mathbf{y})^2} + \varepsilon} \cdot (\mathbf{z}-\mathbf{y}) \cdot (\mathbf{z}-\mathbf{y})^T$$

$$= \nabla_{\mathbf{z}} \mathcal{C}_{BZ}(\mathbf{z}, \mathbf{y}) \cdot \nabla_{\mathbf{z}} \mathcal{C}_{BZ}(\mathbf{z}, \mathbf{y})^T \cdot \frac{\varepsilon}{e^{-(\mathbf{z}-\mathbf{y})^2}}. \quad (4.45)$$

4. EFFICIENT AND FLEXIBLE NONLINEAR OPTIMIZATION

4.5.2.3 Huber and Pseudo-Huber

While the Blake-Zisserman cost function does a good job at reducing the influence of outliers, it also has a property that is very undesirable for smooth non-linear optimization: It is non-convex. This introduces a lot of local minima, and our experiments have also shown that this cost function frequently does not converge to the desired results, unless one is already close to a solution.

A better choice for optimization problems that need to deal with outliers are the Huber and Pseudo-Huber cost functions [34, p. 619]. These functions can be seen as combination between the non-differentiable L_1 norm for outliers with the L_2 norm for inliers. Let b denote the outlier threshold, then the Huber cost function is defined as

$$\mathcal{C}_\mathrm{H}(\mathbf{z}, \mathbf{y}) = \begin{cases} (\mathbf{z} - \mathbf{y})^2 & \text{for } |\mathbf{z} - \mathbf{y}| < b, \\ 2 \cdot b \cdot |\mathbf{z} - \mathbf{y}| & \text{for } |\mathbf{z} - \mathbf{y}| \geq b. \end{cases} \quad (4.46)$$

Since this is a piecewise defined function, it still has one problem: The second-order derivatives are not continuous, which is a disadvantage when applying nonlinear optimization methods. However, the problem can be rectified easily by using the Pseudo-Huber cost function, which has a simple definition and continuous derivatives of all orders:

$$\mathcal{C}_\mathrm{PH}(\mathbf{z}, \mathbf{y}) = 2 \cdot b^2 \cdot \left(\sqrt{\frac{(\mathbf{z} - \mathbf{y})^2}{b^2} + 1} - 1 \right) \quad (4.47)$$

Since we compute the full Hessian matrices of the cost function for our approximation of the objective function Hessian, we prefer this variant over the classic Huber cost function. The function can be seen in Figure 4.6.

4.5 Basic Modules of our Framework

As can be seen in Figure 4.7, the Pseudo-Huber cost function (which performs very similar to the Huber cost function) also leads to reasonable estimates that are closer to the ground truth than the result of using the least squares function. The fit is not as good as when using the Blake-Zisserman function, but in practice, the non-convexity of the Blake-Zisserman function is a much bigger problem.

Computation of the gradient and Hessian of the cost function is not very difficult, but we state the results for completeness:

$$\nabla_z \mathcal{C}_{\text{PH}}(z, y) = \frac{2}{\sqrt{\frac{(z-y)^2}{b^2} + 1}} \cdot (z - y) \tag{4.48}$$

$$\nabla^2_{z,z} \mathcal{C}_{\text{PH}}(z, y) = \frac{2}{\sqrt{\frac{(z-y)^2}{b^2} + 1}} \cdot I_d - \frac{2 \cdot (z - y) \cdot (z - y)^T}{b^2 \cdot \left(\frac{(z-y)^2}{b^2} + 1\right)^{\frac{3}{2}}}$$

$$= \frac{2}{\sqrt{\frac{(z-y)^2}{b^2} + 1}} \cdot I_d - \frac{(\nabla_z \mathcal{C}_{\text{PH}}(z, y)) \cdot (\nabla_z \mathcal{C}_{\text{PH}}(z, y))^T}{2 \cdot b^2 \cdot \sqrt{\frac{(z-y)^2}{b^2} + 1}}$$

$$\tag{4.49}$$

4.5.2.4 Comparison of Robust Cost Functions

A first evaluation of the cost functions discussed previously is provided through Figure 4.7, showing the results of line fitting using each of the cost functions. Fitting has been performed using the LEVMAR package [49] for non-linear optimization. The ground truth line had a slope of -1 and an offset of 0. Noisy measurement data has been generated by adding considerable white noise and some coarse outliers. The result closest to the ground truth was achieved by using the Blake-Zisserman function, the Pseudo-Huber cost function ranks second. The worst result is achieved, as expected, by using the least-squares cost function, which overreacts to the coarse outliers.

4. EFFICIENT AND FLEXIBLE NONLINEAR OPTIMIZATION

However, as we have mentioned earlier, the Blake-Zisserman cost function has a major drawback, which is its strong tendency to introduce local minima as a consequence of its non-convexity. Local minima, however, constitute a major problem, since optimization of functions with local minima is a difficult problem. And indeed, Figure 4.7 shows only half of the truth: The Blake-Zisserman function is a good cost function, but only if one already has a good initial estimate of the actual minimum. If the optimization process is started with a bad initial value, it does not converge towards any usable value at all.

The line fitting problem is a two-dimensional problem, since only the slope and the offset of the line need to be estimated. This makes it possible to analyse the behaviour of the cost functions by plotting the optimization landscape, and the result of this is shown in Figures 4.8 and 4.9 for the Pseudo-Huber and Blake-Zisserman cost, respectively. The x and y coordinates of these images correspond to the slope and offset values, and the color and intensity encode the gradient direction and the gradient magnitude.

The color coding is explained in Figure 4.10, which is an image of a landscape where all gradients point towards the center, and the gradient magnitudes shrink towards the center. This profile represents the "perfect" landscape, assuming that the optimal value is located in the center, since every gradient points directly towards the minimum, and gradient magnitudes only become small in the vicinity of the minimum.

Looking at Figure 4.8, we can see that the profile resembles the reference profile 4.10 very closely, while the profile for the Blake-Zisserman function is drastically different. In particular, it reveals that there are a lot of local minima, as indicated by the black areas surrounding the actual minimum, which confirms our earlier state-

4.5 Basic Modules of our Framework

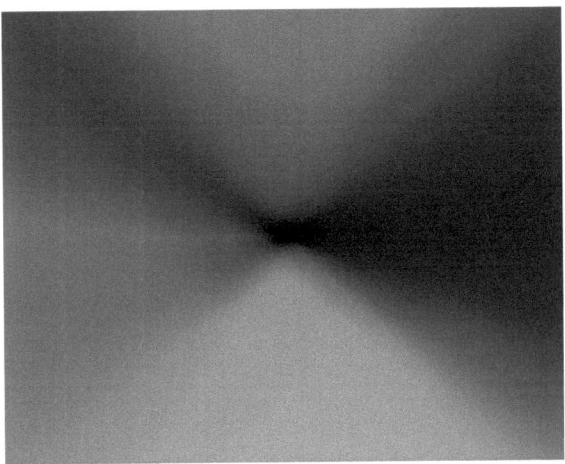

Figure 4.8: Gradient direction (encoded by color) and magnitude (encoded by brightness) for the line fitting problem when using the Pseudo-Huber cost function. Comparison with Figure 4.10 reveals a high degree of similarity to the "ideal" behaviour with respect to convexity.

ment.

Since the intensity-based bundle adjustment problems that we have introduced are non-convex optimization problems even in a least-squares formulation, using the Blake-Zisserman cost function worsens that non-convexity significantly. In our experiments, we made the experience that this cost function is basically unsuitable for intensity-based bundle adjustment. It might still prove useful for refining a solution that is already close to a minimum, and thus it might be applied after an initial fit has been found via the Pseudo-Huber cost function.

4.5.2.5 Cost Functions for Batch Matching

Until now, our discussion of cost functions was limited to the case of comparing two d-dimensional vectors z, y. If we are dealing, e.g., with RGB images, the cost functions would be applied to pairs of

4. EFFICIENT AND FLEXIBLE NONLINEAR OPTIMIZATION

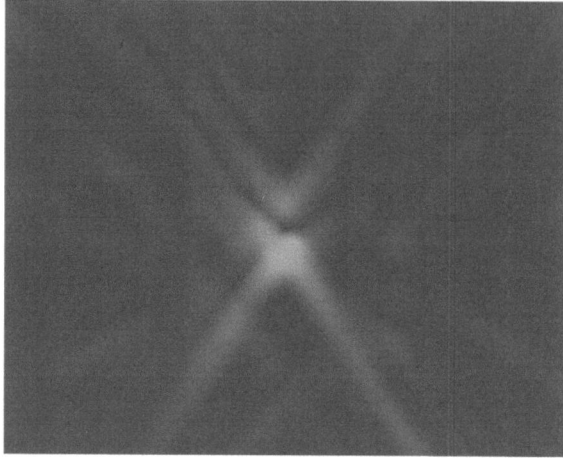

Figure 4.9: Gradient direction (encoded by color) and magnitude (encoded by brightness) for the line fitting problem when using the Blake-Zisserman cost function. The black areas indicate a lot of local minima.

Figure 4.10: Gradient direction and magnitude for a hypothetical cost function that would be optimal in the sense that every gradient points towards the minimum located at the center, and that gradient magnitude becomes smaller as the minimum is approached.

4.5 Basic Modules of our Framework

3-vectors containing red, green and blue intensity values. This does not, however, fit in directly with the architecture of our optimization system, where we expect one vector-valued function f to generate one big vector of measurement predictions whose cost value must be estimated, and the cost function has to work directly on this vector, thus on multiple measurement values simultaneously.

Let us assume now that the reference values y consist of a concatenation of M d-dimensional values, such that

$$\mathbf{y} = \text{vec}(\mathbf{y}_1\ \mathbf{y}_2\ \ldots\ \mathbf{y}_M). \tag{4.50}$$

In the case of intensity-based bundle adjustment, we would have $\mathbf{y}_i = \mathbf{I}_0(\mathbf{p}_j)$. Similarly, assume that the output $\mathbf{z} = \mathbf{f}(\mathbf{x})$ of f is a concatenation of $N \cdot M$ d-dimensional vectors $\mathbf{z}_{i,j}$ with $1 \leq i \leq N$ and $1 \leq j \leq M$, such that

$$\mathbf{z} = \text{vec}\begin{pmatrix} \mathbf{z}_{1,1} & \mathbf{z}_{2,1} & \ldots & \mathbf{z}_{N,1} \\ \mathbf{z}_{1,2} & \mathbf{z}_{2,2} & \ldots & \mathbf{z}_{N,2} \\ \vdots & \vdots & & \vdots \\ \mathbf{z}_{1,M} & \mathbf{z}_{2,M} & \ldots & \mathbf{z}_{N,M} \end{pmatrix} \tag{4.51}$$

where the operator $\text{vec}(\bullet)$ denotes the vectorization of matrices. The value $\mathbf{z}_{i,j}$ corresponds to $\mathbf{I}_i(\pi(\mathbf{K} \cdot \mathbf{T}(\mathbf{a}_i, \mathbf{D}(\mathbf{b}_j))))$ in the basic intensity-based bundle adjustment problem.

Using this notation, we can compute the overall cost associated with vectors z, y as

$$\overline{\mathcal{C}}(\mathbf{z}, \mathbf{y}) = \sum_{i=1}^{N} \sum_{j=1}^{M} \mathcal{C}(\mathbf{z}_{i,j} - \mathbf{y}_j). \tag{4.52}$$

This definition of cost functions is compatible with our framework, and its shape is also familiar from Equation (2.10). Note that the

4. EFFICIENT AND FLEXIBLE NONLINEAR OPTIMIZATION

reference values $\mathbf{y}$ are constant over an image sequence, so $\overline{c}$ will be treated as a function of type $\mathbb{R}^{N \cdot M \cdot d} \to \mathbb{R}$.

The formulas for computing the gradient and Hessian matrix of such cost functions are easily determined as long as the formulas for computing ∇c and $\mathbf{H}_c$ are known. The gradient is then computed by stacking the gradients $\nabla c(\mathbf{z}_{i,j}, \mathbf{y}_i)$ on top of each other, while the Hessian is block-diagonal with blocks $\mathbf{H}_c(\mathbf{z}_{i,j}, \mathbf{y})$ on the diagonal.

4.5.2.6 Another Alternative: Mutual Information

Mutual information is a robust similarity measure based on information theory that is often used for intensity-based matching problems. It has been introduced for visual tracking problems by Viola and Wells [59], where it was shown to be extremely robust to many kinds of perturbations, such as lighting changes etc. We will briefly reproduce some basic theory on mutual information and some details about our specific implementation.

Our optimization framework is laid out for minimizing continuous objective functions, thus we need to use a continuous version mutual information as well. The mutual information of scalar, continuous random variables Z and Y is defined as

$$\mathrm{h}(Z) + \mathrm{h}(Y) - \mathrm{h}(Z,Y), \qquad (4.53)$$

where $\mathrm{h}(Z), \mathrm{h}(Y)$ and $\mathrm{h}(Z,Y)$ denote the entropy of Z, Y, and the joint entropy of Z and Y. Entropy and joint entropy are defined as

4.5 Basic Modules of our Framework

follows:

$$h(p(Z)) = \int_{-\infty}^{\infty} p(Z) \log(p(Z)) \, dZ$$

$$h(p(Z,Y)) = \int_{-\infty}^{\infty} \int_{-\infty}^{\infty} p(Z,Y) \ln(p(Z,Y)) \, dZ \, dY$$

The mutual information is a measure of correlation between the random variables Z and Y. Its value is maximal if the correlation is highest, which means that one of the variables can be perfectly predicted knowing values of the other variable.

Let us assume for now that we are working on single-channel gray-scale images. The random variables Z and Y then represent the intensity values of the reference pixels $\mathbf{y}_i = \mathbf{I}_0(\mathbf{p}_j)$ and the comparison pixels $\mathbf{z}_{i,j} = \mathbf{I}_i(\pi(\mathbf{K} \cdot \mathbf{T}(\mathbf{a}_i, \mathbf{D}(\mathbf{b}_j))))$, where we are using the notation from Equation (2.10). In a discrete setting, we would use a probability mass function to describe the probability of Z and Y taking certain values. Given samples from the images as defined above, such a probability mass function can be approximated very well using histograms of the sample values.

In the our case, we cannot make use of this technique, because histograms are computed using a limited resolution of histogram bins, and such a representation is inherently discrete and thus non-continuous. In these cases, it is a common approach to use kernel-based probability density estimation, such as, e.g., a Parzen window density approximation [60], which has also been applied in the work by Viola and Wells [59]. The basic idea is to approximate the density function via a weighted sum of Gaussian kernels as

$$p(Z) \approx \frac{1}{M} \cdot \sum_{i=1}^{M} G_\psi(z), \qquad (4.54)$$

4. EFFICIENT AND FLEXIBLE NONLINEAR OPTIMIZATION

where G is an appropriate Gaussian kernel with ψ as covariance matrix, and M is the number of samples. The Gaussian kernel typically has the form

$$G_\psi(\mathbf{z}) = (2 \cdot \pi)^{-\frac{M}{2}} \cdot |\psi|^{-\frac{1}{2}} \cdot e^{-\frac{1}{2} z^T \psi^{-1} z}. \tag{4.55}$$

Using the Parzen window estimate, it is possible to specify a formula for continuous approximation of the entropy of a random variable given a number of samples. In our case, we would have M samples drawn from the image values, and we could estimate the entropy associated with the random variable Z as

$$h(Z) \approx \frac{1}{M} \sum_{i=1}^{M} \ln \left(\frac{1}{M} \sum_{j=1}^{M} G_\psi(z_i - z_j) \right) \tag{4.56}$$

From these observations, we derive a MI-based cost function as follows:

$$\mathcal{C}_{\mathrm{MI}}(\mathbf{z}, \mathbf{y}) = \frac{1}{M} \cdot \left(\sum_{i=1}^{M} \ln \left(\frac{1}{M} \sum_{j=1}^{M} G_{\psi_z}(\mathbf{z}_i - \mathbf{z}_j) \right) + \right.$$
$$\sum_{i=1}^{M} \ln \left(\frac{1}{M} \sum_{j=1}^{M} G_{\psi_y}(\mathbf{y}_i - \mathbf{y}_j) \right) +$$
$$\left. \sum_{i=1}^{M} \ln \left(\frac{1}{M} \sum_{j=1}^{M} G_{\psi_{zy}}((\mathbf{z}_i, \mathbf{y}_i) - (\mathbf{z}_j, \mathbf{y}_j)) \right) \right) \tag{4.57}$$

This is our basic formulation for mutual information on gray-scale images. When we are working with multi-channel images, we apply the MI cost function on a per-channel-basis, and add up the results. We omit the formulas for computation of the first and second-order derivatives, as the formulas become quite complicated and lengthy. Results of this can be found in Viola's paper [59], and some results

4.5 Basic Modules of our Framework

on second-order derivatives have been published in the paper by Arbel and Brooks [61].

During our experiments, we have indeed implemented a computation scheme to evaluate the full Hessian of the mutual information cost function. Unfortunately, it turned out that the computational expense for calculation of the Hessian is tremendous, even in a GPU-supported version. While the convergence rate was better using the full Hessian, the overall performance was considerably worse than when using simple gradient descent. We decided not to use the Hessian computation code, and settled for simple gradient descent instead. Note that this can easily be implemented in our framework by using a simple identity matrix as Hessian.

Since mutual information has a reputation of being very robust, we have used it to compare the performance of our light source modeling algorithms against it. It has turned out that mutual information is indeed well suited to deal with images that exhibit uniform brightness changes. However, in the case of a moving light source, the brightness changes are strongly non-uniform, and we were not able to get a reliable reconstruction by merely using a mutual information cost function.

4.5.3 The Lagrangian Term Module

The Lagrangian term module plays a special role within our framework. Mathematically, it represents a scalar function $\lambda^T \cdot h(x)$, so it technically depends on two sets of parameters: The Lagrange multipliers λ, and the parameters x of the function h. The module is itself a container for other scalar functions.

Since the Lagrangian term is a scalar function, one might be tempted to treat it as such within the framework. However, a close look at Figure 4.3 reveals that the Lagrangian term actually needs

4. EFFICIENT AND FLEXIBLE NONLINEAR OPTIMIZATION

to provide some special functionality:

1. Evaluating h, which is actually a vector-valued quantity.

2. Computing the Jacobian of h.

3. Calculation of the Hessian $\nabla^2(\boldsymbol{\lambda}^T \cdot \mathbf{h})$.

These three tasks are quite simple to solve if the gradients and Hessian matrices of the functions h_i contained in a Lagrange term object can be computed.

Evaluation of h is done simply by iterating over the contained function objects and storing their evaluation results in a vector:

$$\mathbf{h}(\mathbf{x}) = (h_1(\mathbf{x})\ h_2(\mathbf{x})\ \ldots\ h_k(\mathbf{x}))^T. \tag{4.58}$$

For computing the Jacobian of h, we can similarly iterate over all functions h_i, compute their gradients, and store the gradient of function i in column i of a matrix. The end result will be the transposed Jacobian of h:

$$\nabla \mathbf{h}(\mathbf{x}) = (\nabla h_1(\mathbf{x})\ \nabla h_2(\mathbf{x})\ \ldots\ \nabla h_k(\mathbf{x})). \tag{4.59}$$

Finally, for computing the Hessian, we note that

$$\nabla^2(\boldsymbol{\lambda}^T \cdot \mathbf{h}(\mathbf{x})) = \nabla^2 \left(\sum_{i=1}^{k} \lambda_i \cdot \mathbf{h}(\mathbf{x}) \right) = \sum_{i=1}^{k} \lambda_i \cdot \nabla^2 \mathbf{h}(\mathbf{x}), \tag{4.60}$$

so that we can again simply iterate over all sub-functions h_i, and add up all Hessian matrices, scaled by λ_i.

5. Modules for Implementing Bundle Adjustment

In the previous chapter, we introduced our framework for flexible and efficient non-linear optimization. However, we did not talk yet about our realization of the intensity-based BA problem stated in Chapter 3 within that framework. This is going to be the main concern of this chapter: We will discuss the details of all the modules that one needs to implement in order to solve our bundle adjustment problems. These modules are essentially implementations of mathematical functions together with their derivatives. In the case of scalar functions, the computation of the gradient and the Hessian are discussed. In the case of non-scalar multi-dimensional functions, we will be concerned with the computation of their Jacobian matrices.

There are three different variants of intensity-based bundle adjustment algorithms that have been realized using this framework, namely:

1. Assuming constant lighting.

2. Assuming a point light source at the camera origin. This is useful when the light source is very close to the camera, and is moving along with it.

3. Using a calibrated light source with non-uniform directional intensity. This can be used in the case of a light source that is not sufficiently close to the camera, and has a non-uniform spatial intensity distribution.

5. MODULES FOR IMPLEMENTING BUNDLE ADJUSTMENT

The different functionality of these algorithms has been implemented within our optimization framework by means of exchangeable modules. This allows for a high degree of re-usability and flexibility. Before we start discussing the separate modules in detail, we will give a schematic overview over each of the algorithms to be discussed herein.

- Surface sampling module: A function that maps a set of surface parameters to a 3D point cloud. Our surface model of choice is a surface induced by an inverse B-spline depth map.

- Surface and normal sampling module: In the variants of our algorithms where lighting is accounted for, it is important to evaluate the surface normals along with the surface points. Mathematically, this is a function that takes a set of surface parameters, and outputs the surface point cloud as well as the normal associated with each point of the cloud.

- Geometry computation module: Performs the rigid transformation of a 3D point cloud to n other frames of reference. It takes as input a 3D point cloud, and n sets of rotation and translation parameters. Rotations will be described as quaternions, and translations via a simple 3D vector, so there are 7 parameters for each view. The output of this function consists of n copies of the original point cloud, each one transformed according to one set of extrinsic parameters provided as input.

- Brightness warping modules: Three modules that compute the brightness warping coefficients for each pixel. Input to the first module is the 3D point cloud together with extrinsic camera parameters and 3D normal vectors associated with each point. The output of that module is used as input to the second module, which performs some intermediate calculations. The third

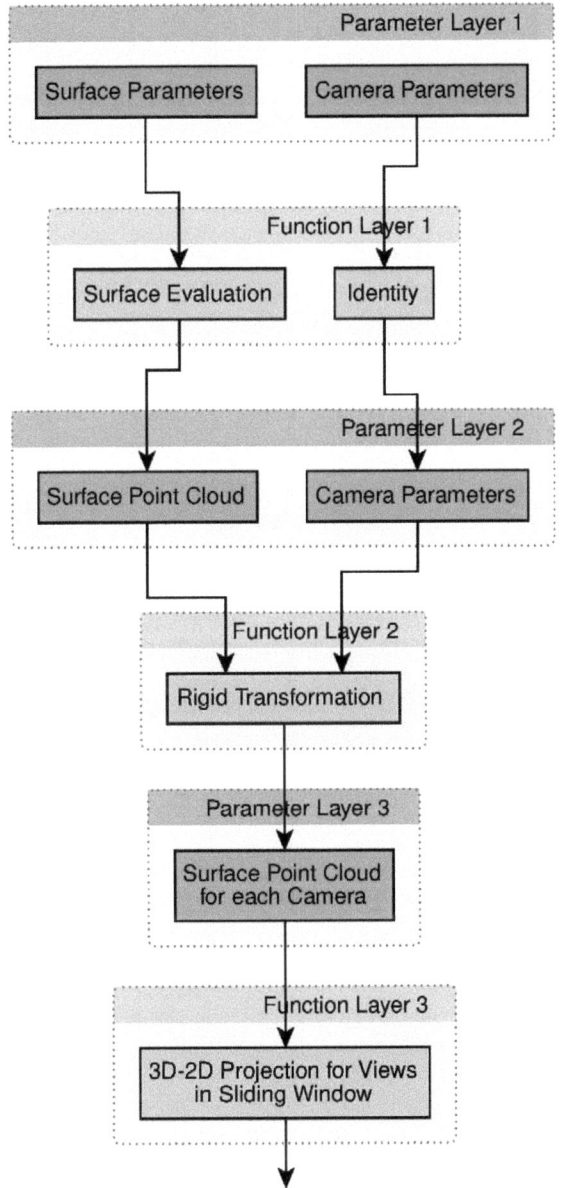

Figure 5.1: Computational graph of the algorithm used for reconstruction and tracking under constant light, first part. Continued in Figure 5.2.

5. MODULES FOR IMPLEMENTING BUNDLE ADJUSTMENT

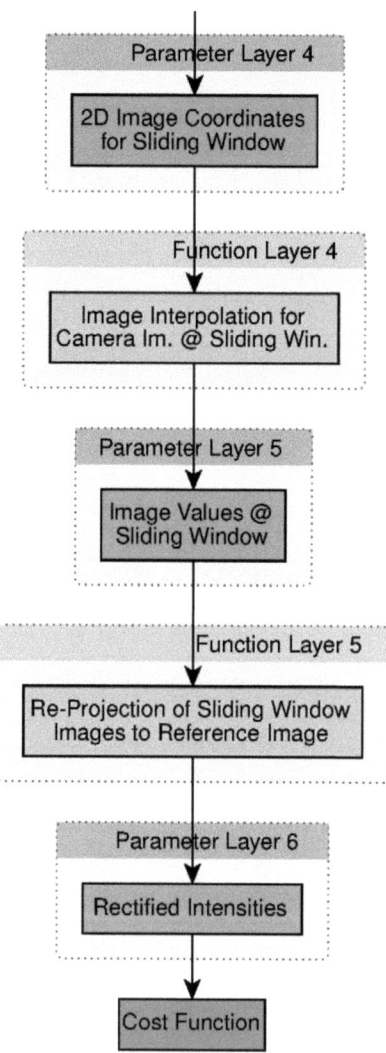

Figure 5.2: Computational graph of the algorithm used for reconstruction and tracking under constant light, second part.

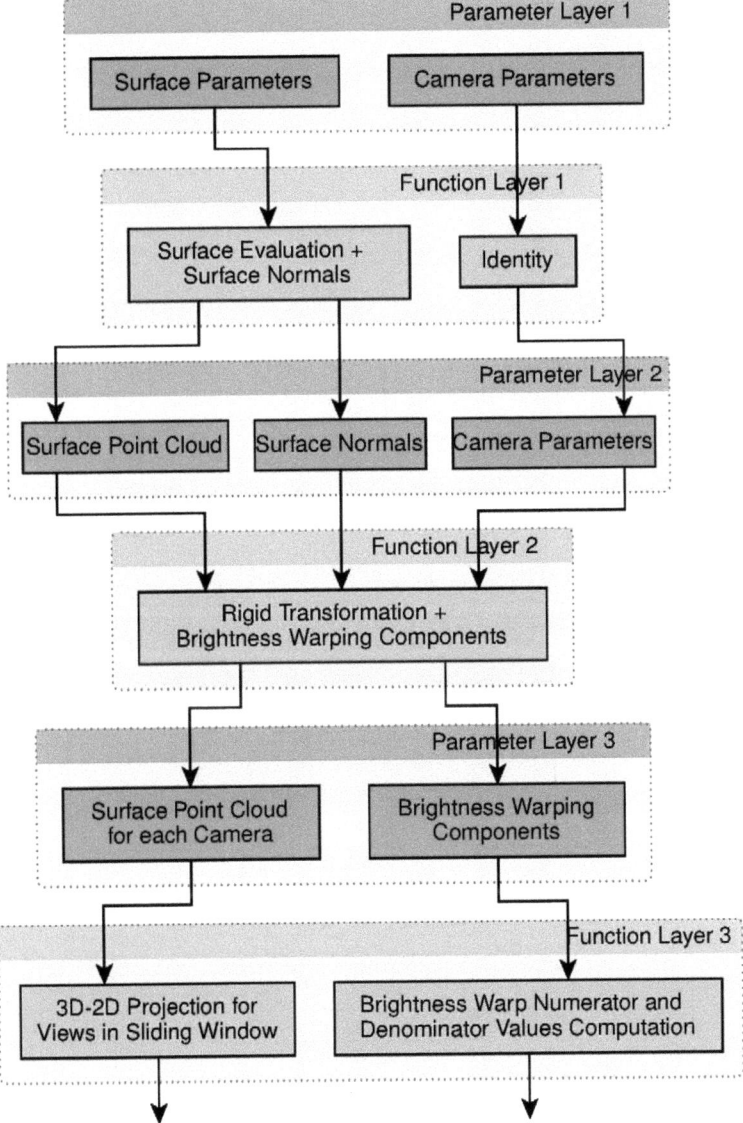

Figure 5.3: Computational graph of the algorithm used for reconstruction and tracking with a point light source at the camera's principal point, first part. Continued in Figure 5.4.

5. MODULES FOR IMPLEMENTING BUNDLE ADJUSTMENT

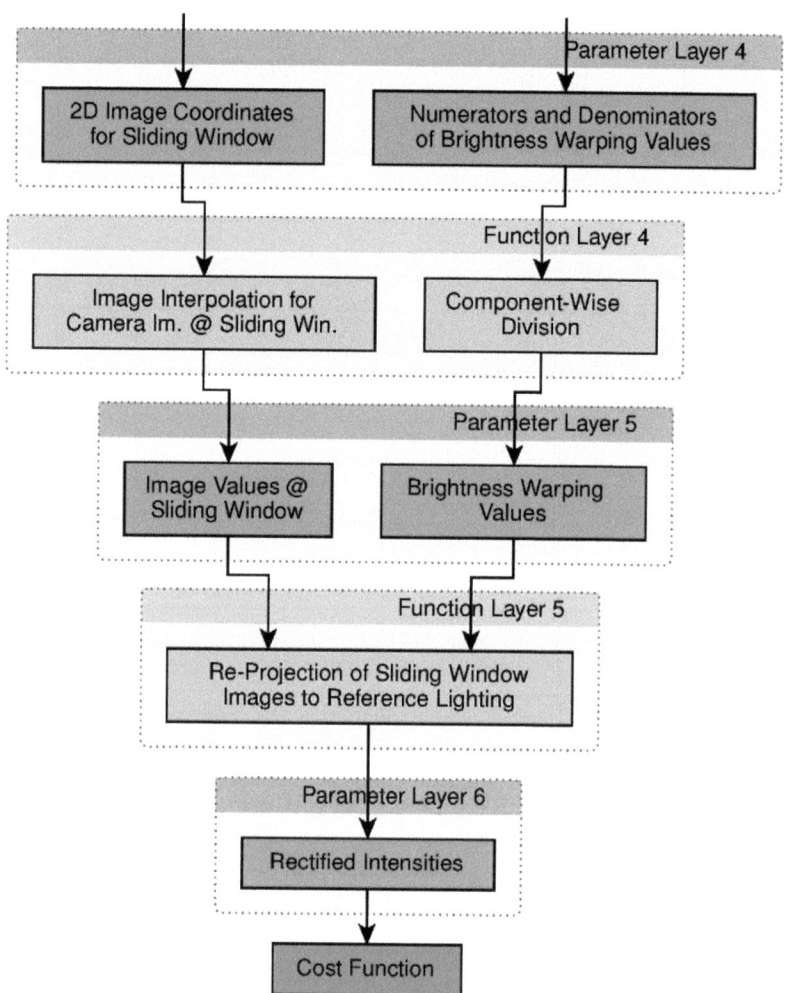

Figure 5.4: Computational graph of the algorithm used for reconstruction and tracking with a point light source at the camera's principal point, second part.

module finally calculates, from the output values of the second module, a vector of brightness warping values that can be used to map the intensity values of some frame i back to the intensity values in the reference frame 0.

- Camera projection module: Takes as input a point cloud, and computes its 2D projection according to a specified camera matrix.

- Image interpolation module: Takes as input n sets of $2D$ coordinates, and interpolates the camera images at the specified image coordinates.

These are the most important functions used for realizing intensity-based bundle adjustment algorithms in our optimization framework. All of the main functions, as well as some smaller helper functions, will be discussed in this chapter.

5.1 Rigid Transformations

As we have discussed in Chapter 1, the representation of a camera is usually split up into intrinsic and extrinsic parameters [34]. The intrinsic parameters describe the projective properties of the camera, while the extrinsic parameters relate the 3D coordinates of points in the scene to the camera's coordinate system. In this section, we will give some details on the aspect of rotation representation for extrinsic parameters.

To specify a rigid transformation of a camera, we need to determine translation and orientation with respect to the scene reference frame. Specifying the translation is straightforward via specification of a three-dimensional vector $t \in \mathbb{R}^3$. When it comes to specifying rotations, however, there are many choices, such as 3×3 ro-

5. MODULES FOR IMPLEMENTING BUNDLE ADJUSTMENT

tation matrices, Euler angles, Axis-Angle representation and many more. We choose to represent rotations by means of unit quaternions, which have a number of desirable properties:

1. They are singularity-free, unlike all three-parameter 3D rotation representations.

2. A quaternion is composed of 4 parameters, which is only one parameter more than needed in a minimal representation, and it is still considerably less than the 9 parameters needed in a rotation matrix representation.

3. Compositions of rotations are performed via quaternion multiplications, which are relatively cheap, yet easy to compute in contrast to some of the other methods.

4. It is quite straightforward to perform spherical interpolation between rotations represented as quaternions.

A drawback of quaternions as rotation representation is that we need to ensure at all times that such a quaternion has unit length. This may or may not be a problem depending on the type of application. We are primarily concerned with optimization problems, where the unity constraint can be implemented easily.

5.1.1 Interpretation of Quaternions as Rotations

The function for mapping a vector of point coordinates $\mathbf{x} \in \mathbb{R}^3$ to a coordinate frame described by translation vector $\mathbf{t} \in \mathbb{R}^3$ and quaternion $\mathbf{q} \in \mathbb{R}^4$ can be computed as

$$\mathbf{T}(\mathbf{t}, \mathbf{q}, \mathbf{x}) = \mathbf{R}(\mathbf{q})^\mathrm{T}(\mathbf{x} - \mathbf{t}), \qquad (5.1)$$

5.1 Rigid Transformations

where $\mathbf{R}(\mathbf{q})$ denotes the 3×3 rotation matrix corresponding to the rotation quaternion $\mathbf{q} = (\check{\mathbf{q}}, q_4) = (q_1, q_2, q_3, q_4)$. In our notation, the fourth component q_4 of the quaternion is the scalar (real) part. To avoid notational difficulties later on, we will use $\hat{q} = q_4$ as another way to specify the scalar component of $\mathbf{q}$. Thus, $\mathbf{q}$ can also be written as $(\check{\mathbf{q}}, \hat{q})$. The rotation matrix corresponding to $\mathbf{q}$ can now be computed as:

$$\mathbf{R}(\mathbf{q}) = (\hat{q}^2 - \check{\mathbf{q}}^T\check{\mathbf{q}})\mathbf{I}_3 + 2(\check{\mathbf{q}}\check{\mathbf{q}}^T + \hat{q}[\check{\mathbf{q}}]_\times), \tag{5.2}$$

with

$$\check{\mathbf{q}} = \begin{pmatrix} q_1 \\ q_2 \\ q_3 \end{pmatrix}, \quad \text{and} \quad [\check{\mathbf{q}}]_\times = \begin{pmatrix} 0 & -q_3 & q_2 \\ q_3 & 0 & -q_1 \\ -q_2 & q_1 & 0 \end{pmatrix}. \tag{5.3}$$

As usual, the operator $[\cdot]_\times$ denotes the conversion of a vector to its corresponding cross product matrix. From this formula, it is also obvious that the inverse (or transposed) rotation matrix is computed through the formula:

$$\mathbf{R}(\mathbf{q})^T = (\hat{q}^2 - \check{\mathbf{q}}^T\check{\mathbf{q}})\mathbf{I}_3 + 2(\check{\mathbf{q}}\check{\mathbf{q}}^T - \hat{q}[\check{\mathbf{q}}]_\times) \tag{5.4}$$

If this representation is to be used in an optimization framework, we are often interested in computing the derivative of above function with respect to parameters $\mathbf{x}, \mathbf{t}, \mathbf{q}$. This is slightly cumbersome, but essentially only a matter of basic calculus. The results are as

5. MODULES FOR IMPLEMENTING BUNDLE ADJUSTMENT

follows:

$$\frac{d\,T(t,q,x)}{d\,x} = R(q)^T \tag{5.5}$$

$$\frac{d\,T(t,q,x)}{d\,t} = -R(q)^T \tag{5.6}$$

$$\frac{d\,T(t,q,x)}{d\,\check{q}} = 2\left([(x-t)\times\check{q} + \hat{q}(x-t)]_\times + \check{q}^T(x-t)\,I_3\right) \tag{5.7}$$

$$\frac{d\,T(t,q,x)}{d\,\hat{q}} = 2\left((x-t)\times\check{q} + \hat{q}(x-t)\right) \tag{5.8}$$

For some applications, we will be interested in the inverse rigid transformation, described by rotation quaternion $q' = q^*$, and translation vector $t' = -R(q)^T \cdot t$. With q^*, we denote the quaternion conjugate, which is defined as $q^* = (-\check{q}, \hat{q})$. It corresponds to the rotation inverse of q. For this case, the rigid transformation would have the specific shape

$$\begin{aligned}T(t',q',x) = R(q')^T(x-t') &= R(q)(x-t') \\ &= R(q)\cdot x + t = T(0,q',x) + t\end{aligned} \tag{5.9}$$

Using this form of the inverse transformation, we can easily determine the derivatives, adapting the results for the forward transformation to the inverse case:

$$\frac{d\,T(t',q',x)}{d\,x} = R(q) \tag{5.10}$$

$$\frac{d\,T(t',q',x)}{d\,t} = I_3 \tag{5.11}$$

$$\frac{d\,T(t',q',x)}{d\,\check{q}} = -2\left([-x\times\check{q} + \hat{q}\cdot x]_\times - \check{q}^T\cdot x\cdot I_3\right) \tag{5.12}$$

$$\frac{d\,T(t',q',x)}{d\,\hat{q}} = 2\left(-x\times\check{q} + \hat{q}\cdot x\right) \tag{5.13}$$

5.1 Rigid Transformations

5.1.2 Quaternions in Multiple View Geometry

Usually, one is not only interested in rigid body transformations of a single point x, but of whole sets of points $\boldsymbol{\xi} = (\mathbf{x}_1, \mathbf{x}_2, \ldots, \mathbf{x}_n) \in \mathbb{R}^{3n}$. Above definitions allow us to formulate this in a concise manner:

$$\mathbf{T}_n(\boldsymbol{\xi}, \mathbf{t}, \mathbf{q}) = \begin{pmatrix} \mathbf{T}(\mathbf{t}, \mathbf{q}, \mathbf{x}_1) \\ \mathbf{T}(\mathbf{t}, \mathbf{q}, \mathbf{x}_2) \\ \vdots \\ \mathbf{T}(\mathbf{t}, \mathbf{q}, \mathbf{x}_n) \end{pmatrix} \qquad (5.14)$$

The derivative of above function w.r.t. $\boldsymbol{\xi}$ is easily derived from earlier formulae. We see that the Jacobian is a block-diagonal matrix with $n \times n$ blocks of size 3×3, and with the rotation matrix $\mathbf{R}(\mathbf{q})^T$ on the diagonal:

$$\frac{\mathrm{d}\,\mathbf{T}_n(\mathbf{t}, \mathbf{q}, \boldsymbol{\xi})}{\mathrm{d}\,\boldsymbol{\xi}} = \begin{pmatrix} \mathbf{R}(\mathbf{q})^T & \mathbf{0}_3 & \cdots & \mathbf{0}_3 \\ \mathbf{0}_3 & \mathbf{R}(\mathbf{q})^T & \ddots & \vdots \\ \vdots & \ddots & \ddots & \mathbf{0}_3 \\ \mathbf{0}_3 & \cdots & \mathbf{0}_3 & \mathbf{R}(\mathbf{q})^T \end{pmatrix} \qquad (5.15)$$

Furthermore, we are also able to specify the form of the derivative w.r.t. $\mathbf{t}, \check{q}$ and $\hat{q}$:

$$\frac{\mathrm{d}\,\mathbf{T}_n(\mathbf{t}, \mathbf{q}, \boldsymbol{\xi})}{\mathrm{d}\,\mathbf{t}} = \begin{pmatrix} -\mathbf{R}(\mathbf{q})^T \\ -\mathbf{R}(\mathbf{q})^T \\ \vdots \\ -\mathbf{R}(\mathbf{q})^T \end{pmatrix}, \quad \text{where } -\mathbf{R}(\mathbf{q})^T \text{ repeats } n \text{ times.}$$

$$(5.16)$$

5. MODULES FOR IMPLEMENTING BUNDLE ADJUSTMENT

We can use the Kronecker matrix product, denoted by $\otimes$, to achieve a more concise notation:

$$\frac{d\,\mathbf{T}_n(\mathbf{t},\mathbf{q},\boldsymbol{\xi})}{d\,\boldsymbol{\xi}} = \mathbf{I}_3 \otimes \mathbf{R}(\mathbf{q})^T, \quad \frac{d\,\mathbf{T}_n(\mathbf{t},\mathbf{q},\boldsymbol{\xi})}{d\,\mathbf{t}} = -\mathbf{1}_n \otimes \mathbf{R}(\mathbf{q})^T. \quad (5.17)$$

Here, $\mathbf{1}_n$ is the n-dimensional column vector $(1,1,\ldots,1)^T$. The Jacobians of $\mathbf{T}_n$ w.r.t. $\check{q}$ and $\hat{q}$ compute as:

$$\frac{d\,\mathbf{T}_n(\mathbf{t},\mathbf{q},\boldsymbol{\xi})}{d\,\check{\mathbf{q}}} = 2 \begin{pmatrix} [(\mathbf{x}_1-\mathbf{t}) \times \check{\mathbf{q}} + \hat{q}(\mathbf{x}_1-\mathbf{t})]_\times + \check{\mathbf{q}}^T(\mathbf{x}_1-\mathbf{t})\mathbf{I}_3 \\ [(\mathbf{x}_2-\mathbf{t}) \times \check{\mathbf{q}} + \hat{q}(\mathbf{x}_2-\mathbf{t})]_\times + \check{\mathbf{q}}^T(\mathbf{x}_2-\mathbf{t})\mathbf{I}_3 \\ \vdots \\ [(\mathbf{x}_n-\mathbf{t}) \times \check{\mathbf{q}} + \hat{q}(\mathbf{x}_n-\mathbf{t})]_\times + \check{\mathbf{q}}^T(\mathbf{x}_n-\mathbf{t})\mathbf{I}_3 \end{pmatrix} \quad (5.18)$$

$$\frac{d\,\mathbf{T}_n(\mathbf{t},\mathbf{q},\boldsymbol{\xi})}{d\,\hat{q}} = 2 \begin{pmatrix} (\mathbf{x}_1-\mathbf{t}) \times \check{\mathbf{q}} + \hat{q}(\mathbf{x}_1-\mathbf{t}) \\ (\mathbf{x}_2-\mathbf{t}) \times \check{\mathbf{q}} + \hat{q}(\mathbf{x}_2-\mathbf{t}) \\ \vdots \\ (\mathbf{x}_n-\mathbf{t}) \times \check{\mathbf{q}} + \hat{q}(\mathbf{x}_n-\mathbf{t}) \end{pmatrix} \quad (5.19)$$

When dealing with observations of a set of n 3D points taken with the same camera, but from m different views

$$\boldsymbol{\tau} = (\mathbf{t}_1,\mathbf{q}_1,\mathbf{t}_2,\mathbf{q}_2,\ldots,\mathbf{t}_m,\mathbf{q}_m),$$

we need to further extend above definitions as follows:

$$\mathbf{T}_{n,m}(\boldsymbol{\tau},\boldsymbol{\xi}) = \begin{pmatrix} \mathbf{T}_n(\boldsymbol{\xi},\mathbf{t}_1,\mathbf{q}_1) \\ \mathbf{T}_n(\boldsymbol{\xi},\mathbf{t}_2,\mathbf{q}_2) \\ \vdots \\ \mathbf{T}_n(\boldsymbol{\xi},\mathbf{t}_m,\mathbf{q}_m) \end{pmatrix} \quad (5.20)$$

Given the preceding elaboration on derivative computation, it is a simple matter then to infer a computation scheme for derivatives

5.2 The Depth Map Model

of $\mathbf{T}_{n,m}$ as well. The block structure of that matrix is as follows:

$$\frac{\mathrm{d}\,\mathbf{T}_{n,m}(\boldsymbol{\xi},\boldsymbol{\tau})}{\mathrm{d}\,\boldsymbol{\xi}} = \begin{pmatrix} \mathbf{I}_n \otimes \mathbf{R}(\mathbf{q}_1)^{\mathrm{T}} \\ \mathbf{I}_n \otimes \mathbf{R}(\mathbf{q}_2)^{\mathrm{T}} \\ \vdots \\ \mathbf{I}_n \otimes \mathbf{R}(\mathbf{q}_n)^{\mathrm{T}} \end{pmatrix} \qquad (5.21)$$

$$\frac{\mathrm{d}\,\mathbf{T}_{n,m}(\boldsymbol{\xi},\boldsymbol{\tau})}{\mathrm{d}\,\boldsymbol{\tau}} = \begin{pmatrix} \frac{\mathrm{d}\,\mathbf{T}_n(\boldsymbol{\xi},\boldsymbol{\tau})}{\mathrm{d}\,\mathbf{x}_1,\mathbf{q}_1} & \mathbf{0}_{3n,7} & \cdots & \mathbf{0}_{3n,7} \\ \mathbf{0}_{3n,7} & \frac{\mathrm{d}\,\mathbf{T}_n(\boldsymbol{\xi},\boldsymbol{\tau})}{\mathrm{d}\,\mathbf{x}_2,\mathbf{q}_2} & \ddots & \vdots \\ \vdots & \ddots & \ddots & \mathbf{0}_{3n,7} \\ \mathbf{0}_{3n,7} & \cdots & \mathbf{0}_{3n,7} & \frac{\mathrm{d}\,\mathbf{T}_n(\boldsymbol{\xi},\boldsymbol{\tau})}{\mathrm{d}\,\mathbf{x}_n,\mathbf{q}_n} \end{pmatrix}. \qquad (5.22)$$

5.2 The Depth Map Model

Common feature-based bundle adjustment methods typically use a point cloud model to represent the reconstructed scene: Every feature is assigned a set of 3D coordinates, and all coordinates are independent of each other. With intensity-based methods, a point cloud representation is likely to cause difficulties, since intensity values are usually not unique, which makes data association practically impossible. Thus, it is desirable to further constrain the scene model, and this is usually done by imposing some kind of shape prior or smoothness constraint on the surface. Typical examples for this technique are planar [62] and non-planar [21, 29, 30] parametric surface tracking methods such as the ones discussed herein.

In this section, we are going to look at some alternatives for representing parametric smooth surfaces, and we will discuss the basics of B-Spline surfaces, which is the representation we have chosen in our implementation. Furthermore, we will discuss some aspects of inverse depth maps, and we will finally show how inverse

5. MODULES FOR IMPLEMENTING BUNDLE ADJUSTMENT

depth maps can be implemented using B-Spline surfaces.

In general, we are dealing with three-dimensional parametric surfaces of the form

$$\mathbf{d} : \mathbb{R}^n \times \mathbb{R}^2 \to \mathbb{R}^3. \tag{5.23}$$

The surface shape is governed by n parameters and the surface function maps surface parameters $\mathbf{p} \in \mathbb{R}^n$ and surface point coordinates $(u, v) \in \mathbb{R}^2$ to three-dimensional coordinates on the surface. In the variant of our algorithm where scene lighting is also taken into account, we will also be interested in computing the surface normals along with the surface values.

As we have mentioned, our surface representation of choice is a bivariate B-Spline model. Still, we shall give a quick overview of other alternatives as well as their advantages and drawbacks.

Generally, one would want the surface model to be sparse in the sense that surface parameters have only local support. This has the advantage that the resulting bundle adjustment equation (2.10) will be sparse and thus feasible to solve. It is well known for feature-based bundle adjustment that the optimization process quickly becomes infeasible for large feature sets if the sparsity of the bundle adjustment equations is not exploited [47].

What would be even worse than the cost of solving dense bundle adjustment equations is the cost of generating a dense Jacobian of the intensity difference function. For a sparse surface model, we would end up with a sparse matrix with $O(m)$ non-zero entries, where m is the number of intensity comparison points. For a dense model, we would need to generate $O(m \cdot n)$ values, which is prohibitively large already for small values of m and n.

The table in Figure 5.5 shows a rough overview over several surface models and their advantages and disadvantages. The rest of this Section is sub-divided into the following parts: First of all,

5.2 The Depth Map Model

Representation	Pros	Cons
B-Spline	Sparse Linear Simple Derivatives	Not very general
Rational B-Spline	Sparse More general	Nonlinear
Radial Basis Functions	Easy interpolation	Dense model

Figure 5.5: Overview of surface representations.

we will introduce B-Spline curves and surfaces, and we will develop some formulas that are relevant for our implementation. Afterwards, we will discuss properties of surfaces induced by direct depth maps and will derive formulas for computation of surface values and surface normals. These formulas will then be adapted to the case of inverse depth maps. Finally, we will combine the formulas for inverse depth surfaces with those for B-Spline surfaces to develop the formulas used in our implementation.

5.2.1 On B-Spline Curves and Surfaces

B-Splines are a well-known parametric model with many applications in computer science. In this Section, we will discuss some aspects of B-Splines that are relevant for our implementation. However, we assume the reader to be familiar with the basic theory of B-splines, as presented, e.g., in [63]. Many different notation schemes are in use for dealing with B-splines, and we will introduce our own notation, which is inspired by the notation used in the documentation of the SISL NURBS library[1].

We start with the formalism for B-spline curves, and we subsequently extend this to B-spline surfaces. According to our notation, the parameters describing a B-spline curve are:

---
[1] http://www.sintef.no/sisl

5. MODULES FOR IMPLEMENTING BUNDLE ADJUSTMENT

- The order k of the curve.

- The number of control points n.

- The dimension d of the domain of the curve.

- The knot vector $\mathbf{t} = (t_1, t_2, \ldots, t_{n+k})^\mathrm{T} \in \mathbb{R}^{n+k}$, which is a non-decreasing sequence of real numbers.

- The control points $\mathbf{p}_i \in \mathbb{R}^d$ of the curve.

- We also denote with $\mathbf{p}$ the vector $(\mathbf{p}_1^\mathrm{T}, \mathbf{p}_2^\mathrm{T}, \ldots, \mathbf{p}_n^\mathrm{T})^\mathrm{T}$ of all control points stacked on top of each other.

- The basis function $_k^i B_\mathbf{t} : \mathbb{R} \to \mathbb{R}$ associated with control point p_i, for order k and knot vector $\mathbf{t}$.

We only consider clamped B-spline curves and surfaces, which imposes the restriction of having k equal knot values at the beginning and end of the knot vector $\mathbf{t}$. Using this notation, we can define a spline curve $\mathbf{c} : \mathbb{R} \to \mathbb{R}^d$ as follows:

$$\mathbf{c}(\mathbf{p}, x) = \sum_{i=1}^{n} \mathbf{p}_i \cdot {}_k^i B_\mathbf{t}(x). \tag{5.24}$$

An example for such a B-spline curve is shown in Figure 5.6. The extension of above definition to a B-spline surface is straightforward:

- The order in first and second parameter direction is specified by k_1, k_2.

- The number of control points in both directions is denoted by n_1, n_2.

- The dimension is d.

5.2 The Depth Map Model

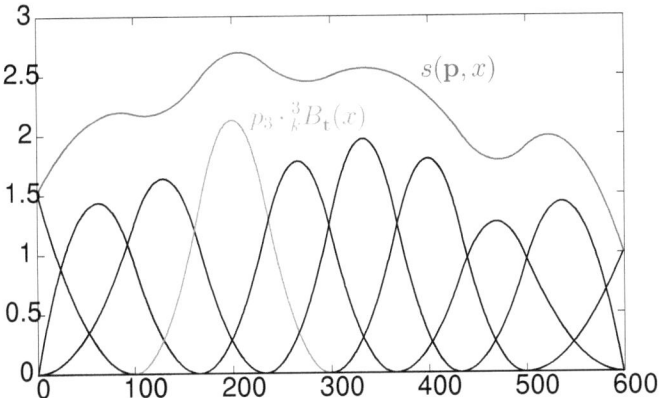

Figure 5.6: Illustration of a typical B-spline curve. The functions drawn in black are the basis functions, multiplied with the respective control point values $\mathbf{p}_i$.

- There are two knot vectors $\mathbf{q}, \mathbf{r}$, again for first respectively second parameter direction.

- The control points are $\mathbf{p}_{ij} \in \mathbb{R}^d$, where $1 \leq i \leq n_1, 1 \leq j \leq n_2$.

- We also denote with $\mathbf{P}$ the following matrix:

$$\mathbf{P} = \begin{pmatrix} \mathbf{p}_{11} & \mathbf{p}_{12} & \cdots & \mathbf{p}_{1n_2} \\ \mathbf{p}_{21} & \mathbf{p}_{22} & \cdots & \mathbf{p}_{2n_2} \\ \vdots & \vdots & & \vdots \\ \mathbf{p}_{n_11} & \mathbf{p}_{n_12} & \cdots & \mathbf{p}_{n_1n_2} \end{pmatrix} \quad (5.25)$$

Each column i of that matrix contains n_1 control points, enumerated along the first coordinate direction and stacked on top of each other.

- With $\mathbf{p}$, we denote the vectorization of $\mathbf{P}$, which is achieved by stacking the column vectors of $\mathbf{P}$ on top of each other into one

5. MODULES FOR IMPLEMENTING BUNDLE ADJUSTMENT

big vector. We write $\mathbf{p} = \text{vec}(\mathbf{P})$, and we have

$$\text{vec}(\mathbf{P}) = \left(\mathbf{p}_{1,1}^T \, \mathbf{p}_{2,1}^T \, \cdots \, \mathbf{p}_{n_1,1}^T \, \mathbf{p}_{1,2}^T \, \mathbf{p}_{2,2}^T \, \cdots \, \mathbf{p}_{n_1,n_2}^T \right)^T. \quad (5.26)$$

The spline surface $\mathbf{s}(\mathbf{p}, u, v) : \mathbb{R}^{n_1 \cdot n_2 \cdot d} \times \mathbb{R}^2 \to \mathbb{R}^d$ is then defined as follows:

$$\mathbf{s}(\mathbf{p}, u, v) = \sum_{i=1}^{n_1} \sum_{j=1}^{n_2} \mathbf{p}_{i,j} \cdot {}_{k_1}^{i}B_\mathbf{q}(u) \cdot {}_{k_2}^{j}B_\mathbf{r}(v). \quad (5.27)$$

5.2.1.1 B-Spline Linearity in Parameters

In most of the problems considered within this work, we are interested in determining surface parameters that best describe the camera measurements. For optimization purposes, it is therefore necessary to compute the derivatives of a B-spline surface with respect to parameters.

It is well-known that B-splines are linear in parameters, which makes the problem of derivative computation almost trivial. This linearity means that if the curve respectively surface evaluation coordinates are fixed, the evaluation of the B-spline is equivalent to a mere matrix-vector multiplication of some basis matrix with the B-spline parameter vector.

For the case of a B-spline curve with $d = 1$, we have

$$c(\mathbf{p}, x) = {}_k^n\mathbf{B_t}(x) \cdot \mathbf{p}, \quad (5.28)$$

where ${}_k^n\mathbf{B_t}(x)$ is defined as n-dimensional row vector

$${}_k^n\mathbf{B_t}(x) = ({}_k^1B_\mathbf{t}(x), {}_k^2B_\mathbf{t}(x), \ldots, {}_k^nB_\mathbf{t}(x)). \quad (5.29)$$

This is easily seen to be equivalent to Equation (5.24). The formula can be generalized to account for the case $d > 1$ as follows: We

5.2 The Depth Map Model

define
$$_k^n\mathbf{B}_{\mathbf{t},d}(x) = {_k^n\mathbf{B}_\mathbf{t}}(x) \otimes \mathbf{I}_d, \tag{5.30}$$

where $\otimes$ denotes the Kronecker matrix product. Then we can use the formula
$$c(\mathbf{p}, x) = {_k^n\mathbf{B}_{\mathbf{t},d}}(x) \cdot \mathbf{p} \tag{5.31}$$

to evaluate the multidimensional spline curve at parameter location x. Note that the resulting matrix exhibits a high degree of sparsity, which is something our optimization framework takes advantage of.

Above result generalizes nicely to the case of evaluation of B-spline curves at multiple parameter locations. Assume that the curve is to be evaluated at parameter positions
$$\mathbf{x} = (x_1, x_2, \ldots, x_m)^\mathrm{T}. \tag{5.32}$$

In this case, we extend the definition of $_k^n\mathbf{B}_{\mathbf{t},d}(x)$ as follows:

$$_k^n\mathbf{B}_{\mathbf{t},d}(\mathbf{x}) = \begin{pmatrix} _k^n\mathbf{B}_{\mathbf{t},d}(x_1) \\ _k^n\mathbf{B}_{\mathbf{t},d}(x_2) \\ \vdots \\ _k^n\mathbf{B}_{\mathbf{t},d}(x_m) \end{pmatrix}, \tag{5.33}$$

so $_k^n\mathbf{B}_{\mathbf{t},d}(\mathbf{x})$ is a $m \times n$-dimensional matrix of vertically stacked row vectors $_k^n\mathbf{B}_{\mathbf{t},d}(x_i)$. Using this generalized matrix instead of the original definition allows us to evaluate the curve at multiple locations merely by multiplying with the B-Spline parameter vector $\mathbf{p}$.

The preceding consideration is easily extended to the case of

5. MODULES FOR IMPLEMENTING BUNDLE ADJUSTMENT

B-spline surfaces. Starting out with Equation (5.27), we have

$$\begin{aligned}
\mathbf{s}(\mathbf{p}, u, v) &= \sum_{i=1}^{n_1} \sum_{j=1}^{n_2} \mathbf{p}_{i,j} \cdot {}_{k_1}^{i}B_{\mathbf{q}}(u) \cdot {}_{k_2}^{j}B_{\mathbf{r}}(v) \\
&= \sum_{i=1}^{n_1} {}_{k_1}^{i}B_{\mathbf{q}}(u) \left(\sum_{j=1}^{n_2} \mathbf{p}_{i,j} \cdot {}_{k_2}^{j}B_{\mathbf{r}}(v) \right) \\
&= \sum_{i=1}^{n_1} {}_{k_1}^{i}B_{\mathbf{q}}(u) \left((\mathbf{p}_{i,1}, \mathbf{p}_{i,2}, \ldots, \mathbf{p}_{i,n_2}) \cdot {}_{k_2}^{n_2}\mathbf{B}_{\mathbf{r}}^{\mathrm{T}}(v) \right) \\
&= {}_{k_1}^{n_1}\mathbf{B}_{\mathbf{q},d}(u) \cdot \mathbf{P} \cdot {}_{k_2}^{n_2}\mathbf{B}_{\mathbf{r}}^{\mathrm{T}}(v).
\end{aligned} \qquad (5.34)$$

Using some properties of vectorizations and the Kronecker product, this can be turned into a matrix-vector equation. More specifically, we are going to use

$$(\mathbf{B}^{\mathrm{T}} \otimes \mathbf{A}) \operatorname{vec}(\mathbf{X}) = \operatorname{vec}(\mathbf{A}\mathbf{X}\mathbf{B}), \qquad (5.35)$$

which can be applied to the surface evaluation problem as follows:

$$\mathbf{s}(\mathbf{p}, u, v) = \operatorname{vec}(\mathbf{s}(\mathbf{p}, u, v)) = \left({}_{k_2}^{n_2}\mathbf{B}_{\mathbf{r}}(v) \otimes {}_{k_1}^{n_1}\mathbf{B}_{\mathbf{q},d}(u) \right) \cdot \operatorname{vec}(\mathbf{P}). \qquad (5.36)$$

Thus, we have turned the problem of evaluating the surface at a location u, v into the problem of evaluating a matrix-vector product.

When evaluation of the spline surface at multiple parameter locations (u_i, v_i) is desired, there exist two possibilities. If the parameter locations are independent of each other, and are specified as vectors

$$\mathbf{u} = (u_1, u_2, \ldots, u_m)^{\mathrm{T}}, \mathbf{v} = (v_1, v_2, \ldots, v_m)^{\mathrm{T}}, \qquad (5.37)$$

we can achieve evaluation of the B-spline surface at locations (u_i, v_i) by stacking basis matrices. We define a symbol for the resulting

5.2 The Depth Map Model

matrix as follows:

$${}^{n_1,n_2}_{k_1,k_2}\mathbf{B}_{\mathbf{q},\mathbf{r},d}(\mathbf{u},\mathbf{v}) = \begin{pmatrix} {}^{n_2}_{k_2}\mathbf{B}_\mathbf{r}(v_1) \otimes {}^{n_1}_{k_1}\mathbf{B}_{\mathbf{q},d}(u_1) \\ {}^{n_2}_{k_2}\mathbf{B}_\mathbf{r}(v_2) \otimes {}^{n_1}_{k_1}\mathbf{B}_{\mathbf{q},d}(u_2) \\ \vdots \\ {}^{n_2}_{k_2}\mathbf{B}_\mathbf{r}(v_m) \otimes {}^{n_1}_{k_1}\mathbf{B}_{\mathbf{q},d}(u_m) \end{pmatrix} \quad (5.38)$$

Evaluating the spline at the parameter locations $\mathbf{u}, \mathbf{v}$ is then possible as a mere matrix-vector multiplication as follows:

$$\begin{pmatrix} \mathbf{s}(\mathbf{p}, u_1, v_1) \\ \mathbf{s}(\mathbf{p}, u_2, v_2) \\ \vdots \\ \mathbf{s}(\mathbf{p}, u_m, v_m) \end{pmatrix} = {}^{n_1,n_2}_{k_1,k_2}\mathbf{B}_{\mathbf{q},\mathbf{r},d}(\mathbf{u},\mathbf{v}) \cdot \mathrm{vec}(\mathbf{P}). \quad (5.39)$$

However, if the B-spline surface is to be sampled on a regular grid of parameter positions, there is a more elegant way to achieve this. Let the parameter coordinates in the first direction be specified as

$$\mathbf{u} = (u_1, u_2, \ldots, u_m), \quad (5.40)$$

and in the second direction as

$$\mathbf{v} = (v_1, v_2, \ldots, v_l). \quad (5.41)$$

Then, the spline surface can be evaluated over the whole lattice by computing

$$\left({}^{n_2}_{k_2}\mathbf{B}_\mathbf{r}(\mathbf{u}) \otimes {}^{n_1}_{k_1}\mathbf{B}_{\mathbf{q},d}(\mathbf{v})\right) \cdot \mathrm{vec}(\mathbf{P}). \quad (5.42)$$

This is the formulation that is used most frequently in our algorithms, and we define the symbol ${}^{n_1,n_2}_{k_1,k_2}\mathbf{L}_{\mathbf{q},\mathbf{r},d}$ to refer to the corresponding matrix:

$${}^{n_1,n_2}_{k_1,k_2}\mathbf{L}_{\mathbf{q},\mathbf{r},d}(\mathbf{u},\mathbf{v}) = {}^{n_2}_{k_2}\mathbf{B}_\mathbf{r}(\mathbf{v}) \otimes {}^{n_1}_{k_1}\mathbf{B}_{\mathbf{q},d}(\mathbf{u}). \quad (5.43)$$

5. MODULES FOR IMPLEMENTING BUNDLE ADJUSTMENT

From the preceding considerations it follows immediately that the derivatives of a B-spline curve resp. surface with respect to parameters **p** is equal to the basis matrix computed above. Alternatively, the derivative values can be deduced directly from equations (5.24) or (5.27), respectively:

$$\frac{d\,c(p,x)}{d\,p_i} = {}^i_{k_1}B_q(x) \cdot I_d, \quad \frac{d\,s(p,u,v)}{d\,p_{ij}} = {}^i_{k_1}B_q(u) \cdot {}^j_{k_2}B_r(v) \cdot I_d. \quad (5.44)$$

5.2.1.2 B-Spline Derivatives w.r.t. Curve Coordinates

Another important problem associated with B-splines is that of differentiation of the B-spline function with respect to the curve resp. surface parameters. This problem appears, e.g., when one has to compute the curve resp. surface tangents, or when we want to compute the length resp. area. Fortunately, this is also rather easily computed, and we can express the corresponding computation concisely as a simple linear transformation on curve resp. surface parameters.

Let us start with the case of curves: When differentiating a spline curve defined by Equation (5.24) with respect to the curve parameter x, it is well known that the result will be another spline curve with the following properties:

- The degree is reduced to $k - 1$.

- The number of control points is reduced to $n - 1$.

- The knot vector will be $(t_2, t_3, \ldots, t_{n+k-1})$, so the first and last entries in the knot vector will have to be discarded.

- The new control points, denoted by q_i, are computed accord-

5.2 The Depth Map Model

ing to the following formula:

$$\mathbf{q}_i = \frac{k-1}{t_{i+k} - t_{i+1}} (\mathbf{p}_{i+1} - \mathbf{p}_i) \qquad (5.45)$$

The computation of the new control points can be concisely formulated in form of a matrix to be multiplied with the original spline parameters. This is easily seen by realizing that both computation of the differences $(\mathbf{p}_{i+1} - \mathbf{p}_i)$ as well as scaling with $\frac{k-1}{t_{i+k}-t_{i+1}}$ are easily expressible as matrix operations, and the combination of both operations will yield another matrix describing the whole operation.

This is best explained using an example. Assume that we have a set of 4 scalar control points $p_i \in \mathbb{R}$, so $d = 1$. Then the matrix computing the differences $p_{i+1} - p_i$ is simply:

$$^4\Delta = \begin{pmatrix} -1 & 1 & 0 & 0 \\ 0 & -1 & 1 & 0 \\ 0 & 0 & -1 & 1 \end{pmatrix} \qquad (5.46)$$

Multiplying the vector of stacked control points against this matrix, we see that the 4 differences will be computed correctly. The overall matrix for computing the curve derivative control points can now be computed by premultiplying the difference computation matrix obtained according to above scheme with the following scaling matrix:

$$^4_k\Sigma_\mathbf{t} = \begin{pmatrix} \frac{k-1}{t_{1+k}-t_{1+1}} & 0 & 0 \\ 0 & \frac{k-1}{t_{2+k}-t_{2+1}} & 0 \\ 0 & 0 & \frac{k-1}{t_{3+k}-t_{3+1}} \end{pmatrix}. \qquad (5.47)$$

This is easily extended to the case of multi-dimensional spline curves. In the case $d = 2$, we can use the following matrix to compute the

5. MODULES FOR IMPLEMENTING BUNDLE ADJUSTMENT

differences:

$$^4\Delta_2 = \begin{pmatrix} -1 & 0 & 1 & 0 & 0 & 0 & 0 & 0 \\ 0 & -1 & 0 & 1 & 0 & 0 & 0 & 0 \\ 0 & 0 & -1 & 0 & 1 & 0 & 0 & 0 \\ 0 & 0 & 0 & -1 & 0 & 1 & 0 & 0 \\ 0 & 0 & 0 & 0 & -1 & 0 & 1 & 0 \\ 0 & 0 & 0 & 0 & 0 & -1 & 0 & 1 \end{pmatrix} \quad (5.48)$$

More generally, we see that these difference matrices have the following shape:

- The size is $(n-1)d \times nd$.

- All entries are 0, except for the diagonal and the d-th superdiagonal.

- The diagonal contains only the value -1.

- The d-th superdiagonal contains only the value 1.

The shape of the difference computation matrix depends on two values, which are the number n of parameters and the number d of dimensions. Thus, we will denote the corresponding difference matrices by $^n\Delta_d$.

Furthermore, the scaling matrix needs to repeat the scaling factors d times. Thus, it has the following shape:

- Size $(n-1)d \times (n-1)d$.

- All values are 0, except for the diagonal.

- The diagonal contains the values $\frac{k-1}{t_{i+k}-t_{i+1}}$, each is repeated d times.

5.2 The Depth Map Model

This matrix is determined by: The number of parameters n, the order of the spline k, the number of dimensions d, and the knot vector t. Scaling matrices constructed according to these values are denoted by ${}_k^n\Sigma_{\mathbf{t},d}$ from now on.

So, all in all, the computation of B-spline derivatives is reduced to multiplying the parameter vector p of the original curve with the matrix $({}_k^n\Sigma_{\mathbf{t},d} \cdot {}^n\Delta_d)$, and interpreting the new parameters as spline curve with $n-1$ control points, degree $k-1$, and knot vector that has been shrinked at beginning and end.

We conclude that the vector

$$\begin{pmatrix} \frac{\mathrm{d}}{\mathrm{d}u_1}\mathbf{c}(\mathbf{p},u_1) \\ \frac{\mathrm{d}}{\mathrm{d}u_2}\mathbf{c}(\mathbf{p},u_2) \\ \ldots \\ \frac{\mathrm{d}}{\mathrm{d}u_n}\mathbf{c}(\mathbf{p},u_n) \end{pmatrix} \quad (5.49)$$

of tangent values for the spline curve is computed by evaluating

$$ {}_{k-1}^{n-1}\mathbf{B}_{\mathbf{t}',d}(\mathbf{u}) \cdot {}_k^n\Sigma_{\mathbf{t},d} \cdot {}^n\Delta_d \cdot \mathbf{p}, \quad (5.50)$$

where t' is the shortened knot vector t as explained above. Note that the vector of tangent values should not be confused with the Jacobian of the function $\mathbf{c}(\mathbf{p},\mathbf{x},\mathbf{y})$, which is a diagonal $n \times n$ matrix. The entries in the diagonal of the Jacobian are exactly the entries of the tangent values vector.

5.2.1.3 B-Spline Derivatives w.r.t. Surface Coordinates

These considerations generalize nicely to B-spline surfaces, where we have to compute the derivative not only with respect to one, but to two different parameter directions. This corresponds to computing the surface tangents in both directions.

5. MODULES FOR IMPLEMENTING BUNDLE ADJUSTMENT

It is possible to directly apply the computation scheme for curve derivatives to surface derivatives with respect to the first parameter direction: Simply compute the matrix product

$${}^{n_1}_{k_1}\mathbf{\Sigma}_{\mathbf{q},d} \cdot {}^{n_1}\mathbf{\Delta}_d \cdot \mathbf{P}, \tag{5.51}$$

where $\mathbf{P}$ is the control point matrix as explained above, and this will yield the parameter matrix for the derivative surface. For the other parameter direction, things are equally simple. The derivative parameters can be computed as

$$\mathbf{P}({}^{n_2}_{k_2}\mathbf{\Sigma}_{\mathbf{r},d} \cdot {}^{n_2}\mathbf{\Delta}_d)^\mathrm{T}. \tag{5.52}$$

Usually, we are not interested in the parameter matrices of the derivative surfaces, but we want to work with parameter vectors instead. This can be achieved by applying the vectorization operator:

$$\mathrm{vec}({}^{n_1}_{k_1}\mathbf{\Sigma}_{\mathbf{q},d} \cdot {}^{n_1}\mathbf{\Delta}_d \cdot \mathbf{P}) \tag{5.53}$$

$$\mathrm{vec}(\mathbf{P}({}^{n_2}_{k_2}\mathbf{\Sigma}_{\mathbf{r},d} \cdot {}^{n_2}\mathbf{\Delta}_d)^\mathrm{T}) \tag{5.54}$$

Again, we are going to use the property $(\mathbf{B}^\mathrm{T} \otimes \mathbf{A})\,\mathrm{vec}(\mathbf{X}) = \mathrm{vec}(\mathbf{AXB})$ of the Kronecker matrix product. It can be applied to above equa-

5.2 The Depth Map Model

tions as follows:

$$\begin{align}
\operatorname{vec}(\,_{k_1}^{n_1}\boldsymbol{\Sigma}_{\mathbf{q},d} \cdot {}^{n_1}\boldsymbol{\Delta}_d \cdot \mathbf{P}) &= \\
\operatorname{vec}((\,_{k_1}^{n_1}\boldsymbol{\Sigma}_{\mathbf{q},d} \cdot {}^{n_1}\boldsymbol{\Delta}_d) \cdot \mathbf{P} \cdot \mathbf{I}_{n_2}) &= \\
(\mathbf{I}_{n_2}^{\mathrm{T}} \otimes (\,_{k_1}^{n_1}\boldsymbol{\Sigma}_{\mathbf{q},d} \cdot {}^{n_1}\boldsymbol{\Delta}_d))\,\operatorname{vec}(\mathbf{P}) &= \\
(\mathbf{I}_{n_2} \otimes (\,_{k_1}^{n_1}\boldsymbol{\Sigma}_{\mathbf{q},d} \cdot {}^{n_1}\boldsymbol{\Delta}_d))\,\operatorname{vec}(\mathbf{P}), & \quad (5.55) \\
\operatorname{vec}(\mathbf{P}(\,_{k_2}^{n_2}\boldsymbol{\Sigma}_{\mathbf{r},d} \cdot {}^{n_2}\boldsymbol{\Delta}_d)^{\mathrm{T}}) &= \\
\operatorname{vec}(\mathbf{I}_{dn_1} \cdot \mathbf{P}(\,_{k_2}^{n_2}\boldsymbol{\Sigma}_{\mathbf{r},d} \cdot {}^{n_2}\boldsymbol{\Delta}_d)^{\mathrm{T}}) &= \\
((\,_{k_2}^{n_2}\boldsymbol{\Sigma}_{\mathbf{r},d} \cdot {}^{n_2}\boldsymbol{\Delta}_d) \otimes \mathbf{I}_{dn_1})\,\operatorname{vec}(\mathbf{P}) & \quad (5.56)
\end{align}$$

Pre-multiplying above matrices with appropriate B-spline basis matrices will allow evaluation of tangent values through a simple matrix-vector product, and it will be convenient to define abbreviations for these tangent evaluation matrices as follows:

$$\,_{k_1,k_2}^{n_1,n_2}\mathcal{B}_{\mathbf{u},\mathbf{q},\mathbf{r},d}(\mathbf{u},\mathbf{v}) = \,_{k_1-1,k_2}^{n_1-1,n_2}\mathbf{B}_{\mathbf{q}',\mathbf{r},d}(\mathbf{u},\mathbf{v}) \cdot (\mathbf{I}_{n_2} \otimes (\,_{k_1}^{n_1}\boldsymbol{\Sigma}_{\mathbf{q},d} \cdot {}^{n_1}\boldsymbol{\Delta}_d)), \tag{5.57}$$

$$\,_{k_1,k_2}^{n_1,n_2}\mathcal{B}_{\mathbf{v},\mathbf{q},\mathbf{r},d}(\mathbf{u},\mathbf{v}) = \,_{k_1,k_2-1}^{n_1,n_2-1}\mathbf{B}_{\mathbf{q},\mathbf{r}',d}(\mathbf{u},\mathbf{v}) \cdot ((\,_{k_2}^{n_2}\boldsymbol{\Sigma}_{\mathbf{r},d} \cdot {}^{n_2}\boldsymbol{\Delta}_d) \otimes \mathbf{I}_{dn_1}). \tag{5.58}$$

If we want to compute all derivative surface parameter values for both parameter directions using one matrix-vector product, we can stack the above matrices vertically into one matrix

$$\,_{k_1,k_2}^{n_1,n_2}\mathcal{B}_{\mathrm{uv},\mathbf{q},\mathbf{r},d}(\mathbf{u},\mathbf{v}) = \begin{pmatrix} \,_{k_1,k_2}^{n_1,n_2}\mathcal{B}_{\mathbf{u},\mathbf{q},\mathbf{r},d}(\mathbf{u},\mathbf{v}) \\ \,_{k_1,k_2}^{n_1,n_2}\mathcal{B}_{\mathbf{v},\mathbf{q},\mathbf{r},d}(\mathbf{u},\mathbf{v}) \end{pmatrix}. \tag{5.59}$$

Note that this matrix is extremely sparse, and it is definitely beneficial to exploit that whereever possible. Multiplication with the vector $\operatorname{vec}(\mathbf{P})$ directly yields the tangent values of the surface in both directions, stacked on top of each other. In the case of evaluation

5. MODULES FOR IMPLEMENTING BUNDLE ADJUSTMENT

parameters being on a regular grid, we can simply use the lattice basis matrices $\mathbf{L}$ instead of the general basis matrices $\mathbf{B}$. Since evaluation of spline surfaces on a regular grid is what we actually use in our implementation, we introduce additional notation for that specific case. The tangent computation matrices will in that case be denoted as

$$_{k_1,k_2}^{n_1,n_2}\mathcal{L}_{\mathbf{u},\mathbf{q},\mathbf{r},d}(\mathbf{u},\mathbf{v}) = {}_{k_1-1,k_2}^{n_1-1,n_2}\mathbf{L}_{\mathbf{q}',\mathbf{r},d}(\mathbf{u},\mathbf{v}) \cdot (\mathbf{I}_{n_2} \otimes (_{k_1}^{n_1}\mathbf{\Sigma}_{\mathbf{q},d} \cdot {}^{n_1}\mathbf{\Delta}_d)), \quad (5.60)$$

$$_{k_1,k_2}^{n_1,n_2}\mathcal{L}_{\mathbf{v},\mathbf{q},\mathbf{r},d}(\mathbf{u},\mathbf{v}) = {}_{k_1,k_2-1}^{n_1,n_2-1}\mathbf{L}_{\mathbf{q},\mathbf{r}',d}(\mathbf{u},\mathbf{v}) \cdot ((_{k_2}^{n_2}\mathbf{\Sigma}_{\mathbf{r},d} \cdot {}^{n_2}\mathbf{\Delta}_d) \otimes \mathbf{I}_{dn_1}). \quad (5.61)$$

The stacked matrices will be defined analogously as

$$_{k_1,k_2}^{n_1,n_2}\mathcal{L}_{\mathbf{uv},\mathbf{q},\mathbf{r},d}(\mathbf{u},\mathbf{v}) = \begin{pmatrix} _{k_1,k_2}^{n_1,n_2}\mathcal{L}_{\mathbf{u},\mathbf{q},\mathbf{r},d}(\mathbf{u},\mathbf{v}) \\ _{k_1,k_2}^{n_1,n_2}\mathcal{L}_{\mathbf{v},\mathbf{q},\mathbf{r},d}(\mathbf{u},\mathbf{v}) \end{pmatrix}. \quad (5.62)$$

5.2.2 Surfaces Induced by Depth Maps

The particular surface model used in most of our developments is an inverse B-Spline depth map. Before we continue with describing that specific type of depth map in detail, there are some properties of depth maps that we want to discuss here in a more general setting, so that our formulas can be used for other types of surface models as well.

For our treatment of surface models, it is most convenient to interpret a parametric depth map $z(\mathbf{p}, u, v)$ as a function that assigns depth values to pixel coordinates in some image. Since this is technically not a full 3D model, it is also often called a 2.5D surface model.

One of the most important operations on depth maps is the computation of 3D coordinates of a point with known pixel coordinates u, v, given the depth map z. To achieve this, we make use

5.2 The Depth Map Model

of the fact that the inverse camera matrix $\mathbf{K}^{-1}$ maps homogeneous pixel coordinates $(u, v, 1)^\mathrm{T}$ to 3D spatial coordinates that lie along the viewing ray associated with pixel coordinates $(u, v)^\mathrm{T}$ at depth 1. This allows us to define the three-dimensional surface $\mathbf{d}_z(u, v)$ that is induced by a parametric depth map $z(\mathbf{p}, u, v)$ as

$$\mathbf{d}_z(\mathbf{p}, u, v) = z(\mathbf{p}, u, v) \left(\mathbf{K}^{-1} \cdot \begin{pmatrix} u \\ v \\ 1 \end{pmatrix} \right). \tag{5.63}$$

This will be the basis for further analysis of surfaces that are based on depth maps. We are later going to be interested in the derivatives of functions of this kind with respect to $\mathbf{p}, u$, and v.

Often, it is convenient to evaluate the surface at several parameter locations u_j, v_j simultaneously. Let m be the number of surface parameter locations to be evaluated, and let $\mathbf{u} \in \mathbb{R}^m, \mathbf{v} \in \mathbb{R}^m$ be the surface coordinates of those locations. Define $\mathbf{z}(\mathbf{p}, \mathbf{u}, \mathbf{v})$ as the vector of depth values for the coordinate pairs (u_j, v_j):

$$\mathbf{z}(\mathbf{p}, \mathbf{u}, \mathbf{v}) = \Big(z(\mathbf{p}, u_1, v_1) \quad z(\mathbf{p}, u_2, v_2) \quad \ldots \quad z(\mathbf{p}, u_m, v_m) \Big)^\mathrm{T}. \tag{5.64}$$

In the following, let $\mathrm{diag}(\mathbf{z})$ denote the diagonal matrix created from a vector $\mathbf{z}$ by setting the diagonal elements equal to the elements of $\mathbf{z}$. Thus, $\mathrm{diag}(\mathbf{z}(\mathbf{p}, \mathbf{u}, \mathbf{v}))$ is the matrix with all depth values in its diagonal. Then, we note that the product of matrices

$$\mathbf{K}^{-1} \begin{pmatrix} \mathbf{u}^\mathrm{T} \\ \mathbf{v}^\mathrm{T} \\ \mathbf{1}_{1,m} \end{pmatrix} \mathrm{diag}(\mathbf{z}(\mathbf{p}, \mathbf{u}, \mathbf{v})) \tag{5.65}$$

evaluates to a $3 \times m$ matrix containing the surface values $\mathbf{d}_z(\mathbf{p}, u_j, v_j)$ as columns. Since that expression is bound to appear very often in

5. MODULES FOR IMPLEMENTING BUNDLE ADJUSTMENT

the following elaborations, it will be convenient to define the shorthand term

$$\mathcal{K}(\mathbf{u}, \mathbf{v}) = \mathbf{K}^{-1} \begin{pmatrix} \mathbf{u}^\mathrm{T} \\ \mathbf{v}^\mathrm{T} \\ \mathbf{1}_{1,m} \end{pmatrix}, \qquad (5.66)$$

allowing us to compactly write down above expression as

$$\mathcal{K}(\mathbf{u}, \mathbf{v}) \cdot \mathrm{diag}(\mathbf{z}(\mathbf{p}, \mathbf{u}, \mathbf{v})). \qquad (5.67)$$

Alternatively, we can write this as

$$\mathcal{K}(\mathbf{u}, \mathbf{v}) \circ (\mathbf{1}_{3,1} \cdot (\mathbf{z}(\mathbf{p}, \mathbf{u}, \mathbf{v}))^\mathrm{T}), \qquad (5.68)$$

where $\circ$ denotes the Hadamard product, which is the componentwise product of matrices. This alternative formula will be useful later on for computing derivatives. Note that modern linear algebra libraries, like the Eigen library used in our implementation, provide efficient implementations for evaluating both variants of this expression. For more information on the Hadamard product, see [64].

Above expression can be interpreted as a matrix-valued function that performs the mapping that we are looking for, since it takes surface parameters and surface locations to 3D point coordinates. However, we want to avoid matrix-valued functions, and we will instead look at the vectorization of that function, thereby generalizing equation (5.63) as

$$\mathbf{d}_z(\mathbf{p}, \mathbf{u}, \mathbf{v}) = \mathrm{vec}(\mathcal{K}(\mathbf{u}, \mathbf{v})) \circ \mathrm{vec}(\mathbf{1}_{3,1} \cdot (\mathbf{z}(\mathbf{p}, \mathbf{u}, \mathbf{v}))^\mathrm{T}) \qquad (5.69)$$

to the case of vector-valued evaluation positions $\mathbf{u}, \mathbf{v}$. It is easily verified that for $m = 1$, this definition coincides with the original definition from equation (5.63). The function $\mathbf{d}_z(\mathbf{p}, \mathbf{u}, \mathbf{v})$ maps surface

5.2 The Depth Map Model

parameters and surface locations to a vector of m 3D surface points that are stacked on top of each other. Each of these surface values is a 3D vector, so formally $\mathbf{d}_z$ is a mapping of type

$$\mathbf{d}_z : \mathbb{R}^n \times \mathbb{R}^m \times \mathbb{R}^m \to \mathbb{R}^{3m}. \tag{5.70}$$

5.2.2.1 Derivatives w.r.t. Surface Parameters

Using the Hadamard product in the surface definition allows a simple and concise formulation of the computation of various derivatives of the surface. Before we continue giving details on those computation schemes, we would like to discuss two properties of Hadamard products. The first concerns the derivative of the product of two vectors. It reads as follows:

$$\frac{d}{d\mathbf{a}}(\mathbf{a} \circ \mathbf{b}) = \mathrm{diag}(\mathbf{b}), \quad \frac{d}{d\mathbf{b}}(\mathbf{a} \circ \mathbf{b}) = \mathrm{diag}(\mathbf{a}), \tag{5.71}$$

which is easily verified. Based on this observation, we can formulate a product rule for the Hadamard product of vector-valued functions:

$$\frac{d}{d\mathbf{x}}(\mathbf{a}(\mathbf{x}) \circ \mathbf{b}(\mathbf{x})) = \mathrm{diag}(\mathbf{b}(\mathbf{x}))\frac{d\mathbf{a}(\mathbf{x})}{d\mathbf{x}} + \mathrm{diag}(\mathbf{a}(\mathbf{x}))\frac{d\mathbf{b}(\mathbf{x})}{d\mathbf{x}}, \tag{5.72}$$

which is also easily verified. Using the first of these two observations, we are able to deduce that the derivatives of the surface with respect to parameters are computed as

$$\begin{aligned}\frac{d}{d\mathbf{p}}\mathbf{d}_z(\mathbf{p}, \mathbf{u}, \mathbf{v}) &= \mathrm{diag}(\mathrm{vec}(\mathcal{K}(\mathbf{u}, \mathbf{v}))) \cdot \frac{d}{d\mathbf{p}}\mathrm{vec}(\mathbf{1}_{3,1} \cdot (\mathbf{z}(\mathbf{p}, \mathbf{u}, \mathbf{v}))^T) \\ &= \mathrm{diag}(\mathrm{vec}(\mathcal{K}(\mathbf{u}, \mathbf{v}))) \cdot \frac{d}{d\mathbf{p}}(\mathbf{I}_m \otimes \mathbf{1}_{3,1}) \cdot \mathbf{z}(\mathbf{p}, \mathbf{u}, \mathbf{v}) \\ &= \mathrm{diag}(\mathrm{vec}(\mathcal{K}(\mathbf{u}, \mathbf{v}))) \cdot (\mathbf{I}_m \otimes \mathbf{1}_{3,1}) \cdot \frac{d}{d\mathbf{p}}\mathbf{z}(\mathbf{p}, \mathbf{u}, \mathbf{v}).\end{aligned} \tag{5.73}$$

5. MODULES FOR IMPLEMENTING BUNDLE ADJUSTMENT

5.2.2.2 Tangents

Tangents of surfaces are generally computed by differentiating the surface function with respect to surface coordinates. This is also true for surfaces that are induced by depth maps, and we can compute tangents ^uT_z and ^vT_z in first and second parameter direction as

$$^uT_z(\mathbf{p}, u, v) := \frac{\mathrm{d}}{\mathrm{d}u}\mathbf{d}_z(\mathbf{p}, u, v), \quad ^vT_z(\mathbf{p}, u, v) := \frac{\mathrm{d}}{\mathrm{d}v}\mathbf{d}_z(\mathbf{p}, u, v) \quad (5.74)$$

at specific locations u, v, based on Definition (5.63). For the case of multiple surface locations at which we want to determine tangent vectors, it is tempting to simply differentiate the surface function (5.69) with respect to u or v. However, proceeding like this will yield blockdiagonal matrices that contain the tangent vectors, which is inconvenient. Again, we would like to avoid matrix-valued functions, and instead compute a stacked vector of tangents.

Therefore, we define functions

$$^u\mathbf{T}_z(\mathbf{p}, \mathbf{u}, \mathbf{v}) = \begin{pmatrix} ^uT_z(\mathbf{p}, u_1, v_1) \\ ^uT_z(\mathbf{p}, u_2, v_2) \\ \vdots \\ ^uT_z(\mathbf{p}, u_m, v_m) \end{pmatrix}, \quad ^v\mathbf{T}_z(\mathbf{p}, \mathbf{u}, \mathbf{v}) = \begin{pmatrix} ^vT_z(\mathbf{p}, u_1, v_1) \\ ^vT_z(\mathbf{p}, u_2, v_2) \\ \vdots \\ ^vT_z(\mathbf{p}, u_m, v_m) \end{pmatrix}$$
(5.75)

for computing the vector of stacked tangents in first and second coordinate directions. In what follows, we will only give details for the computation of ^uT_z and $^u\mathbf{T}_z$. It is trivial to adapt those formulas to the case of ^vT_z and $^v\mathbf{T}_z$.

We start by computing the derivative of $\mathbf{d}_z$ with respect to u,

5.2 The Depth Map Model

based on (5.63):

$$\frac{\mathrm{d}}{\mathrm{d}u}\mathbf{d}_z(\mathbf{p}, u, v) = \frac{\mathrm{d}}{\mathrm{d}u}z(\mathbf{p}, u, v) \cdot \mathbf{K}^{-1} \cdot \begin{pmatrix} x \\ y \\ 1 \end{pmatrix} + \mathbf{K}_\mathbf{X}^{-1} \cdot z(\mathbf{p}, u, v), \quad (5.76)$$

where $\mathbf{K}_\mathbf{X}^{-1}$ is the first column of $\mathbf{K}^{-1}$. For the depth map tangents, we will now define the shorthands

$$^{u}\mathcal{T}_z(\mathbf{p}, u, v) = \frac{\mathrm{d}}{\mathrm{d}x}z(\mathbf{p}, u, v), \quad ^{v}\mathcal{T}_z(\mathbf{p}, u, v) = \frac{\mathrm{d}}{\mathrm{d}y}z(\mathbf{p}, u, v), \quad (5.77)$$

in order to keep our presentation as concise as possible. Note that $^{u}\mathcal{T}_z$ and $^{v}\mathcal{T}_z$ are scalar-valued functions. As we have done for depth map values, we also define abbreviations for stacked tangent values:

$$^{u}\mathcal{T}_z(\mathbf{p}, \mathbf{u}, \mathbf{v}) = \begin{pmatrix} \frac{\mathrm{d}}{\mathrm{d}u}z(\mathbf{p}, u_1, v_1) \\ \frac{\mathrm{d}}{\mathrm{d}u}z(\mathbf{p}, u_2, v_2) \\ \vdots \\ \frac{\mathrm{d}}{\mathrm{d}u}z(\mathbf{p}, u_m, v_m) \end{pmatrix}, \quad ^{v}\mathcal{T}_z(\mathbf{p}, \mathbf{u}, \mathbf{v}) = \begin{pmatrix} \frac{\mathrm{d}}{\mathrm{d}v}z(\mathbf{p}, u_1, v_1) \\ \frac{\mathrm{d}}{\mathrm{d}v}z(\mathbf{p}, u_2, v_2) \\ \vdots \\ \frac{\mathrm{d}}{\mathrm{d}v}z(\mathbf{p}, u_m, v_m) \end{pmatrix}$$
(5.78)

These definitions allow us to formulate the computation scheme in a more concise way. Furthermore, routines for computing $^{u}\mathcal{T}_z$ and $^{v}\mathcal{T}_z$ are usually available in implementations. When z is, e.g., a B-spline surface, the computation of these tangent values is simply a matrix-vector multiplication, since B-spline derivatives with respect to surface position are again B-splines. Formula (5.76) shows how to compute the tangent of a surface at a specific location. Using the

5. MODULES FOR IMPLEMENTING BUNDLE ADJUSTMENT

introduced abbreviations, it can be restated as

$$^{u}T_z(\mathbf{p}, u, v) = {}^{u}\mathcal{J}_z(\mathbf{p}, u, v) \cdot \mathbf{K}^{-1} \cdot \begin{pmatrix} u \\ v \\ 1 \end{pmatrix} + \mathbf{K}_\mathbf{X}^{-1} \cdot z(\mathbf{p}, u, v). \qquad (5.79)$$

It is possible to extend this computation scheme for computation of $^{u}\mathbf{T}_z$:

$$^{u}\mathbf{T}_z(\mathbf{p}, \mathbf{u}, \mathbf{v}) = \mathrm{diag}(\mathrm{vec}(\mathcal{K}(\mathbf{u}, \mathbf{v}))) \cdot (\mathbf{I}_m \otimes \mathbf{1}_{3,1}) \cdot {}^{u}\mathcal{J}_z(\mathbf{p}, \mathbf{u}, \mathbf{v}) +$$
$$(\mathbf{I}_m \otimes \mathbf{K}_\mathbf{X}^{-1}) \cdot \mathbf{z}(\mathbf{p}, \mathbf{u}, \mathbf{v}). \qquad (5.80)$$

Note that since **u** and **v** stay constant in practice, the matrices

$$\mathrm{diag}(\mathrm{vec}(\mathcal{K}(\mathbf{u}, \mathbf{v}))) \cdot (\mathbf{I}_m \otimes \mathbf{1}_{3,1}), \quad (\mathbf{I}_m \otimes \mathbf{K}_\mathbf{X}^{-1}) \qquad (5.81)$$

stay constant as well and can easily be precomputed.

5.2.2.3 Normals

The surface normals are computed as cross product between the tangent vectors in both surface directions. Looking at the original definition (5.63), the surface normal at a single surface location u, v can be determined as

$$\begin{aligned}
\mathbf{n}_z(\mathbf{p}, u, v) &= \frac{\mathrm{d}}{\mathrm{d}u}\mathbf{d}_z(\mathbf{p}, u, v) \times \frac{\mathrm{d}}{\mathrm{d}v}\mathbf{d}_z(\mathbf{p}, u, v) \\
&= \mathbf{K}_\mathbf{X}^{-1} \times \mathbf{K}_\mathbf{Y}^{-1} \cdot z(\mathbf{p}, u, v)^2 \\
&\quad - \mathbf{K}_\mathbf{Y}^{-1} \times (\mathbf{K}^{-1}(u, v, 1)^\mathrm{T}) \cdot z(\mathbf{p}, u, v) \cdot {}^{u}\mathcal{J}_z(\mathbf{p}, u, v) \\
&\quad + \mathbf{K}_\mathbf{X}^{-1} \times (\mathbf{K}^{-1}(u, v, 1)^\mathrm{T}) \cdot z(\mathbf{p}, u, v) \cdot {}^{v}\mathcal{J}_z(\mathbf{p}, u, v)
\end{aligned}$$

5.2 The Depth Map Model

This can be put in a more concise form. We define 3×3 matrices $\widetilde{\mathbf{K}}(u,v)$ as

$$\widetilde{\mathbf{K}}(u,v) = \left(\mathbf{K}_\mathbf{X}^{-1} \times \mathbf{K}_\mathbf{Y}^{-1} | -\mathbf{K}_\mathbf{Y}^{-1} \times (\mathbf{K}^{-1}(u,v,1)^T) | \mathbf{K}_\mathbf{X}^{-1} \times (\mathbf{K}^{-1}(u,v,1)^T)\right) \quad (5.82)$$

and a function $\mathcal{N}_z(\mathbf{p}, u, v)$ as

$$\mathcal{N}_z(\mathbf{p}, u, v) = \begin{pmatrix} z(\mathbf{p}, u, v) \\ {}^u\mathcal{J}_z(\mathbf{p}, u, v) \\ {}^v\mathcal{J}_z(\mathbf{p}, u, v) \end{pmatrix}. \quad (5.83)$$

The foregoing definitions allow us to establish a formula for normal evaluation at surface coordinates (u, v) concisely as

$$\mathbf{n}_z(\mathbf{p}, u, v) = \widetilde{\mathbf{K}}_i \cdot z(\mathbf{p}, u, v) \cdot \mathcal{N}_z(\mathbf{p}, u, v). \quad (5.84)$$

Now we are ready to generalize the computation scheme to simultaneous evaluation of $m > 1$ normals. We define two more abbreviations $\widetilde{\mathbf{K}}(\mathbf{u}, \mathbf{v})$ and $\mathcal{N}_z(\mathbf{p}, \mathbf{u}, \mathbf{v})$:

$$\widetilde{\mathbf{K}}(\mathbf{u}, \mathbf{v}) = \begin{pmatrix} \widetilde{\mathbf{K}}(u_1, v_1) & 0 & \cdots & 0 \\ 0 & \widetilde{\mathbf{K}}(u_2, v_2) & \ddots & \vdots \\ \vdots & \ddots & \ddots & 0 \\ 0 & \cdots & 0 & \widetilde{\mathbf{K}}(u_m, v_m) \end{pmatrix}, \quad (5.85)$$

$$\mathcal{N}_z(\mathbf{p}, \mathbf{u}, \mathbf{v}) = \begin{pmatrix} \mathcal{N}_z(\mathbf{p}, u_1, v_1) \\ \mathcal{N}_z(\mathbf{p}, u_2, v_2) \\ \vdots \\ \mathcal{N}_z(\mathbf{p}, u_m, v_m) \end{pmatrix}. \quad (5.86)$$

5. MODULES FOR IMPLEMENTING BUNDLE ADJUSTMENT

In the following formulas, we will leave away u and v to facilitate a more concise presentation. This is also supported by realizing that u and v are, in our case, constant values. This means that the blockdiagonal matrix $\widetilde{\mathbf{K}}$ also remains constant, since the camera calibration matrix is constant as well. Thus, the matrix $\widetilde{\mathbf{K}}$ only needs to be computed once and can be re-used for repeated normal evaluation.

With these definitions, the computation of normals can be done by evaluating

$$\mathbf{n}_z(\mathbf{p}) = \widetilde{\mathbf{K}} \cdot (\mathrm{diag}(\mathbf{z}(\mathbf{p})) \otimes \mathbf{I}_3) \cdot \mathcal{N}_z(\mathbf{p}) \qquad (5.87)$$

which is essentially a sparse-dense product between the constant, precalculated matrix $\widetilde{\mathbf{K}}$ and the dense, parameter-dependent vector $(\mathrm{diag}(\mathbf{z}(\mathbf{p})) \otimes \mathbf{I}_3) \cdot \mathcal{N}_z(\mathbf{p})$.

All in all, we now have an efficient computation scheme for the surface normals. When using this formulation in an optimization problem, it is also important to be able to compute the derivative of this normal computation function with respect to parameters.

Differentiating $\mathbf{n}_z(\mathbf{p}, u, v)$ as specified in (5.84) with respect to $\mathbf{p}$ yields the following result:

$$\frac{\mathrm{d}}{\mathrm{d}\mathbf{p}} \mathbf{n}_z(\mathbf{p}, u, v) = \widetilde{\mathbf{K}}_i \cdot \left(D_i(\mathbf{p}) \cdot \frac{\mathrm{d}}{\mathrm{d}\mathbf{p}} \mathcal{N}_z(\mathbf{p}, u, v) + \mathcal{N}_z(\mathbf{p}, u, v) \cdot \frac{\mathrm{d}}{\mathrm{d}\mathbf{p}} z(\mathbf{p}, u, v) \right) \qquad (5.88)$$

Note that $\mathcal{N}_z(\mathbf{p}, u, v) \cdot \frac{\mathrm{d}}{\mathrm{d}\mathbf{p}} z(\mathbf{p}, u, v)$ is an outer product, which can alternatively be computed as

$$\mathrm{diag}(\mathcal{N}_z(\mathbf{p}, u, v)) \cdot \left(\frac{\mathrm{d}}{\mathrm{d}\mathbf{p}} z(\mathbf{p}, u, v) \otimes \mathbf{1}_{3,1} \right). \qquad (5.89)$$

5.2 The Depth Map Model

For computing the full derivative of $\mathbf{n}_z(\mathbf{p})$, this suggests the following formula:

$$\frac{\mathrm{d}}{\mathrm{d}\mathbf{p}}\mathbf{n}_z(\mathbf{p}) = \widetilde{\mathbf{K}} \cdot \left((\mathrm{diag}(\mathbf{z}(\mathbf{p})) \otimes \mathbf{I}_3) \cdot \frac{\mathrm{d}}{\mathrm{d}\mathbf{p}}\mathcal{N}_z(\mathbf{p}) + \mathrm{diag}(\mathcal{N}_z(\mathbf{p})) \cdot \left(\frac{\mathrm{d}}{\mathrm{d}\mathbf{p}}\mathbf{z}(\mathbf{p}) \otimes \mathbf{1}_{3,1} \right) \right). \tag{5.90}$$

A note on efficient evaluation of the preceding formula: Often, implementations provide ways to directly compute $\mathbf{z}$, $^{\mathrm{u}}\mathcal{J}_z$, and $^{\mathrm{v}}\mathcal{J}_z$. Thus, it would be trivial to compute the stacked vector

$$(\mathbf{z}(\mathbf{p})^{\mathrm{T}}, \mathcal{J}_\mathbf{x}(\mathbf{p})^{\mathrm{T}}, \mathcal{J}_\mathbf{y}(\mathbf{p})^{\mathrm{T}})^{\mathrm{T}}, \tag{5.91}$$

which we will now abbreviate as $\mathcal{N}_z^*$. Creating the vector $\mathcal{N}_z$, as defined above, from the vector $\mathcal{N}_z^*$ involves rearranging its values, which incurs a small, but avoidable performance penalty. By exploiting the characteristics of the so-called commutation matrix, we are able to establish a formula that works directly with $\mathcal{N}_z^*$, thus avoiding that penalty.

More details about the commutation matrix can be found in the paper by Magnus and Neudecker [65], and we adopt their notation here, except for using the letter $\mathbf{C}$ instead of $\mathbf{K}$ to denote commutation matrices. This is to avoid any confusion with camera matrices. In our case, $\mathbf{C}_{m,n}$ denotes the commutation matrix with the property

$$\mathrm{vec}(\mathbf{A}^{\mathrm{T}}) = \mathbf{C}_{m,n} \cdot \mathrm{vec}(\mathbf{A}), \tag{5.92}$$

where $\mathbf{A} \in \mathbb{R}^{m \times n}$. The commutation matrix is thus useful for relating the vectorization of a matrix with the vectorization of its transpose. A commutation matrix $\mathbf{C}_{m,n}$ has size $mn \times mn$, and its inverse is $\mathbf{C}_{n,m}$, such that $\mathbf{C}_{m,n} \cdot \mathbf{C}_{n,m} = \mathbf{I}_{mn}$. Furthermore, for matrices $\mathbf{A} \in \mathbb{R}^{m \times n}$, $\mathbf{B} \in \mathbb{R}^{k \times l}$, it establishes a relation between $\mathbf{A} \otimes \mathbf{B}$

5. MODULES FOR IMPLEMENTING BUNDLE ADJUSTMENT

and $\mathbf{B} \otimes \mathbf{A}$ as follows:

$$\mathbf{C}_{k,m} \cdot (\mathbf{A} \otimes \mathbf{B}) \cdot \mathbf{C}_{l,n} = \mathbf{B} \otimes \mathbf{A}. \tag{5.93}$$

Now we can formulate a relationship between $\mathcal{N}_z^*$ and $\mathcal{N}_z$ as follows:

$$\mathcal{N}_z(\mathbf{p}) = \mathrm{vec}((\mathbf{z}(\mathbf{p}), {}^{\mathrm{u}}\mathcal{J}_z(\mathbf{p}), {}^{\mathrm{v}}\mathcal{J}_z(\mathbf{p}))^{\mathrm{T}}). \tag{5.94}$$

Using the commutation matrix, this can be changed into

$$\mathcal{N}_z(\mathbf{p}) = \mathbf{C}_{m,3} \cdot \mathrm{vec}((\mathbf{z}(\mathbf{p}), {}^{\mathrm{u}}\mathcal{J}_z(\mathbf{p}), {}^{\mathrm{v}}\mathcal{J}_z(\mathbf{p}))) = \mathbf{C}_{m,3} \cdot \mathcal{N}_z^*(\mathbf{p}). \tag{5.95}$$

Going back to formula (5.87), we see that normals can be computed from $\mathcal{N}_z^*$ as

$$\mathbf{n}_z(\mathbf{p},\mathbf{u},\mathbf{v}) = \widetilde{\mathbf{K}} \cdot (\mathrm{diag}(\mathbf{z}(\mathbf{p})) \otimes \mathbf{I}_3) \cdot \mathbf{C}_{m,3} \cdot \mathcal{N}_z^*(\mathbf{p}). \tag{5.96}$$

This can be further changed into

$$\mathbf{n}_z(\mathbf{p},\mathbf{u},\mathbf{v}) = \widetilde{\mathbf{K}} \cdot \mathbf{C}_{3,m} \cdot (\mathbf{I}_3 \otimes \mathrm{diag}(\mathbf{z}(\mathbf{p}))) \cdot \mathbf{C}_{3,m} \cdot \mathbf{C}_{m,3} \cdot \mathcal{N}_z^*(\mathbf{p}), \tag{5.97}$$

which we can simplify to

$$\mathbf{n}_z(\mathbf{p},\mathbf{u},\mathbf{v}) = \widetilde{\mathbf{K}} \cdot \mathbf{C}_{3,m} \cdot (\mathbf{I}_3 \otimes \mathrm{diag}(\mathbf{z}(\mathbf{p}))) \cdot \mathcal{N}_z^*(\mathbf{p}). \tag{5.98}$$

Note that $\widetilde{\mathbf{K}} \cdot \mathbf{C}_{3,m}$ remains constant and can be precomputed, as long as x and y remain constant. Thus, we see that the effect of reordering $\mathcal{N}_z^*$ can basically be achieved by reordering $\widetilde{\mathbf{K}}$ instead.

The formula for computation of derivatives can also be adapted to compute derivatives from $\mathcal{N}_z^*$ instead of $\mathcal{N}_z$. Formula (5.90) then

5.2 The Depth Map Model

becomes

$$\frac{\mathrm{d}}{\mathrm{d}\mathbf{p}}\mathbf{n}_z(\mathbf{p}) = \widetilde{\mathbf{K}} \cdot \mathbf{C}_{3,m} \cdot \left((\mathbf{I}_3 \otimes \mathrm{diag}(\mathbf{z}(\mathbf{p}))) \cdot \frac{\mathrm{d}}{\mathrm{d}\mathbf{p}}\mathcal{N}_z^*(\mathbf{p}) + \mathrm{diag}(\mathcal{N}_z^*(\mathbf{p})) \cdot \left(\mathbf{1}_{3,1} \otimes \frac{\mathrm{d}}{\mathrm{d}\mathbf{p}}\mathbf{z}(\mathbf{p}) \right) \right). \quad (5.99)$$

5.2.3 Surfaces Induced by Inverse Depth Maps

It is well-known that inverse depth parameterization schemes are well-suited for 3D reconstruction problems. Intuitively, they reflect the fact that distant points can be measured with lower accuracy than closer ones.

Since this is a general idea that can be applied to virtually any depth map model, it makes sense to adapt the formulas developed for general depth models to this case. We are going to decouple the depth inversion step from the depth model, which will lead to slightly modified formulas for surface, tangent, and normal computation.

In the following, we will assume that $z(\mathbf{p}, u, v)$ is the inverse depth map, which means that $\frac{1}{z(\mathbf{p},u,v)}$ is the actual depth map. As in the case of general depth map models, this definition can be extended to encompass simultaneous evaluation at locations (u_i, v_i) specified as vectors $\mathbf{u}, \mathbf{v}$.

For that case, we are going to make use of the Hadamard inverse. Since the Hadamard product is the component-wise product between matrices, the Hadamard inverse is the component-wise inverse of matrices. For a matrix $\mathbf{M} \in \mathbb{R}^{m \times n}$, we denote its Hadamard inverse as $\widehat{\mathbf{M}}$, and we formally define the inverse in a component-wise fashion as

$$\widehat{\mathbf{M}}_{i,j} = \mathbf{M}_{i,j}^{-1}. \quad (5.100)$$

This is consistent with the notation used in [64]. It should be clear

5. MODULES FOR IMPLEMENTING BUNDLE ADJUSTMENT

that evaluating

$$\widehat{z}(\mathbf{p}, \mathbf{u}, \mathbf{v}) \qquad (5.101)$$

is equivalent to evaluating the depth map at all locations specified by $\mathbf{u}, \mathbf{v}$ simultaneously. Using this concise notation, the general surface formulation from equation (5.63) turns into

$$\mathbf{d}_{\widehat{z}}(\mathbf{p}, u, v) = \widehat{z}(\mathbf{p}, u, v) \left(\mathbf{K}^{-1} \cdot \begin{pmatrix} x \\ y \\ 1 \end{pmatrix} \right), \qquad (5.102)$$

and for simultaneous evaluation of multiple surface locations, we can use

$$\mathbf{d}_{\widehat{z}}(\mathbf{p}, \mathbf{u}, \mathbf{v}) = \mathrm{vec}(\mathcal{K}(\mathbf{u}, \mathbf{v})) \circ \mathrm{vec}(\mathbf{1}_{3,1} \cdot (\widehat{\mathbf{z}}(\mathbf{p}, \mathbf{u}, \mathbf{v}))^{\mathrm{T}}), \qquad (5.103)$$

which is easily derived from equation (5.69).

5.2.3.1 Derivatives w.r.t. Surface Parameters

The formulas for evaluating a surface that is defined as an inverse depth map have been really straightforward so far. When computing derivatives, things become a little bit more complicated. In what fallows, we are going to need a formula for differentiating the Hadamard inverse function. It is easily seen that the derivative of the Hadamard inverse of some vector a computes as

$$\frac{\mathrm{d}}{\mathrm{d}\,\mathbf{a}} \widehat{\mathbf{a}} = -\mathrm{diag}(\widehat{\mathbf{a}})^2, \qquad (5.104)$$

which is analogous to the scalar rule $\frac{\mathrm{d}}{\mathrm{d}\,x} \frac{1}{x} = -(\frac{1}{x})^2$. This rule can now be applied to formula (5.73), and we end up with the following

5.2 The Depth Map Model

result:

$$\frac{\mathrm{d}}{\mathrm{d}\mathbf{p}}\mathbf{d}_{\widehat{z}}(\mathbf{p},\mathbf{u},\mathbf{v}) = -\operatorname{diag}(\operatorname{vec}(\mathcal{K}(\mathbf{u},\mathbf{v}))) \cdot (\mathbf{I}_m \otimes \mathbf{1}_{3,1}) \cdot$$
$$\operatorname{diag}(\widehat{\mathbf{z}}(\mathbf{p},\mathbf{u},\mathbf{v}))^2 \cdot \frac{\mathrm{d}}{\mathrm{d}\mathbf{p}}\mathbf{z}(\mathbf{p},\mathbf{u},\mathbf{v}). \quad (5.105)$$

If z is linear in parameters, and $\frac{\mathrm{d}}{\mathrm{d}\mathbf{p}}\mathbf{z}$ is a sparse matrix, the evaluation can be done in an especially efficient way. Details on this technique will be provided in Section 5.9.

5.2.3.2 Tangents

Let us reconsider equation (5.76) for computation of the tangents of a depth-map induced surface. The formula given there is

$$^{u}\mathbf{T}_z(\mathbf{p},\mathbf{u},\mathbf{v}) = \operatorname{diag}(\operatorname{vec}(\mathcal{K}(\mathbf{u},\mathbf{v}))) \cdot (\mathbf{I}_m \otimes \mathbf{1}_{3,1}) \cdot {}^{u}\mathcal{J}_z(\mathbf{p},\mathbf{u},\mathbf{v}) +$$
$$(\mathbf{I}_m \otimes \mathbf{K}_\mathbf{X}^{-1}) \cdot \mathbf{z}(\mathbf{p},\mathbf{u},\mathbf{v}).$$

When using an inverse depth map, this computation scheme is easily modified by replacing z with $\widehat{z}$. We then need to determine a relationship between ${}^{u}\mathcal{J}_{\widehat{z}}$ and ${}^{u}\mathcal{J}_z$. This relationship is:

$$^{u}\mathcal{J}_{\widehat{z}} = \begin{pmatrix} \frac{\mathrm{d}}{\mathrm{d}u}\widehat{z}(\mathbf{p},u_1,v_1) \\ \frac{\mathrm{d}}{\mathrm{d}u}\widehat{z}(\mathbf{p},u_2,v_2) \\ \vdots \\ \frac{\mathrm{d}}{\mathrm{d}u}\widehat{z}(\mathbf{p},u_m,v_m) \end{pmatrix}$$

$$= -\operatorname{diag}(\widehat{\mathbf{z}}(\mathbf{p},\mathbf{u},\mathbf{v}))^2 \cdot \begin{pmatrix} \frac{\mathrm{d}}{\mathrm{d}u}z(\mathbf{p},u_1,v_1) \\ \frac{\mathrm{d}}{\mathrm{d}u}z(\mathbf{p},u_2,v_2) \\ \vdots \\ \frac{\mathrm{d}}{\mathrm{d}u}z(\mathbf{p},u_m,v_m) \end{pmatrix}$$

$$= -\operatorname{diag}(\widehat{\mathbf{z}}(\mathbf{p},\mathbf{u},\mathbf{v}))^2 \cdot {}^{u}\mathcal{J}_z(\mathbf{p},\mathbf{u},\mathbf{v}).$$

5. MODULES FOR IMPLEMENTING BUNDLE ADJUSTMENT

This allows us to state the tangent computation formula as

$$^u\mathbf{T}_z(\mathbf{p}, \mathbf{u}, \mathbf{v}) = -\operatorname{diag}(\operatorname{vec}(\mathcal{K}(\mathbf{u}, \mathbf{v}))) \cdot (\mathbf{I}_m \otimes \mathbf{1}_{3,1})$$
$$\cdot \operatorname{diag}(\widehat{\mathbf{z}}(\mathbf{p}, \mathbf{u}, \mathbf{v}))^2 \cdot {}^u\mathcal{J}_z(\mathbf{p}, \mathbf{u}, \mathbf{v}) + (\mathbf{I}_m \otimes \mathbf{K}_\mathbf{X}^{-1}) \cdot \widehat{\mathbf{z}}(\mathbf{p}, \mathbf{u}, \mathbf{v}).$$

5.2.3.3 Normals

The computation of normals can also be adopted to the special case of inverse depth maps. We start by recapitulating the original formulas (5.87) and (5.98) for computing normals:

$$\mathbf{n}_z(\mathbf{p}, \mathbf{u}, \mathbf{v}) = \widetilde{\mathbf{K}} \cdot (\operatorname{diag}(\mathbf{z}(\mathbf{p}, \mathbf{u}, \mathbf{v})) \otimes \mathbf{I}_3) \cdot \mathcal{N}_z(\mathbf{p}, \mathbf{u}, \mathbf{v}),$$
$$\mathbf{n}_z(\mathbf{p}, \mathbf{u}, \mathbf{v}) = \widetilde{\mathbf{K}} \cdot \mathbf{C}_{3,m} \cdot (\mathbf{I}_3 \otimes \operatorname{diag}(\mathbf{z}(\mathbf{p}, \mathbf{u}, \mathbf{v}))) \cdot \mathcal{N}_z^*(\mathbf{p}, \mathbf{u}, \mathbf{v}).$$

We will only show how $\mathcal{N}_{\hat{z}}^*$ changes in the case of an inverse depth map, since this is the practically more relevant case. Through the relationship $\mathcal{N}_{\hat{z}}(\mathbf{p}) = \mathbf{C}_{m,3} \cdot \mathcal{N}_{\hat{z}}^*(\mathbf{p})$, these considerations can be translated to $\mathcal{N}_{\hat{z}}$. The original definition of $\mathcal{N}_{\hat{z}}^*$ is:

$$\mathcal{N}_z^*(\mathbf{p}) = \begin{pmatrix} \mathbf{z}(\mathbf{p}) \\ {}^u\mathcal{J}_z(\mathbf{p}) \\ {}^v\mathcal{J}_z(\mathbf{p}) \end{pmatrix}.$$

In the section about tangents, we have seen that

$$^x\mathcal{J}_{\hat{z}} = -\operatorname{diag}(\widehat{\mathbf{z}}(\mathbf{p}))^2 \cdot {}^u\mathcal{J}_z(\mathbf{p}). \qquad (5.106)$$

This implies the relationship

$$\mathcal{N}_{\hat{z}}^*(\mathbf{p}) = \begin{pmatrix} \widehat{\mathbf{z}}(\mathbf{p}) \\ -\widehat{\mathbf{z}}(\mathbf{p})^{\circ 2} \circ {}^u\mathcal{J}_z(\mathbf{p}) \\ -\widehat{\mathbf{z}}(\mathbf{p})^{\circ 2} \circ {}^v\mathcal{J}_z(\mathbf{p}) \end{pmatrix}, \qquad (5.107)$$

5.2 The Depth Map Model

where the superscript $\circ n$ denotes the Hadamard exponential of a vector, which is the component-wise exponential. This in turn leads to the formula

$$\mathbf{n}_{\hat{z}}(\mathbf{p}, \mathbf{u}, \mathbf{v}) = \widetilde{\mathbf{K}} \cdot \mathbf{C}_{3,m} \cdot \operatorname{diag}\begin{pmatrix} \widehat{\mathbf{z}}(\mathbf{p})^{\circ 2} \\ -\widehat{\mathbf{z}}(\mathbf{p})^{\circ 3} \\ -\widehat{\mathbf{z}}(\mathbf{p})^{\circ 3} \end{pmatrix} \cdot \begin{pmatrix} \mathbf{1}_m \\ {}^{\mathrm{u}}\mathfrak{J}_z(\mathbf{p}) \\ {}^{\mathrm{v}}\mathfrak{J}_z(\mathbf{p}) \end{pmatrix}. \quad (5.108)$$

Differentiating this formula with respect to **p** yields the following result (we omit some details of the computation):

$$\frac{\mathrm{d}}{\mathrm{d}\mathbf{p}}\mathbf{n}_{\hat{z}}(\mathbf{p}) = \widetilde{\mathbf{K}} \cdot \mathbf{C}_{3,m} \cdot \left[\operatorname{diag}\begin{pmatrix} \widehat{\mathbf{z}}(\mathbf{p})^{\circ 3} \\ \widehat{\mathbf{z}}(\mathbf{p})^{\circ 3} \\ \widehat{\mathbf{z}}(\mathbf{p})^{\circ 3} \end{pmatrix} \cdot \frac{\mathrm{d}}{\mathrm{d}\mathbf{p}} \begin{pmatrix} -2\mathbf{z}(\mathbf{p}) \\ -({}^{\mathrm{u}}\mathfrak{J}_z(\mathbf{p})) \\ -({}^{\mathrm{v}}\mathfrak{J}_z(\mathbf{p})) \end{pmatrix} \right.$$

$$\left. + \operatorname{diag}\begin{pmatrix} \mathbf{0}_m \\ \widehat{\mathbf{z}}(\mathbf{p})^{\circ 4} \circ {}^{\mathrm{u}}\mathfrak{J}_z(\mathbf{p}) \\ \widehat{\mathbf{z}}(\mathbf{p})^{\circ 4} \circ {}^{\mathrm{v}}\mathfrak{J}_z(\mathbf{p}) \end{pmatrix} \cdot \frac{\mathrm{d}}{\mathrm{d}\mathbf{p}} \begin{pmatrix} \mathbf{0}_m \\ 3\mathbf{z}(\mathbf{p}) \\ 3\mathbf{z}(\mathbf{p}) \end{pmatrix} \right] \quad (5.109)$$

Again, this formula can be implemented in an especially efficient way if z is a B-spline surface. We will give details later on.

5.2.4 Inverse Depth Maps using B-Splines

Finally, we are ready to describe the inverse B-Spline depth map model used in our implementation. Combining the results from the previous section, it is quite a simple matter now to derive all necessary formulas. The functionality of the associated module is as follows:

1. It accepts a $n \cdot m$-dimensional vector **p** of spline surface parameters, as described in Equation (5.26).

2. The output of the module is a point cloud of M 3D points

5. MODULES FOR IMPLEMENTING BUNDLE ADJUSTMENT

$d_{\hat{s}}(\mathbf{p}, u, v)$, evaluated at the reference surface point coordinates (u_j, v_j), where j ranges from 1 to M. The surface coordinates are chosen, in our case, to lie on a regular grid, such that the underlying B-Spline surface can be evaluated using the respective basis matrices $\mathbf{L}, \mathcal{L}_u, \mathcal{L}_v$ as defined in Equations (5.43) and (5.62).

3. Optionally, the module outputs the normal vectors $\mathbf{n}_{\hat{s}}$ of the surface. They are useful for implementing lighting calculations.

4. Furthermore, the module computes the Jacobian of the point cloud and, if required, of the surface normals, with respect to surface parameters.

We have developed all the formulas required to compute these values for the general case of arbitrary inverse depth maps, and we will now specialize these formulas to the case of inverse B-Spline depth maps.

We will start with the evaluation of the point cloud from the surface parameters. For this case, Equation (5.103) can be applied directly:

$$\mathbf{d}_{\hat{s}}(\mathbf{p}, \mathbf{u}, \mathbf{v}) = \mathrm{vec}(\mathcal{K}(\mathbf{u}, \mathbf{v})) \circ \mathrm{vec}(1_{3,1} \cdot (\widehat{\mathbf{s}}(\mathbf{p}, \mathbf{u}, \mathbf{v}))^T), \quad (5.110)$$

where $\mathbf{s}(\mathbf{p}, \mathbf{u}, \mathbf{v})$ is evaluated by computing the matrix-vector product $\mathbf{L} \cdot \mathbf{p}$.

The computation of the surface normals at the evaluation positions $\mathbf{u}, \mathbf{v}$ can be done by adapting Equation (5.108) to the case of B-Spline surfaces. Leaving away the parameters $\mathbf{u}, \mathbf{v}$ for brevity, the

5.2 The Depth Map Model

formula becomes:

$$\mathbf{n}_{\hat{s}}(\mathbf{p}) = \widetilde{\mathbf{K}} \cdot \mathbf{C}_{3,m} \cdot \operatorname{diag} \begin{pmatrix} \hat{\mathbf{s}}(\mathbf{p})^{\circ 2} \\ -\hat{\mathbf{s}}(\mathbf{p})^{\circ 3} \\ -\hat{\mathbf{s}}(\mathbf{p})^{\circ 3} \end{pmatrix} \cdot \begin{pmatrix} \mathbf{1}_m \\ \mathcal{L}_\mathrm{u} \cdot \mathbf{p} \\ \mathcal{L}_\mathrm{v} \cdot \mathbf{p} \end{pmatrix}. \tag{5.111}$$

For computing the Jacobian of the point cloud with respect to surface parameters, we can use Formula (5.105):

$$\frac{\mathrm{d}}{\mathrm{d}\mathbf{p}}\mathbf{d}_{\hat{s}}(\mathbf{p},\mathbf{u},\mathbf{v}) = -\operatorname{diag}(\operatorname{vec}(\mathcal{K}(\mathbf{u},\mathbf{v}))) \cdot (\mathbf{I}_m \otimes \mathbf{1}_{3,1}) \cdot \\ \operatorname{diag}(\hat{\mathbf{s}}(\mathbf{p},\mathbf{u},\mathbf{v}))^2 \cdot \mathbf{L}. \tag{5.112}$$

And finally, the most difficult part is the computation of the Jacobian of the surface normals. Formula (5.109) can be adapted to the case of a B-Spline depth map as follows:

$$\frac{\mathrm{d}}{\mathrm{d}\mathbf{p}}\mathbf{n}_{\hat{s}}(\mathbf{p}) = \widetilde{\mathbf{K}} \cdot \mathbf{C}_{3,m} \cdot \left[\operatorname{diag} \begin{pmatrix} \hat{\mathbf{s}}(\mathbf{p})^{\circ 3} \\ \hat{\mathbf{s}}(\mathbf{p})^{\circ 3} \\ \hat{\mathbf{s}}(\mathbf{p})^{\circ 3} \end{pmatrix} \cdot \begin{pmatrix} -2\mathbf{L} \\ -\mathcal{L}_\mathrm{u} \\ -\mathcal{L}_\mathrm{v} \end{pmatrix} \right. \\ \left. + \operatorname{diag} \begin{pmatrix} \mathbf{0}_m \\ \hat{\mathbf{s}}(\mathbf{p})^{\circ 4} \circ (\mathcal{L}_\mathrm{u} \cdot \mathbf{p}) \\ \hat{\mathbf{s}}(\mathbf{p})^{\circ 4} \circ (\mathcal{L}_\mathrm{v} \cdot \mathbf{p}) \end{pmatrix} \cdot \begin{pmatrix} \mathbf{0}_m \\ 3\mathbf{L} \\ 3\mathbf{L} \end{pmatrix} \right] \tag{5.113}$$

Using these formulas, the depth map surface module can be implemented. The evaluation of the Jacobian matrices is done according to the technique described in Section 5.9 in order to avoid computation of matrix products between sparse matrices.

5. MODULES FOR IMPLEMENTING BUNDLE ADJUSTMENT

5.3 Perspective Projection

According to our presentation in Chapter 1, the perspective projection of a point b is computed as $\pi(\mathbf{K} \cdot b)$, where π represents the perspective divide, and $\mathbf{K}$ is the matrix containing the intrinsic camera parameters. Our module for perspective projection evaluates this function for a set of points $\mathbf{b}_i \in \mathbb{R}^3$ that it receives as input. In addition to computing the actual perspective projection, the module allows to specify a constant rigid transformation using a rotation matrix $\mathbf{R}$ and a translation vector $\mathbf{t}$, so that the overall computation performed by the module for one point is

$$\mathbf{g}(\mathbf{b}_i) = \pi(\mathbf{K} \cdot (\mathbf{R} \cdot (\mathbf{b}_i - \mathbf{t}))) \tag{5.114}$$

This additional constant rigid transformation is useful for the case of a calibrated point light source, since the point cloud has to be transformed into the frame of reference of the light source. This transformation is, just like the rigid transformation between a pair of stereo cameras, a constant rigid transformation.

The overall function $\mathbf{f}$ is then a function $\mathbb{R}^{3 \cdot M} \to \mathbb{R}^{2 \cdot M}$, where M is the number of points to be transformed and projected. Letting $\mathbf{b}$ denote the vector $(\mathbf{b}_1^T, \mathbf{b}_2^T, \ldots, \mathbf{b}_M^T)^T$ consisting of all vectors $\mathbf{b}_i$ stacked on top of each other, the function is then defined as

$$\mathbf{f}(\mathbf{b}) = \begin{pmatrix} \mathbf{g}(\mathbf{b}_1) \\ \mathbf{g}(\mathbf{b}_2) \\ \vdots \\ \mathbf{g}(\mathbf{b}_M) \end{pmatrix} \tag{5.115}$$

The derivatives can be determined easily if the derivatives of $\mathbf{g}$ are known. Let $\mathbf{b}'_i = (\mathbf{b}_i - \mathbf{t})$, and let $\mathbf{K}^* = \mathbf{K} \cdot \mathbf{R}$. Furthermore,

5.3 Perspective Projection

let us denote with $\mathbf{K}_1^*, \mathbf{K}_2^*, \mathbf{K}_3^*$ the first, second and third rows of $\mathbf{K}^*$. Then, the derivative of g is computed as

$$\frac{d}{d\,\mathbf{b}_i}\mathbf{g}(\mathbf{b}_i) = \mathbf{J}_\mathbf{g}(\mathbf{b}_i) = \begin{pmatrix} (\mathbf{K}_3^* \cdot \mathbf{b}_i') \cdot \mathbf{K}_1^* - (\mathbf{K}_1^* \cdot \mathbf{b}_i') \cdot \mathbf{K}_3^* \\ (\mathbf{K}_3^* \cdot \mathbf{b}_i') \cdot \mathbf{K}_2^* - (\mathbf{K}_2^* \cdot \mathbf{b}_i') \cdot \mathbf{K}_3^* \end{pmatrix} \cdot \frac{1}{(\mathbf{K}_3^* \cdot \mathbf{b}_i')^2} \quad (5.116)$$

For computing the overall Jacobian of f, these derivatives are arranged into a block-diagonal matrix as follows:

$$\mathbf{J}_\mathbf{f}(\mathbf{b}) = \begin{pmatrix} \mathbf{J}_\mathbf{g}(\mathbf{b}_1) & 0 & \cdots & 0 \\ 0 & \mathbf{J}_\mathbf{g}(\mathbf{b}_2) & \ddots & \vdots \\ \vdots & \ddots & \ddots & 0 \\ 0 & \cdots & 0 & \mathbf{J}_\mathbf{g}(\mathbf{b}_M) \end{pmatrix} \quad (5.117)$$

Our implementation of this module is a bit more general, since it also allows the user to project the same point cloud to multiple views with possibly different camera matrices and extrinsic transformations. In that case, let us denote the camera matrices for the views with $\mathbf{K}_j$, the rotation matrices with $\mathbf{R}_j$, and the translation vectors with $\mathbf{t}_j$. Furthermore, assume that there are N views, and let us define

$$\mathbf{g}_j(\mathbf{b}_i) = \pi(\mathbf{K}_j \cdot (\mathbf{R}_j \cdot (\mathbf{b}_i - \mathbf{t}_j))), \quad (5.118)$$

$$\mathbf{f}_j(\mathbf{b}) = \begin{pmatrix} \mathbf{g}_j(\mathbf{b}_1) \\ \mathbf{g}_j(\mathbf{b}_2) \\ \vdots \\ \mathbf{g}_j(\mathbf{b}_M) \end{pmatrix}. \quad (5.119)$$

Finally, we can re-define f as a function of type $\mathbb{R}^{3 \cdot M} \to \mathbb{R}^{2 \cdot N \cdot M}$ as

5. MODULES FOR IMPLEMENTING BUNDLE ADJUSTMENT

follows:
$$\mathbf{f}(\mathbf{b}) = \begin{pmatrix} \mathbf{f}_1(\mathbf{b}) \\ \mathbf{f}_2(\mathbf{b}) \\ \vdots \\ \mathbf{f}_N(\mathbf{b}) \end{pmatrix}. \qquad (5.120)$$

Note that this definition also makes sense for $N = 1$, and then coincides with our initial definition. The Jacobian now also looks a bit different:

$$\mathbf{J}_{\mathbf{f}_j}(\mathbf{b}) = \begin{pmatrix} \mathbf{J}_{\mathbf{g}_j}(\mathbf{b}_1) & 0 & \cdots & 0 \\ 0 & \mathbf{J}_{\mathbf{g}_j}(\mathbf{b}_2) & \ddots & \vdots \\ \vdots & \ddots & \ddots & 0 \\ 0 & \cdots & 0 & \mathbf{J}_{\mathbf{g}_j}(\mathbf{b}_M) \end{pmatrix}, \quad \mathbf{J}_\mathbf{f}(\mathbf{b}) = \begin{pmatrix} \mathbf{J}_{\mathbf{f}_1}(\mathbf{b}) \\ \mathbf{J}_{\mathbf{f}_2}(\mathbf{b}) \\ \vdots \\ \mathbf{J}_{\mathbf{f}_N}(\mathbf{b}) \end{pmatrix}.$$
$$(5.121)$$

5.4 Image Interpolation

Images recorded by common cameras are discrete, meaning that the image value $\overline{\mathcal{I}}(u, v)$ of some image $\overline{\mathcal{I}}$ at pixel coordinates (u, v) is only defined if and only if $(u, v) \in \mathbb{Z}^2$, and if u and v are within the image boundaries which depend on the camera's resolution.

For our optimization problems, this is quite bad news because our optimization approach only works with continuous, differentiable functions. This is a well-known problem, and it is typically solved by employing image sub-sampling methods that turn the discrete image function $\overline{\mathcal{I}}$ into a continuous one by means of interpolation. The most common interpolation methods are nearest neighbour, bi-linear, and bi-cubic interpolation, in order of increasing quality.

For optical flow methods, it is recommended to use bi-cubic filtering, as mentioned in the paper by Sun et al. [42]. As we have

5.4 Image Interpolation

mentioned in Chapter 1, our algorithms are actually very close in spirit to optical flow algorithms, which makes bi-cubic filtering seem a good choice for our algorithms as well. In our implementation, we are making use of the well-known OPENCV[1] library for performing image sub-sampling using the `remap` function. We will not go into details on cubic spline interpolation methods here, and refer the interested reader to [66].

In the following, we shall denote $\mathcal{J}$ to be the continuous image approximating $\overline{\mathcal{J}}$ by applying the bi-cubic interpolation scheme. Our image interpolation module performs simultaneous interpolation of the M reference points in each of the N images that currently are in the sliding window. First of all, we will define functions $^i\mathbf{f}$ that interpolate a set of M points in image i as follows:

$$^i\mathbf{f}(^i\mathbf{u},^i\mathbf{v}) = \begin{pmatrix} \mathcal{J}_i(^i\mathbf{u}_1,^i\mathbf{v}_1) \\ \mathcal{J}_i(^i\mathbf{u}_2,^i\mathbf{v}_2) \\ \vdots \\ \mathcal{J}_i(^i\mathbf{u}_M,^i\mathbf{v}_M) \end{pmatrix} \qquad (5.122)$$

Here, $(^i\mathbf{u}_j,^i\mathbf{v}_j)$ are sets of pixel coordinates at which the images in the window are to be evaluated, where j denotes the point index and i the image index. These sub-functions can now be used to define the overall functionality of our module as

$$\mathbf{f}(^1\mathbf{u},^1\mathbf{v},^2\mathbf{u},^2\mathbf{v},\ldots,^N\mathbf{u},^N\mathbf{v}) = \begin{pmatrix} ^1\mathbf{f}(^1\mathbf{u},^1\mathbf{v}) \\ ^2\mathbf{f}(^2\mathbf{u},^2\mathbf{v}) \\ \vdots \\ ^N\mathbf{f}(^N\mathbf{u},^N\mathbf{v}) \end{pmatrix}. \qquad (5.123)$$

Thus, the function **f** computes the stacked, interpolated image val-

---

[1] http://opencv.willowgarage.com

5. MODULES FOR IMPLEMENTING BUNDLE ADJUSTMENT

ues at the specified positions.

For computing derivatives of f, there are two main approaches: The first, straightforward one is to take the mathematical definition of bi-cubic sub-sampling and compute the analytic derivatives. An early implementation of our image sub-sampling module actually used this method. However, as Brooks and Arbel point out [61], it is more efficient to compute the derivative image once and for all and subsequently apply a sub-sampling scheme on that image. Our experiments also confirmed that this technique does not interfere with the image alignment process and is much faster.

For computing the image derivatives, it has been suggested to use a 5-point filter [42]. We will denote the derivative images obtained that way with $\overline{\mathcal{J}}_u$ and $\overline{\mathcal{J}}_v$ for the first and second image coordinate direction, respectively. The interpolated images (we use bi-cubic interpolation here as well) will be denoted with $\mathcal{J}_u$ and $\mathcal{J}_v$. Then the Jacobian of $^i\mathcal{J}$ is approximated as

$$\mathbf{J}_{\mathcal{J}}(u,v) \approx \begin{pmatrix} \mathcal{J}_u(u,v) & \mathcal{J}_v(u,v) \end{pmatrix} =: \mathbf{J}^*_{\mathcal{J}}(u,v) \qquad (5.124)$$

Thus, we compute an approximation to the Jacobian of functions $^i\mathbf{f}$ as

$$\mathbf{J}_{i\mathbf{f}}(^i\mathbf{u},{^i\mathbf{v}}) \approx \begin{pmatrix} \mathbf{J}^*_{i\mathcal{J}}(^i\mathbf{u}_1,{^i\mathbf{v}}_1) & 0 & \cdots & 0 \\ 0 & \mathbf{J}^*_{i\mathcal{J}}(^i\mathbf{u}_2,{^i\mathbf{v}}_2) & \ddots & \vdots \\ \vdots & \ddots & \ddots & 0 \\ 0 & \cdots & 0 & \mathbf{J}^*_{i\mathcal{J}}(^i\mathbf{u}_M,{^i\mathbf{v}}_M) \end{pmatrix}$$

$$=: \mathbf{J}^*_{i\mathbf{f}}(^i\mathbf{u},{^i\mathbf{v}}), \quad (5.125)$$

5.5 Brightness Warping

and an approximation to the Jacobian of f as

$$\mathbf{J_f} \approx \begin{pmatrix} \mathbf{J}^*_{1\mathbf{f}}(^1\mathbf{u},^1\mathbf{v}) & 0 & \cdots & 0 \\ 0 & \mathbf{J}^*_{2\mathbf{f}}(^2\mathbf{u},^2\mathbf{v}) & \ddots & \vdots \\ \vdots & \ddots & \ddots & 0 \\ 0 & \cdots & 0 & \mathbf{J}^*_{N\mathbf{f}}(^N\mathbf{u},^N\mathbf{v}) \end{pmatrix}. \quad (5.126)$$

5.5 Brightness Warping

In this Section, we are going to discuss the modules involved in computing the brightness warping function $^{l_t}_{B}w_j(\mathbf{p}, \mathbf{a}_i)$ as introduced in Chapter 1, Equation (3.10). Since the involved formulas are rather complex, the computation process is broken up into three steps, represented by three modules. Before we continue with the discussion of those modules, let us analyse the structure of the correction factors. First of all, we note that the factors can be reshaped such that the cosines of $\alpha_{k,j}$ and $\alpha_{0,j}$ are computed using the dot product formula:

$$^{l_t}_{B}w_j(\mathbf{p}, \mathbf{a}_i) = \frac{|\mathbf{d}_{l_t}(\mathbf{p}, \mathbf{a}_i, u_j, v_j)|^2}{\cos\alpha(\mathbf{p}, \mathbf{a}_i, u_j, v_j)} \cdot \frac{\cos\alpha(\mathbf{p}, \mathbf{a}_0, u_j, v_j)}{|\mathbf{d}_{l_t}(\mathbf{p}, \mathbf{a}_0, u_j, v_j)|^2} = \frac{|\mathbf{d}_{l_t}(\mathbf{p}, \mathbf{a}_i, u_j, v_j)|^3 \cdot \mathbf{d}_{l_t}(\mathbf{p}, \mathbf{a}_0, u_j, v_j)^T \cdot \mathbf{n}_z(\mathbf{p}, u_j, v_j)}{|\mathbf{d}_{l_t}(\mathbf{p}, \mathbf{a}_0, u_j, v_j)|^3 \cdot \mathbf{d}_{l_t}(\mathbf{p}, \mathbf{a}_i, u_j, v_j)^T \cdot \mathbf{n}_z(\mathbf{p}, u_j, v_j)} \quad (5.127)$$

The surface computation module outputs a 3D point cloud along with the associated normals, which are subsequently used as input to this formula, along with the vector a of extrinsic camera parameters. Let the 3D points be denoted by x_j, and the associated normals by n_j, and let x and n be vectors containing all points resp. normals, stacked on top of each other. Above formula can then be

5. MODULES FOR IMPLEMENTING BUNDLE ADJUSTMENT

written as

$${}^{l_t}_B w_j(\mathbf{a}_i, \mathbf{x}, \mathbf{n}) = \frac{|\mathbf{T}(\widetilde{\mathbf{a}}_i, l_t) - \mathbf{x}_j|^3 \cdot (\mathbf{T}(\widetilde{\mathbf{a}}_0, l_t) - \mathbf{x}_j)^\mathrm{T} \cdot \mathbf{n}_j}{|\mathbf{T}(\widetilde{\mathbf{a}}_0, l_t) - \mathbf{x}_j|^3 \cdot (\mathbf{T}(\widetilde{\mathbf{a}}_i, l_t) - \mathbf{x}_j)^\mathrm{T} \cdot \mathbf{n}_j} \quad (5.128)$$

In our case, $\mathbf{a}_0$ are extrinsic parameters that correspond to the identity transformation, thus we can further simplify the formula into

$$^{l_t}_B w_j(\mathbf{a}_i, \mathbf{x}, \mathbf{n}) = \frac{|\mathbf{T}(\widetilde{\mathbf{a}}_i, l_t) - \mathbf{x}_j|^3 \cdot (l_t - \mathbf{x}_j)^\mathrm{T} \cdot \mathbf{n}_j}{|l_t - \mathbf{x}_j|^3 \cdot (\mathbf{T}(\widetilde{\mathbf{a}}_i, l_t) - \mathbf{x}_j)^\mathrm{T} \cdot \mathbf{n}_j}. \quad (5.129)$$

Using this simplified formula, we can now give an overview of the three modules that we are using to implement the brightness warping function. These are as follows:

1. The first module performs computation of the values

$$\begin{aligned}
^1\mathbf{y}_{i,j} &= \mathbf{f}_1(\mathbf{a}_i, \mathbf{x}_j) = \mathbf{T}(\widetilde{\mathbf{a}}_i, l_t) - \mathbf{x}_j, \\
^2\mathbf{y}_j &= \mathbf{f}_2(\mathbf{x}_j, \mathbf{n}_j) = \mathbf{n}_j \cdot |l_t - \mathbf{x}_j|^3, \\
^3 y_j &= f_3(\mathbf{x}_j, \mathbf{n}_j) = (l_t - \mathbf{x}_j)^\mathrm{T} \cdot \mathbf{n}_j,
\end{aligned} \quad (5.130)$$

and stacks the computation results on top of each other. We will call these values the *brightness warping components*.

2. Afterwards, these values are used by the second module to compute the numerator and denominator values of (5.129) as

$$\begin{aligned}
^1 z_{i,j} &= g_1(^1\mathbf{y}_{i,j}, {}^3 y_j) = |^1\mathbf{y}_{i,j}|^3 \cdot {}^3 y_j, \\
^2 z_{i,j} &= g_2(^1\mathbf{y}_{i,j}, {}^2\mathbf{y}_j) = {}^1\mathbf{y}_{i,j}^\mathrm{T} \cdot {}^2\mathbf{y}_j.
\end{aligned} \quad (5.131)$$

Again, these values are stacked on top of each other. We will call these values the *brightness warping numerators and denominators*.

3. Finally, the brightness warping values are computed by per-

5.5 Brightness Warping

forming a component-wise division of the values g_1, g_2. Using the notation $\widehat{v}$ to denote the inverse of some scalar v, the corresponding formula is

$$h({}^1z_{i,j}, {}^2z_{i,j}) = {}^1z_{i,j} \cdot {}^2\widehat{z}_{i,j}. \quad (5.132)$$

These values finally are the brightness warping values that can be used to map intensities from some frame back to the template image.

These modules are employed in both of our light-modelling algorithms. Figure 5.7 shows how they typically work together. Note that they are also part of our algorithm diagrams shown in Figures 5.3 and 5.4. The functions themselves have already been defined, but to provide a complete specification of the modules, we still have to discuss formulas for computation of the derivatives of these functions.

We start with the derivatives of the brightness warping components, denoted by functions $\mathbf{f}_1(\mathbf{a}_i, \mathbf{x}_j)$, $\mathbf{f}_2(\mathbf{x}_j, \mathbf{n}_j)$, and $\mathbf{f}_3(\mathbf{x}_j, \mathbf{n}_j)$. All of these derivatives are quite simple to compute, except maybe for the function $\mathbf{f}_1(\mathbf{a}_i, \mathbf{x}_j)$, where we need to compute the derivative of $\mathbf{T}(\widetilde{\mathbf{a}}_i, \mathbf{l}_t)$. This is the inverse rigid transformation corresponding to $\mathbf{a}_i$, such that

$$\mathbf{T}(\widetilde{\mathbf{a}}_i, \mathbf{T}(\mathbf{a}_i, \mathbf{x})) = \mathbf{x}. \quad (5.133)$$

The computation of this derivative has already been discussed in Section 5.1 about rigid transformations, so we will refer the reader to formulas (5.10) through (5.13).

5. MODULES FOR IMPLEMENTING BUNDLE ADJUSTMENT

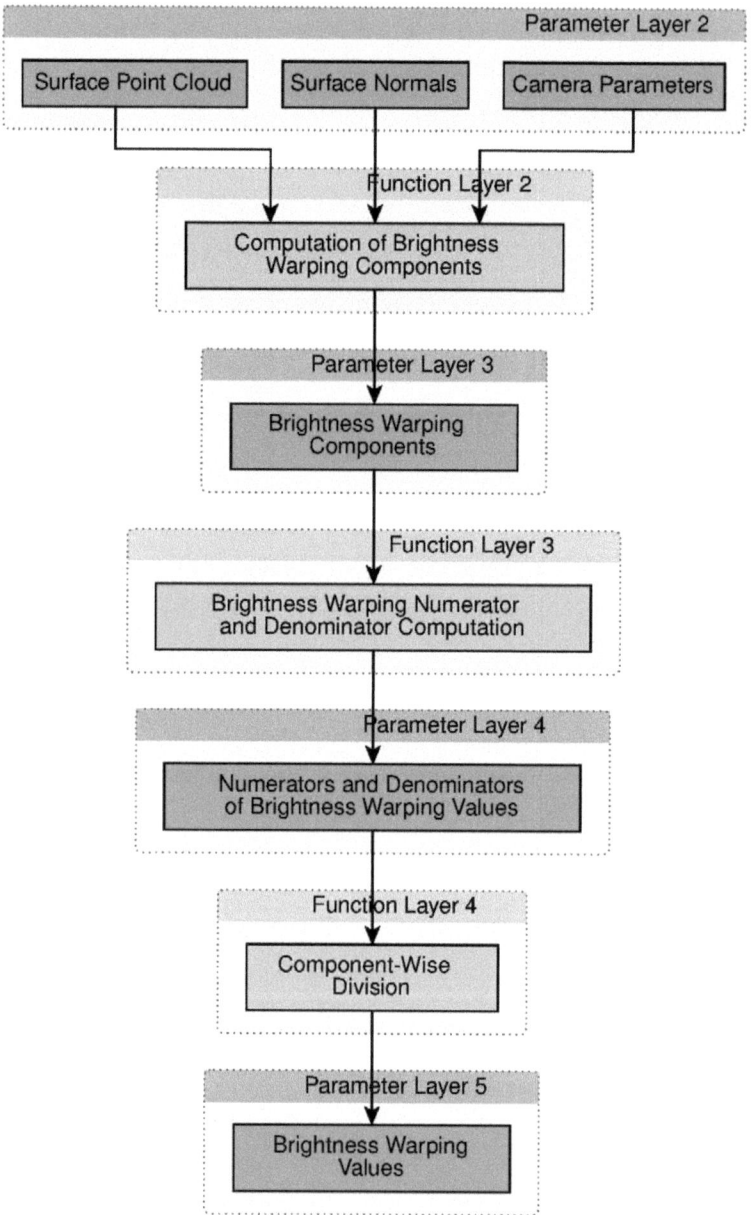

Figure 5.7: Computational graph showing the typical interaction of modules involved in computing the brightness warping functions.

5.5 Brightness Warping

All other derivatives are quite easy to determine, and we state only the results here:

$$\frac{d}{d\mathbf{x}_j}\mathbf{f}_1(\mathbf{a}_i, \mathbf{x}_j) = \mathbf{I}_3 \tag{5.134}$$

$$\frac{d}{d\mathbf{x}_j}\mathbf{f}_2(\mathbf{x}_j, \mathbf{n}_j) = -3 \cdot |\mathbf{l}_t - \mathbf{x}_j| \cdot (\mathbf{n}_j \cdot (\mathbf{l}_t - \mathbf{x}_j)^{\mathrm{T}}) \tag{5.135}$$

$$\frac{d}{d\mathbf{n}_j}\mathbf{f}_2(\mathbf{x}_j, \mathbf{n}_j) = |\mathbf{l}_t - \mathbf{x}_j|^3 \cdot \mathbf{I}_3 \tag{5.136}$$

$$\frac{d}{d\mathbf{x}_j}f_3(\mathbf{x}_j, \mathbf{n}_j) = -\mathbf{n}_j^{\mathrm{T}} \tag{5.137}$$

$$\frac{d}{d\mathbf{n}_j}f_3(\mathbf{x}_j, \mathbf{n}_j) = -\mathbf{x}_j^{\mathrm{T}} \tag{5.138}$$

The derivatives for the functions g_1 and g_2 are then

$$\frac{d}{d\,^1\mathbf{y}_{i,j}}g_1(^1\mathbf{y}_{i,j}, {}^3y_j) = 3 \cdot |^1\mathbf{y}_{i,j}| \cdot {}^3y_j \cdot {}^1\mathbf{y}_{i,j}^{\mathrm{T}} \tag{5.139}$$

$$\frac{d}{d\,^3y_j}g_1(^1\mathbf{y}_{i,j}, {}^3y_j) = |^1\mathbf{y}_{i,j}|^3 \tag{5.140}$$

$$\frac{d}{d\,^1\mathbf{y}_{i,j}}g_2(^1\mathbf{y}_{i,j}, {}^2\mathbf{y}_j) = {}^2\mathbf{y}_j^{\mathrm{T}} \tag{5.141}$$

$$\frac{d}{d\,^2\mathbf{y}_j}g_2(^1\mathbf{y}_{i,j}, {}^2\mathbf{y}_j) = {}^1\mathbf{y}_{i,j}^{\mathrm{T}} \tag{5.142}$$

Finally, the derivatives of $h(^1z_{i,j}, {}^2z_{i,j})$ are determined as

$$\frac{d}{d\,^1z_{i,j}}h(^1z_{i,j}, {}^2z_{i,j}) = {}^2\widehat{z}_{i,j} \tag{5.143}$$

$$\frac{d}{d\,^2z_{i,j}}h(^1z_{i,j}, {}^2z_{i,j}) = -\frac{^1z_{i,j}}{^2z_{i,j}^2}. \tag{5.144}$$

In our implementation, the modules actually embody stacks of the functions introduced here, such that they simultaneously compute values for a set of M points and N views of a scene. The extension of our functions that have been defined on a per-view,

5. MODULES FOR IMPLEMENTING BUNDLE ADJUSTMENT

per-point basis to the case of multiple views and multiple points can be done analogously to the case of rigid transformations, and we will not go into detail here.

Notice that Figures 5.3 and 5.4 actually do not show the brightness warping component computation as a separate module, which might be unexpected. The reason for this is that we have simply extended the already present rigid transformation module to compute the brightness warping components as well, which is more efficient than implementing the module separately.

5.6 Unit Quaternion Constraints

As we have explained earlier, our optimization framework implements equality constraints by means of the Lagrange Term module, which expects constraints to be specified by means of scalar function modules. When formulated as a scalar constraint, the condition for ensuring that a 4-dimensional sub-vector of some parameter vector c is

$$h_i(\mathbf{c}) = 1 - [\mathbf{c}]_{i:i+3}^2, \tag{5.145}$$

where the notation $[\mathbf{x}]_{i:j}$ represents the sub-vector $(\mathbf{x}_i, \mathbf{x}_{i+1}, \ldots, \mathbf{x}_j)^\mathrm{T}$ of $\mathbf{x}$. Using the value of i that represents the position of the rotation quaternion to be constrained within $\mathbf{c}$, this is exactly the constraint that we need. Note that $h_i(\mathbf{c}) = 0$ if and only if $[\mathbf{c}]_{i:i+3}^2 = 1$.

In our case, the overall parameter vector to be constrained is the vector $\mathbf{c} = (\mathbf{a}_\mathcal{V}, \mathbf{p})$, where $\mathbf{a}_\mathcal{V}$ contains the extrinsic parameters for the views in the sliding window. Let $\mathcal{V} = \{\mathcal{V}_1, \mathcal{V}_2, \ldots, \mathcal{V}_N\}$, where N is the number of views in the sliding window. Then the vector $\mathbf{a}_\mathcal{V}$ would be composed of sub-vectors $\mathbf{a}_{\mathrm{t},\mathcal{V}_1}$ and $\mathbf{a}_{\mathrm{q},\mathcal{V}_1}$ representing translation vector and rotation quaternion, respectively. Formally,

5.7 A Scale Uniqueness Constraint

the shape of $\mathbf{a}_\mathcal{V}$ would then be

$$\mathbf{a}_\mathcal{V} = (\mathbf{a}_{t,\mathcal{V}_1}^T, \mathbf{a}_{q,\mathcal{V}_1}^T, \mathbf{a}_{t,\mathcal{V}_2}^T, \mathbf{a}_{q,\mathcal{V}_2}^T, \ldots, \mathbf{a}_{t,\mathcal{V}_N}^T, \mathbf{a}_{q,\mathcal{V}_N}^T)^T,$$

and we would need N constraints $h_{(i-1)\cdot 7+4}(\mathbf{c})$ with $1 \leq i \leq N$ to enforce unit length on all rotation quaternions for all views.

The derivatives of this constraint function are:

$$\nabla h_i(\mathbf{c}) = \begin{pmatrix} \mathbf{0}_{i-1} \\ 2 \cdot [\mathbf{c}]_{i:i+3} \\ \mathbf{0}_{N-i-4} \end{pmatrix}, \tag{5.146}$$

$$\mathbf{H}_{h_i}(\mathbf{c}) = \begin{pmatrix} \mathbf{0}_{i-1,i-1} & \mathbf{0}_{i-1,4} & \mathbf{0}_{i-1,N-i-4} \\ \mathbf{0}_{4,i-1} & 2 \cdot \mathbf{I}_4 & \mathbf{0}_{4,N-i-4} \\ \mathbf{0}_{N-i-4,i-1} & \mathbf{0}_{N-i-4,i-1} & \mathbf{0}_{N-i-4,N-i-4} \end{pmatrix}. \tag{5.147}$$

5.7 A Scale Uniqueness Constraint

As we have mentioned in the introduction, our algorithms, except for the one using calibrated light, perform reconstructions only up to scale. Since it is not possible to retrieve the scale, we at least need to make sure that it is unique. Otherwise, we would introduce an artificial degree of freedom into our optimization problem, making it infeasible to solve.

Scale uniqueness can be achieved easily by constraining the inverse depth map to have a certain average value as follows:

$$c = \frac{\sum_{j=1}^{M} z(\mathbf{p}, u_j, v_j)}{M}, \tag{5.148}$$

where $c \in \mathbb{R}$ is an arbitrary constant, and the values $z(\mathbf{p}, u_j, v_j)$ are the *inverse* depth values. As we have explained above, we are using

5. MODULES FOR IMPLEMENTING BUNDLE ADJUSTMENT

an inverse B-Spline depth map, which means that above constraint is, within the SQP framework, equivalent to

$$h(\mathbf{a}_V, \mathbf{p}) = \mathbf{1}_{1,M} \cdot \mathbf{L} \cdot \mathbf{p} - M \cdot c, \tag{5.149}$$

where $\mathbf{L}$ is the B-spline basis matrix. This constraint is linear in parameters, and its derivatives are easily computed as

$$\nabla h(\mathbf{a}_V, \mathbf{p}) = \begin{pmatrix} \mathbf{0}_{7 \cdot N} \\ (\mathbf{1}_{1,M} \cdot \mathbf{L})^\mathrm{T} \end{pmatrix}, \tag{5.150}$$

and the Hessian matrix of this constraint is simply the 0 matrix.

5.8 Regularization

Our algorithms, as presented up to now, are already capable of performing the task of reconstruction and motion recovery quite well in case of suitable data. However, there is one major drawback that has a strongly adverse effect on the performance of the system: In case of very small camera displacements, large changes to the depth map result in almost no changes in the 2D re-projected intensities. This gives the system a lot of undesired freedom to play around with parameters, and it frequently leads to the depth map blowing up if the first few images of a tracking sequence do not exhibit enough baseline. Basically, there is not enough information contained in the images to allow recovery of the depth map, so the system should not even try to perform the recovery.

This problem is well-known, and it can effectively be rectified by adding a regularization term to the image alignment objective. Recently, total variation regularization and some variants thereof [67] have been applied with great success to many problems [41, 68, 69] in computer vision. This type of regularization is also applicable to

5.8 Regularization

our problem and serves, in that context, to restrain the surface from being distorted. A particularly nice, slightly more practical explanation of regularization is given in the paper by Sun et al. [42] on optical flow principles.

The basic idea for this type of regularization is the addition of a penalty term to the original objective function $E(\mathbf{a}, \mathbf{b})$ as defined in Equation (2.10). In the case of total variation regularization, the penalty term is typically chosen as

$$\int_P |\nabla z(\mathbf{p}, x, y)| \, dx \, dy, \tag{5.151}$$

such that the actual objective function to be optimized becomes

$$E(\mathbf{a}, \mathbf{b}) + \lambda \int_P |\nabla z(\mathbf{p}, x, y)| \, dx \, dy, \tag{5.152}$$

where λ is a weighting term for the regularization. Note that the integral term is only useful for mathematical analysis, but is almost always replaced with a discrete sum in actual implementations, where the underlying function D is typically also defined as a discrete function on a grid. In our case, we will approximate the integral in a very similar manner, using a variant of Simpson's formula.

We have developed a similar regularizer for our algorithm. The concept behind the regularizer is quite simple. First of all, we argue that we should regularize the inverse depth map, and not the actual surface. The reason for this is that we do not want to punish depth variations at higher depth more than depth variations at closer depths. The problem with direct depth regularization is shown in Figure 5.8.

The well-known formula for evaluating the area of some 3D sur-

5. MODULES FOR IMPLEMENTING BUNDLE ADJUSTMENT

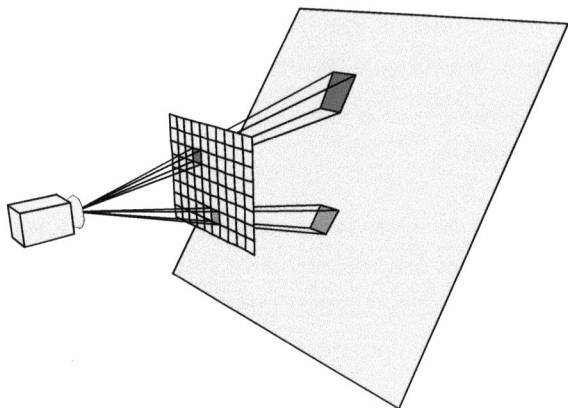

Figure 5.8: Schematic illustration showing the problem with direct depth regularization: When observing a simple slanted plane, the depth associated with a pixel, and thus the accociated area, varies greatly over the whole image. This leads to nonuniform regularization of different parts of the plane, which is undesireable.

face $\mathbf{S} : \mathbb{R}^2 \to \mathbb{R}^3$ is

$$\iint_P |\mathbf{S}_x(x,y) \times \mathbf{S}_y(x,y)| \, dx \, dy, \tag{5.153}$$

where $P \subseteq \mathbb{R}^2$ is the parameter space over which we want to integrate, and $\mathbf{S}_x$ and $\mathbf{S}_y$ denote the surface derivatives in the first and second parameter direction, respectively. Since we want to do regularization based on inverse depths, our definition of the surface to be regularized is

$$\mathbf{S}(\mathbf{p}, x, y) = \begin{pmatrix} x \\ y \\ s(\mathbf{p}, x, y) \end{pmatrix}, \tag{5.154}$$

where the function s is the B-Spline surface function as defined in Equation (5.27). Computing the directional derivatives with respect to x and y is rather trivial, since computation of spline derivatives

5.8 Regularization

has been shown to be a simple linear function in Section 5.2.1.

Applying Formula (5.153) leads to the following integral to be evaluated:

$$\iint_P \sqrt{1 + s_x(\mathbf{p}, x, y)^2 + s_y(\mathbf{p}, x, y)^2}\, dx\, dy, \tag{5.155}$$

Replacing the 1 in above formula with a constant α yields a regularization term that is similar to the Huber regularization term as discussed by Pock et al. [70]. The evaluation of such an integral is rather difficult, and it is much simpler to approximate it using, e.g., Simpson's quadrature rule. This is also especially convenient in our case, since the surface is any ways sampled at fixed parameter locations.

More specifically, our approximation of the integral is based on the following composite formulation of Simpson's rule [71]:

$$\int_a^b f(x)\, dx \approx \frac{h}{48}\bigg[17f(x_1) + 59f(x_2) + 43f(x_3) + 49f(x_4)$$
$$+ 48 \sum_{i=5}^{n-4} f(x_i) + 49f(x_{n-3}) + 43f(x_{n-2}) + 59f(x_{n-1}) + 17f(x_n)\bigg], \tag{5.156}$$

where the values $x_1, x_2, \ldots, x_n$ are spaced equally in the interval $[a, b]$. This formulation holds for the case of a function $f : \mathbb{R} \to \mathbb{R}$ with one-dimensional real domain. Note that this corresponds to a simple dot product between the weighting constants with a vector of sampling values of the function f. Letting

$$\mathbf{f} = (f(x_1), f(x_2), \ldots, f(x_n))^\mathrm{T} \in \mathbb{R}^n$$

be a vector of sampling values, and letting $\mathbf{w}_n$ denote the vector $\frac{1}{48}(17, 59, 43, 49, 48, 48, \ldots, 48, 49, 43, 59, 17)^\mathrm{T} \in \mathbb{R}^n$ of weights used

5. MODULES FOR IMPLEMENTING BUNDLE ADJUSTMENT

in the formula, we can thus rephrase (5.156) as

$$\int_a^b f(x)\,dx \approx \mathbf{w}_n^\mathrm{T} \cdot \mathbf{f}. \qquad (5.157)$$

Extending this formula to the case of a double integral over a two-dimensional real domain $\mathbb{R}^2$ is possible by applying it twice. Let us define a matrix $\mathbf{F}$ of function samples such that

$$\mathbf{F} = \begin{pmatrix} f(x_1, y_1) & f(x_1, y_2) & \cdots & f(x_1, y_m) \\ f(x_2, y_1) & f(x_2, y_2) & \cdots & f(x_2, y_m) \\ \vdots & \vdots & \ddots & \vdots \\ f(x_n, y_1) & f(x_n, y_2) & \cdots & f(x_n, y_m) \end{pmatrix}, \qquad (5.158)$$

where $x_1, x_2, \ldots, x_n$ and $y_1, y_2, \ldots, y_n$ are spaced equally over the intervals $[a, b]$ and $[c, d]$, respectively. Then, we can formulate the following approximation formula for the two-dimensional integral over f:

$$\int_a^b \int_c^d f(x, y)\,dx\,dy \approx \mathbf{w}_n^\mathrm{T} \cdot \mathbf{F} \cdot \mathbf{w}_m. \qquad (5.159)$$

Within our framework, it is more convenient to work with the vectorization of $\mathbf{F}$, in which case the formula is expressed simply as

$$\mathbf{w}_n^\mathrm{T} \cdot \mathbf{F} \cdot \mathbf{w}_m = (\mathbf{w}_n^\mathrm{T} \otimes \mathbf{w}_m^\mathrm{T}) \cdot \mathrm{vec}(\mathbf{F}), \qquad (5.160)$$

via the well-known rule $\mathrm{vec}(\mathbf{AXB}) = (\mathbf{B}^\mathrm{T} \otimes \mathbf{A}) \cdot \mathrm{vec}(\mathbf{X})$. Applied to the case of Formula (5.156), the integral approximation boils down to evaluating above expression for the case

$$f(x, y) = \sqrt{1 + s_x(\mathbf{p}, x, y)^2 + s_y(\mathbf{p}, x, y)^2}. \qquad (5.161)$$

In our case, the evaluation of the values s_x and s_y is done through simple matrix-vector products, and we are thus able to specify a

5.8 Regularization

concise computation scheme for the vector $\text{vec}(\mathbf{F})$ that is formed from the entries of f. We have discussed the computation of spline tangent values at length in Section 5.2.1, and we have seen there that those values can easily be computed using some basis matrices $\mathcal{L}_x$ and $\mathcal{L}_y$. Making use of Hadamard products, the formula we seek is

$$\text{vec}(\mathbf{F}) = \left((\mathcal{L}_x \cdot \mathbf{p})^{\circ 2} + (\mathcal{L}_y \cdot \mathbf{p})^{\circ 2} + \mathbf{1}_{N,1}\right)^{\circ \frac{1}{2}}, \quad (5.162)$$

where $N = n \cdot m$ is the number of evaluation locations. Overall, our regularization function is then defined as

$$R(\mathbf{p}) = (\mathbf{w}_n^T \otimes \mathbf{w}_m^T) \cdot \left((\mathcal{L}_x \cdot \mathbf{p})^{\circ 2} + (\mathcal{L}_y \cdot \mathbf{p})^{\circ 2} + \mathbf{1}_{N,1}\right)^{\circ \frac{1}{2}}. \quad (5.163)$$

As usual, it is necessary to compute the derivatives of the regularization term to make it usable within our optimization framework. The gradient of the regularization function is easily computed as follows:

$$\frac{d}{d\mathbf{p}}R(\mathbf{p}) = (\mathbf{w}_n^T \otimes \mathbf{w}_m^T) \cdot \text{diag}\left((\mathcal{L}_x \cdot \mathbf{p})^{\circ 2} + (\mathcal{L}_y \cdot \mathbf{p})^{\circ 2} + \mathbf{1}_{N,1}\right)^{\circ(-\frac{1}{2})} \cdot$$

$$\left(\text{diag}(\mathcal{L}_x \cdot \mathbf{p}) \quad \text{diag}(\mathcal{L}_y \cdot \mathbf{p})\right) \cdot \begin{pmatrix} \mathcal{L}_x \\ \mathcal{L}_y \end{pmatrix} = \nabla_{\mathbf{p}} R(\mathbf{p})^T \quad (5.164)$$

Computing the Hessian is a bit more involved. We start by rearranging the gradient computation formula as follows:

$$\nabla_{\mathbf{p}} R(\mathbf{p}) = \begin{pmatrix} \mathcal{L}_x^T & \mathcal{L}_y^T \end{pmatrix} \cdot \text{diag} \begin{pmatrix} \mathbf{w}_n \otimes \mathbf{w}_m \\ \mathbf{w}_n \otimes \mathbf{w}_m \end{pmatrix} \cdot \begin{pmatrix} \text{diag}(\mathcal{L}_x \cdot \mathbf{p}) \\ \text{diag}(\mathcal{L}_y \cdot \mathbf{p}) \end{pmatrix} \cdot$$

$$\left((\mathcal{L}_x \cdot \mathbf{p})^{\circ 2} + (\mathcal{L}_y \cdot \mathbf{p})^{\circ 2} + \mathbf{1}_{N,1}\right)^{\circ(-\frac{1}{2})}. \quad (5.165)$$

The formula is thus reshaped into a chain multiplication of four com-

5. MODULES FOR IMPLEMENTING BUNDLE ADJUSTMENT

ponents: Two constant matrices, a stack of two parameter-dependent diagonal matrices and a parameter-dependent vector. The main challenge when computing the derivative of this expression, and thus the Hessian matrix of R, is the computation of the derivative of the matrix-vector product of the two rightmost terms. To compute this derivative, we define a helper function h as follows:

$$\mathbf{h}(\mathbf{q},\mathbf{r}) = \begin{pmatrix} \mathrm{diag}(\mathcal{L}_x \cdot \mathbf{q}) \\ \mathrm{diag}(\mathcal{L}_y \cdot \mathbf{q}) \end{pmatrix} \cdot \left((\mathcal{L}_x \cdot \mathbf{r})^{\circ 2} + (\mathcal{L}_y \cdot \mathbf{r})^{\circ 2} + \mathbf{1}_{N,1}\right)^{\circ(-\tfrac{1}{2})} =$$

$$\mathrm{diag}\begin{pmatrix} (\mathcal{L}_x \cdot \mathbf{r})^{\circ 2} + (\mathcal{L}_y \cdot \mathbf{r})^{\circ 2} + \mathbf{1}_{N,1} \\ (\mathcal{L}_x \cdot \mathbf{r})^{\circ 2} + (\mathcal{L}_y \cdot \mathbf{r})^{\circ 2} + \mathbf{1}_{N,1} \end{pmatrix}^{\circ(-\tfrac{1}{2})} \cdot \begin{pmatrix} \mathcal{L}_x \\ \mathcal{L}_y \end{pmatrix} \cdot \mathbf{q}, \quad (5.166)$$

where q and r are both vectors of the same dimension as the number of surface parameters, so they have the same dimension as p. Note that h is a slightly generalized version of the matrix-vector product of the two rightmost terms in (5.165). Computing the derivatives of $\mathbf{h}(\mathbf{q},\mathbf{r})$ with respect to q and r will be a simple matter based on (5.166), and we will be able to compute the derivative of $\mathbf{h}(\mathbf{q},\mathbf{r})$ based on the partial results using the chain rule. The derivatives are:

$$\frac{\mathrm{d}}{\mathrm{d}\mathbf{q}}\mathbf{h}(\mathbf{q},\mathbf{r}) = \mathrm{diag}\begin{pmatrix} (\mathcal{L}_x \cdot \mathbf{r})^{\circ 2} + (\mathcal{L}_y \cdot \mathbf{r})^{\circ 2} + \mathbf{1}_{N,1} \\ (\mathcal{L}_x \cdot \mathbf{r})^{\circ 2} + (\mathcal{L}_y \cdot \mathbf{r})^{\circ 2} + \mathbf{1}_{N,1} \end{pmatrix}^{\circ(-\tfrac{1}{2})} \cdot \begin{pmatrix} \mathcal{L}_x \\ \mathcal{L}_y \end{pmatrix}$$
(5.167)

$$\frac{\mathrm{d}}{\mathrm{d}\mathbf{r}}\mathbf{h}(\mathbf{q},\mathbf{r}) =$$
$$-\begin{pmatrix} \mathrm{diag}(\mathcal{L}_x \cdot \mathbf{q}) \\ \mathrm{diag}(\mathcal{L}_y \cdot \mathbf{q}) \end{pmatrix} \cdot \mathrm{diag}\left((\mathcal{L}_x \cdot \mathbf{r})^{\circ 2} + (\mathcal{L}_y \cdot \mathbf{r})^{\circ 2} + \mathbf{1}_{N,1}\right)^{\circ(-\tfrac{3}{2})} \cdot$$
$$\left(\mathrm{diag}(\mathcal{L}_x \cdot \mathbf{r}) \cdot \mathcal{L}_x + \mathrm{diag}(\mathcal{L}_y \cdot \mathbf{r}) \cdot \mathcal{L}_y\right).$$

Using the fact that $\mathbf{h}(\mathbf{p},\mathbf{p}) = \mathbf{h}((\mathbf{I}_N \mathbf{I}_N)^{\mathrm{T}} \cdot \mathbf{p})$, we can compute the desired derivative of $\mathbf{h}(\mathbf{p}, \mathbf{p})$ using the chain rule as

$$\operatorname{diag}\begin{pmatrix}(\mathcal{L}_x \cdot \mathbf{p})^{\circ 2} + (\mathcal{L}_y \cdot \mathbf{p})^{\circ 2} + \mathbf{1}_{N,1} \\ (\mathcal{L}_x \cdot \mathbf{p})^{\circ 2} + (\mathcal{L}_y \cdot \mathbf{p})^{\circ 2} + \mathbf{1}_{N,1}\end{pmatrix}^{\circ(-\frac{1}{2})} \cdot \begin{pmatrix}\mathcal{L}_x \\ \mathcal{L}_y\end{pmatrix} -$$

$$\begin{pmatrix}\operatorname{diag}(\mathcal{L}_x \cdot \mathbf{p}) \\ \operatorname{diag}(\mathcal{L}_y \cdot \mathbf{p})\end{pmatrix} \cdot \operatorname{diag}\left((\mathcal{L}_x \cdot \mathbf{p})^{\circ 2} + (\mathcal{L}_y \cdot \mathbf{p})^{\circ 2} + \mathbf{1}_{N,1}\right)^{\circ(-\frac{3}{2})} \cdot$$

$$\begin{pmatrix}\operatorname{diag}(\mathcal{L}_x \cdot \mathbf{p}) & \operatorname{diag}(\mathcal{L}_y \cdot \mathbf{p})\end{pmatrix} \cdot \begin{pmatrix}\mathcal{L}_x \\ \mathcal{L}_y\end{pmatrix}. \quad (5.168)$$

Combining this result with the linear part of Formula (5.165) yields the overall formula for computing the Hessian matrix of the regularization term:

$$\mathbf{H}_R(\mathbf{p}) = \begin{pmatrix}\mathcal{L}_x^T & \mathcal{L}_y^T\end{pmatrix} \cdot \operatorname{diag}\begin{pmatrix}\mathbf{w}_n \otimes \mathbf{w}_m \\ \mathbf{w}_n \otimes \mathbf{w}_m\end{pmatrix} \cdot$$

$$\left(\operatorname{diag}\begin{pmatrix}(\mathcal{L}_x \cdot \mathbf{p})^{\circ 2} + (\mathcal{L}_y \cdot \mathbf{p})^{\circ 2} + \mathbf{1}_{N,1} \\ (\mathcal{L}_x \cdot \mathbf{p})^{\circ 2} + (\mathcal{L}_y \cdot \mathbf{p})^{\circ 2} + \mathbf{1}_{N,1}\end{pmatrix}^{\circ(-\frac{1}{2})}\right.$$

$$-\begin{pmatrix}\operatorname{diag}(\mathcal{L}_x \cdot \mathbf{p}) \\ \operatorname{diag}(\mathcal{L}_y \cdot \mathbf{p})\end{pmatrix} \cdot$$

$$\operatorname{diag}\left((\mathcal{L}_x \cdot \mathbf{p})^{\circ 2} + (\mathcal{L}_y \cdot \mathbf{p})^{\circ 2} + \mathbf{1}_{N,1}\right)^{\circ(-\frac{3}{2})} \cdot$$

$$\left.\begin{pmatrix}\operatorname{diag}(\mathcal{L}_x \cdot \mathbf{p}) \\ \operatorname{diag}(\mathcal{L}_y \cdot \mathbf{p})\end{pmatrix}^T\right) \cdot \begin{pmatrix}\mathcal{L}_x \\ \mathcal{L}_y\end{pmatrix}. \quad (5.169)$$

5.9 Efficient Sparse-Sparse Matrix Products

The optimization framework that has been introduced in Chapter 4 makes sure that the sparse matrix chain products that are needed to compute the overall derivatives are evaluated in a very efficient way. However, as we have seen in this Chapter, the evaluation of sparse

5. MODULES FOR IMPLEMENTING BUNDLE ADJUSTMENT

Jacobian and Hessian matrices can be a quite complex problem in itself. The more complicated Jacobian/Hessian computation formulas consist themselves of products of several sparse matrices. However, because the surface model underlying most of our computations is linear in parameters (see Section 5.2.1.1), many of the Jacobian and Hessian computation formulas are of the following shape:

$$\mathbf{J}(\mathbf{p}) = \mathbf{A} \cdot \mathbf{X}(\mathbf{p}) \cdot \mathbf{B}, \qquad (5.170)$$

where $\mathbf{A}$ and $\mathbf{B}$ are some constant matrices (often these are related to the B-Spline basis matrices), and $\mathbf{X}(\mathbf{p})$ is a parameter-dependent matrix. All of the matrices have a constant sparsity structure that is not dependent on $\mathbf{p}$. An example for this is Equation (5.169).

The straightforward way to evaluate that matrix product would be simply carrying out the chained matrix product: We could use the algorithms developed for the optimization framework to determine an optimal bracketing and pre-compute multiplication tables, which would probably provide decent performance. However, there is an even faster way: Accessing the non-zero entries of $\mathbf{J}(\mathbf{p})$ as dense vector, it is possible to compute the values of those entries directly as a sparse-dense matrix-vector product. Carrying out sparse-dense products is usually an operation that is at least as fast as carrying out a pre-recorded matrix multiplication, but does not require any special preparation.

Before we can start to present the theory behind our idea, we need to discuss some technical details of the data structure underlying sparse matrices. Our description will be based on the compressed column storage (CCS) scheme used by the Eigen library for linear algebra. The ideas are, however, certainly applicable to other sparse matrix storage schemes as well. For an overview of sparse matrix storage schemes and some basic concepts, see [72].

5.9 Efficient Sparse-Sparse Matrix Products

To give the reader an idea about the CCS scheme, we will provide an example. Consider the matrix

$$\mathbf{M} = \begin{pmatrix} 1 & 0 & 0 \\ 0 & 0 & 5 \\ 4 & 0 & 7 \end{pmatrix}. \tag{5.171}$$

In CCS format, such a matrix is represented by a collection of three arrays, which we will denote by $\mathtt{val}(\mathbf{M}), \mathtt{rowidx}(\mathbf{M}), \mathtt{colidx}(\mathbf{M})$. The array $\mathtt{val}(\mathbf{M})$ stores the non-zero values contained in the matrix. In our example, we would have $\mathtt{val}(\mathbf{M}) = (1, 4, 5, 7)^\mathrm{T}$. For each element, we also need to know its position in the matrix. The row index of each element is stored in the array $\mathtt{rowidx}(\mathbf{M})$, which would be $(0, 2, 1, 2)^\mathrm{T}$ in our example. Finally, the array $\mathtt{colidx}(\mathbf{M})$ stores for each column of the matrix the index into $\mathtt{val}(\mathbf{M})$ at which it starts. For the example, we have $\mathtt{colidx}(\mathbf{M}) = (0, 2, 2)^\mathrm{T}$. Typically, it is more efficient to access and manipulate the array of sparse matrix values directly instead of using general matrix multiplication algorithms.

To develop our idea for computing the values of the val array directly, we need to define some mathematical tools that provide a link between the array-based implementation of sparse matrices on computers and the mathematical formulas. Intuitively, we need a way to express the val operator in a mathematical way. This is easily achieved as follows: The vectorization of a sparse matrix $\mathbf{M}$ will in general yield a sparse vector $\mathrm{vec}(\mathbf{M})$. The val operator is now seen to be a mapping that removes the 0 entries from that sparse vector. This means that val is a linear operator on the vectorization of $\mathbf{M}$, and can thus be expressed as a matrix-vector multiplication.

5. MODULES FOR IMPLEMENTING BUNDLE ADJUSTMENT

In our example, we would have

$$\text{val}(\mathbf{M}) = (1, 4, 5, 7)^\text{T} = \begin{pmatrix} 1 & 0 & 0 & 0 & 0 & 0 & 0 & 0 \\ 0 & 0 & 1 & 0 & 0 & 0 & 0 & 0 \\ 0 & 0 & 0 & 0 & 0 & 0 & 1 & 0 \\ 0 & 0 & 0 & 0 & 0 & 0 & 0 & 1 \end{pmatrix} \cdot \text{vec}(\mathbf{M}).$$

(5.172)

Thus, it is possible to implement the val operator as a multiplication of $\text{vec}(\mathbf{M})$ with a matrix of certain shape that selects the non-zero entries of the vectorization of $\mathbf{M}$. More formally, let $\mathbf{M}$ be a sparse matrix with n rows, m columns, and N non-zero entries. Then we define the matrix $\chi(\mathbf{M})$ as follows:

1. The size of $\chi(\mathbf{M})$ is $N \times (n \cdot m)$.

2. All entries are 0 except for those in rows i and corresponding columns $\text{rowidx}(\text{vec}(\mathbf{M}))_i$, which are set to 1 (with $0 \leq i < N$).

Another notable property of these matrices is that their transpose reverses the mapping, such that $\chi(\mathbf{M})^\text{T} \cdot \chi(\mathbf{M}) \cdot \text{vec}(\mathbf{M}) = \text{vec}(\mathbf{M})$.

Now we are finally ready to discuss our technique. We start by vectorizing the original equation $\mathbf{J}(\mathbf{p}) = \mathbf{A} \cdot \mathbf{X}(\mathbf{p}) \cdot \mathbf{B}$, which yields the formula

$$\text{vec}(\mathbf{J}(\mathbf{p})) = (\mathbf{B}^\text{T} \otimes \mathbf{A}) \cdot \text{vec}(\mathbf{X}(\mathbf{p})). \tag{5.173}$$

Since $\text{vec}(\mathbf{X}(\mathbf{p}))$ is a sparse vector, some of the columns of the Kronecker product $\mathbf{B}^\text{T} \otimes \mathbf{A}$ will be irrelevant for the computation. Mathematically, this can be explained by observing

$$(\mathbf{B}^\text{T} \otimes \mathbf{A}) \cdot \text{vec}(\mathbf{X}(\mathbf{p})) = ((\mathbf{B}^\text{T} \otimes \mathbf{A}) \cdot \chi(\mathbf{X}(\mathbf{p})^\text{T}) \cdot (\chi(\mathbf{X}(\mathbf{p})) \cdot \text{vec}(\mathbf{X}(\mathbf{p}))),$$

(5.174)

since $((\mathbf{B}^\text{T} \otimes \mathbf{A}) \cdot \chi(\mathbf{X}(\mathbf{p})^\text{T})$ is equal to the matrix $\mathbf{B}^\text{T} \otimes \mathbf{A}$ without the columns corresponding to the zero entries of $\text{vec}(\mathbf{X}(\mathbf{p}))$.

5.9 Efficient Sparse-Sparse Matrix Products

Now, since we want to find the entries of val($\mathbf{J}(\mathbf{p})$), we apply the matrix $\chi(\mathbf{J}(\mathbf{p}))$ as follows:

$$\text{vec}(\mathbf{J}(\mathbf{p})) = ((\mathbf{B}^T \otimes \mathbf{A}) \cdot \chi(\mathbf{X}(\mathbf{p})^T) \cdot (\chi(\mathbf{X}(\mathbf{p})) \cdot \text{vec}(\mathbf{X}(\mathbf{p}))) \Leftrightarrow$$
$$\chi(\mathbf{J}(\mathbf{p})) \cdot \text{vec}(\mathbf{J}(\mathbf{p})) =$$
$$(\chi(\mathbf{J}(\mathbf{p})) \cdot (\mathbf{B}^T \otimes \mathbf{A}) \cdot \chi(\mathbf{X}(\mathbf{p})^T) \cdot (\chi(\mathbf{X}(\mathbf{p})) \cdot \text{vec}(\mathbf{X}(\mathbf{p})). \quad (5.175)$$

Finally, we see that the vector val($\mathbf{J}(\mathbf{p})$) of values contained in the sparse matrix $\mathbf{J}(\mathbf{p})$ can be computed by evaluating a sparse-dense matrix-vector product, with a sparse matrix of

$$\chi(\mathbf{J}(\mathbf{p})) \cdot (\mathbf{B}^T \otimes \mathbf{A}) \cdot \chi(\mathbf{X}(\mathbf{p})^T) \quad (5.176)$$

and a dense vector of $\chi(\mathbf{X}(\mathbf{p})) \cdot \mathbf{X}(\mathbf{p}) = \text{val}(\mathbf{X}(\mathbf{p}))$. Since the sparsity structure of all the involved matrices is static, the matrices $\chi(\mathbf{J}(\mathbf{p}))$ and $\chi(\mathbf{X}(\mathbf{p}))$ remain the same, and the whole expression $(\chi(\mathbf{J}(\mathbf{p})) \cdot (\mathbf{B}^T \otimes \mathbf{A}) \cdot \chi(\mathbf{X}(\mathbf{p})^T)$ is thus constant.

As an example, consider the following simple formula:

$$\mathbf{J}(\mathbf{p}) = \mathbf{A} \cdot \text{diag}(\mathbf{p})^2 \cdot \mathbf{B}. \quad (5.177)$$

According to our elaboration above, we might calculate the values of val($\mathbf{J}$) directly using the constant matrix

$$\mathbf{D} = \chi(\mathbf{J}(\mathbf{p})) \cdot (\mathbf{B}^T \otimes \mathbf{A}) \cdot \chi(\text{diag}(\mathbf{p})^2). \quad (5.178)$$

We would then compute the values as a simple sparse-dense matrix-vector product using

$$\text{val}(\mathbf{J}) = \mathbf{D} \cdot \text{val}(\text{diag}(\mathbf{p})^2). \quad (5.179)$$

Note that this product can be evaluated efficiently since val$(\text{diag}(\mathbf{p})^2)$

5. MODULES FOR IMPLEMENTING BUNDLE ADJUSTMENT

is simply the component-wise squared vector $\mathbf{p}$.

In general, we can say that this computation scheme is only efficient if the computation of $(\chi(\mathbf{X}(\mathbf{p})) \cdot \text{vec}(\mathbf{X}(\mathbf{p})) = \texttt{val}(\mathbf{X}(\mathbf{p}))$ is efficient. This is, however, always the case in our modules. One example is the formula for computing the Hessian of the regularization term, which is specified in Formula (5.169): The middle, parameter-dependent matrix corresponding to the matrix $\mathbf{X}(\mathbf{p})$ in our computation scheme, would be the matrix

$$\left(\text{diag} \begin{pmatrix} (\mathcal{L}_x \cdot \mathbf{p})^{\circ 2} + (\mathcal{L}_y \cdot \mathbf{p})^{\circ 2} + \mathbf{1}_{N,1} \\ (\mathcal{L}_x \cdot \mathbf{p})^{\circ 2} + (\mathcal{L}_y \cdot \mathbf{p})^{\circ 2} + \mathbf{1}_{N,1} \end{pmatrix}^{\circ(-\frac{1}{2})} - \begin{pmatrix} \text{diag}(\mathcal{L}_x \cdot \mathbf{p}) \\ \text{diag}(\mathcal{L}_y \cdot \mathbf{p}) \end{pmatrix} \cdot \right.$$

$$\left. \text{diag}\left((\mathcal{L}_x \cdot \mathbf{p})^{\circ 2} + (\mathcal{L}_y \cdot \mathbf{p})^{\circ 2} + \mathbf{1}_{N,1}\right)^{\circ(-\frac{3}{2})} \cdot \begin{pmatrix} \text{diag}(\mathcal{L}_x \cdot \mathbf{p}) \\ \text{diag}(\mathcal{L}_y \cdot \mathbf{p}) \end{pmatrix}^{\text{T}} \right)$$

(5.180)

The structure of that matrix is quite simple: It is a 2×2 block matrix consisting of large diagonal matrices. Thus, computing the vector $\texttt{val}(\mathbf{X}(\mathbf{p}))$ is possible quite easily using simple component-wise vector-vector operations.

6. Light Source Calibration

In the previous Chapter, we have described an algorithm that makes use of an explicit light model assuming a point-shaped light with a non-uniform intensity distribution. For this algorithm to be of any use at all, we need to provide some means to calibrate the light source, by which we mean determining the light source's position along with its intensity profile. Figure 6.1 visualizes the situation.

We are assuming that the light source to be calibrated is the only source of light in the scene, and we also assume that it is small compared to the scene structures observed. By small, we mean that the extent of the light source can be neglected, such that the rays coming from the source appear to originate from only one point. This is an important prerequisite for treating the light source as an inverse camera.

Camera-to-light calibration methods are quite common in the area of structured light [73], and they typically rely on usage of a projector that is able to project a specific pattern onto the scene. In our case, we do not assume that we are able to project a pattern of choice onto the scene. Rather, we see the non-uniform intensity distribution of a light source as a nuisance that we wish to compensate. The method that we are proposing is able to cope with the calibration problem without requiring projection of specific patterns through the light source.

Our algorithm computes the position of the light source and its intensity profile from a number of images of a calibration pattern at

6. LIGHT SOURCE CALIBRATION

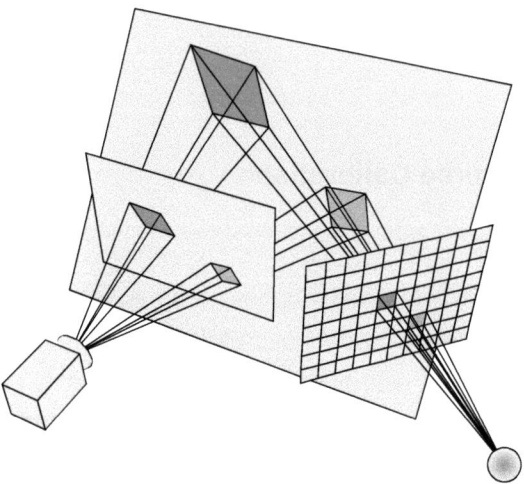

Figure 6.1: Example scene showing how the light source in a scene is treated as an inverse camera: All the light rays emerge from a common projection center, and they might have different intensities.

different positions. It is a two-step process that first tries to find the light source's projection center, and then determines its light intensity profile. The calibration pattern is a simple white rectangle surrounded by a black border, such that the rectangle can be detected easily in images.

Since we treat the light source as an inverse camera, the situation is actually very similar to the calibration of a stereo camera pair. The intrinsic parameters associated with the light source will be chosen to match the parameters of the camera. Furthermore, we will determine translation l_t and rotation l_r describing the pose of the light source relative to the camera, corresponding to the extrinsic parameters of stereo calibration. Calibrating the rotation of a light source might seem confusing at first sight, since a light source usually emits light in all directions. However, realizing that the camera will only see a limited section of the full light profile, it makes sense to choose the rotation of the light source to point towards

Figure 6.2: Top: Two example calibration images, Bottom Left: Recovered light intensity profile, Bottom Right: Projected image. The recovered area corresponds roughly to the lower right quarter of the projected image.

6. LIGHT SOURCE CALIBRATION

the calibrated region. Thus, the rotation will be chosen such that the light source "camera" looks towards the calibration patterns that have been seen by the actual camera.

Our algorithm makes strong use of the image formation laws for Lambertian surfaces that we have described in Chapter 3. Furthermore, we assume that the camera intrinsics and distortion have been calibrated and images rectified accordingly. Also, we need to know the radiometric response of the camera as well as its vignetting profile. There are many calibration methods available [74, 75, 76, 77] for determining these quantities. In our case, all cameras we were using were set to operate in raw mode, thus their response was already linear, and we only needed to determine the vignetting profile. This has been done according to the method described in the paper by Goldman and Chen [75], Section 6.1.

6.1 Estimation of the Projection Center

First off, let us recall the Lambertian law of reflection that we have already discussed in Section 3.2 on light source modelling. We shall adapt the formulas presented there to our calibration scenario. Consider a situation where we are looking at a calibration plane that is specified trough normal $\mathbf{n}$ and distance d in Hessian normal form, such that

$$\mathbf{n}^T \cdot \mathbf{x} - d = 0 \tag{6.1}$$

describes the plane in 3D space. Then, the intensity of some point $\mathbf{x}$ on that plane, as observed in image i, can be calculated as

$$\mathfrak{I}_i(\pi(\mathbf{K} \cdot \mathbf{x})) = \mathbf{d} \cdot \frac{\mathbf{n}^T \cdot (\mathbf{l}_t - \mathbf{x})}{|\mathbf{n}| \cdot |\mathbf{l}_t - \mathbf{x}|} \cdot \frac{1}{|\mathbf{l}_t - \mathbf{x}|^2}, \tag{6.2}$$

6.1 Estimation of the Projection Center

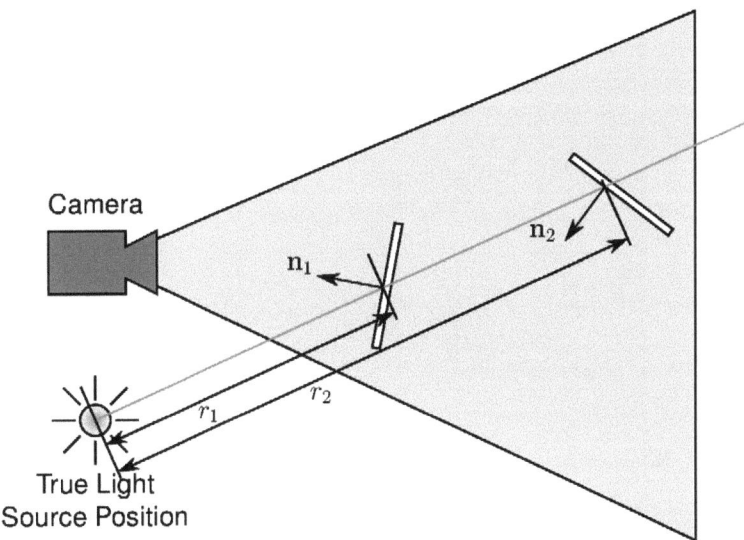

Figure 6.3: The same light ray passing through two calibration planes.

where d is a value depending on surface albedo and light intensity, and $\pi(\mathbf{K} \cdot \mathbf{x})$ is the perspective projection of $\mathbf{x}$ to pixel coordinates. The first of the two fraction terms corresponds to the cosine of the angle between incoming light and surface normal, and the second accounts for light attenuation over distance. This assumes that the intensity, as reported by the camera, is not affected by non-linear camera response or camera vignetting, that the plane's reflectance is Lambertian, and that the light source exhibits inverse squared attenuation over distance.

Note that the quantity d is one of the actual values that we want to calibrate: Since the calibration pattern is of uniform white color, the only other reason for changing values of d would be the light intensity. It is a simple matter to rearrange above equation to calculate d, so if the light source position is known, we would already be able to calculate the intensity of that specific ray.

Now consider the situation shown in Figure 6.3, showing a case

6. LIGHT SOURCE CALIBRATION

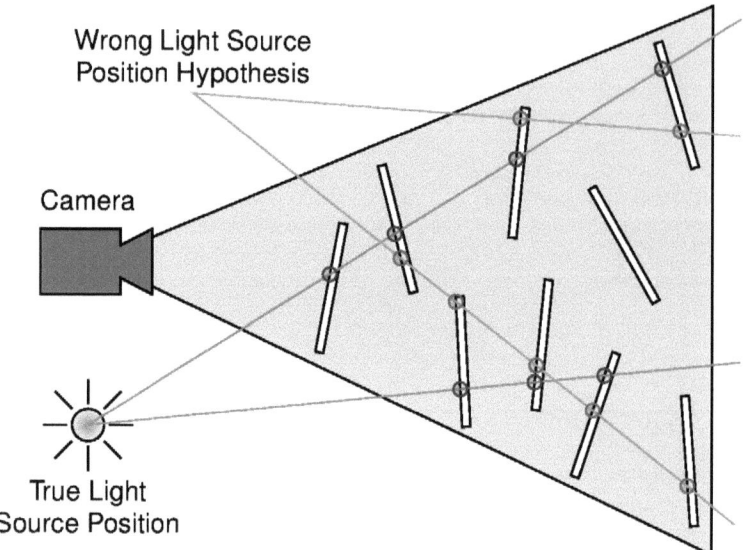

Figure 6.4: Schematic view of the calibration situation, showing the camera and a number of calibration planes. For the correct light source position, the intensity values at the ray-plane intersections will behave according to the Lambertian reflectance law (blue circles). In the other case, the behaviour will differ considerably from that predicted by the reflectance law (red circles).

where two images of calibration planes at different positions have been taken, and there is a light ray that hits them both. We have seen that the value d can be determined using only one measurement associated with one light ray. Now we have two measurements, so we are also able to compute two values of d that should be equal in the ideal case. We can calculate an optimal value for d in the least-squares sense. Then, the discrepancy between the intensity values predicted by the Lambertian reflectance law and the actual measurements are used as error quantifier.

Of course, the scheme is not restricted to only two calibration patterns. Generally, the calibration results will improve with the number of calibration images used. Figure 6.4 illustrates the situation when using more than two calibration patterns.

6.1 Estimation of the Projection Center

In the following, we assume that we have recorded M calibration images $\mathfrak{I}_1, \mathfrak{I}_2, \ldots, \mathfrak{I}_M$. Each of these images shows the calibration plane, and it is a simple matter to detect that plane and determine its location relative to the camera, e.g., using the functions `findContours` and `solvePnP` from the OPENCV library[1]. The planes will be represented in Hessian normal form, and we will denote their normals and distances with $\mathbf{n}_i$ and d_i. Furthermore, let $\mathbf{x}_j \in \mathbb{R}^3$ denote points that are located on the calibration rectangles, where j ranges from 1 to N, and N is the total number of points.

We will formulate the problem of finding the projection center as an optimization problem on the variable $\mathbf{l}_t$, defining an objective function $o(\mathbf{l}_t)$ on the 3D coordinates $\mathbf{l}_t$. The objective function rewards a configuration where the calibration pattern brightness values behave according to the Lambertian reflectance law, and penalizes configurations where the brightness values differ from what is computed by the Lambertian law.

The basic idea is as follows: For a candidate light position $\mathbf{l}_t$, each of the 3D points $\mathbf{x}_j$ induces a ray from the candidate light position to the point $\mathbf{x}_j$. Intersections between the calibration planes and these rays can subsequently computed, and we shall denote by $\mathbf{y}_{i,j}$ the intersection of the ray induced by $\mathbf{x}_j$ with the calibration plane in image $\mathfrak{I}_i$. It might happen that the line-plane intersection lies outside the calibration rectangle, so we also need a indicator variable $v_{i,j}$ to indicate whether this is the case. The value of $v_{i,j}$ will be equal to 1 if the intersection is inside the rectangle, and 0 otherwise. We will denote the distance between $\mathbf{l}_t$ and $\mathbf{y}_{i,j}$ with $r_{i,j}$, and the corresponding cosine between the calibration plane normal and the light ray is denoted by $c_{i,j}$.

---

[1] http://opencv.willowgarage.com/

6. LIGHT SOURCE CALIBRATION

For each ray, we now have M equations of type

$$\mathfrak{I}_i(\pi(\mathbf{K}\cdot\mathbf{y}_{i,j})) = \mathbf{d}_{i,j}\cdot\frac{c_{i,j}}{r_{i,j}^2}. \tag{6.3}$$

Theoretically, the values $\mathbf{d}_{i,j}$ should all be the same for all images i and one specific ray j. We can calculate a least-squares solution $\widetilde{\mathbf{d}}_j$ representing that common value for each ray j by minimizing the objective

$$\sum_{i=1}^{M} v_{i,j}\cdot\left(\mathfrak{I}_i(\pi(\mathbf{K}\cdot\mathbf{y}_{i,j})) - \widetilde{\mathbf{d}}_j\cdot\frac{c_{i,j}}{r_{i,j}^2}\right)^2. \tag{6.4}$$

The solution to this minimization process can be calculated as

$$\widetilde{\mathbf{d}}_j = \frac{\sum_{i=1}^{M} v_{i,j}\cdot\left(\mathfrak{I}_i(\pi(\mathbf{K}\cdot\mathbf{y}_{i,j}))\cdot\frac{c_{i,j}}{r_{i,j}^2}\right)}{\sum_{i=1}^{M} v_{i,j}\cdot\left(\frac{c_{i,j}}{r_{i,j}^2}\right)^2}. \tag{6.5}$$

Note that choosing the points $\mathbf{x}_j$ to lie on the calibration rectangles makes sure that each ray hits at least one of those rectangles, and prevents situations where $\widetilde{\mathbf{d}}_j$ cannot be determined at all because all $v_{i,j}$ are equal to 0. Now we are ready to formulate the objective function as follows:

$$o(\mathbf{l}_t) = \frac{\sum_{j=1}^{N}\sum_{i=1}^{M} v_{i,j}\cdot\left(\widetilde{\mathbf{d}}_j\cdot\frac{c_{i,j}}{r_{i,j}^2} - \mathfrak{I}_i(\pi(\mathbf{K}\cdot\mathbf{y}_{i,j}))\right)}{\sum_{j=1}^{N}\sum_{i=1}^{M} v_{i,j}}. \tag{6.6}$$

This can be interpreted as the average weighted error for each pixel between the predicted intensity by the Lambertian reflectance law and the measured intensity, using the optimal value $\widetilde{\mathbf{d}}_j$ as computed above.

6.2 Optimization of the Objective

The objective function (6.6) is a quite complex, non-convex, non-continuous function. Optimization of such functions using a non-linear optimization technique, such as the one introduced in Chapter 4, is difficult, if not impossible. However, there are other optimization techniques available that are better suited for the problem at hand.

Both the non-convexity as well as the non-continuity can be addressed by using probabilistic optimization methods, such as simulated annealing [78]. Recently, Papazov and Burschka [79] have shown how such techniques can be applied to the problem of rigid point set registration. We were able to apply their method to optimize our objective function with great success. We have also tried out a classic non-linear method, using the LEVMAR package, without success.

The probabilistic method requires the parameter space to be a box, such that is has upper and lower bounds in each parameter direction. We assume that the light source is rather close to the camera, and restrict the parameter space of the light source position to a box around the camera's principal point, with extents just big enough to reach the closest point of any calibration rectangle seen in the calibration images. Figure 6.5 shows the situation schematically.

Since the objective function is quite expensive to evaluate, and around 10000 function evaluations of the function are required to find a minimum, we need to limit the number of rays that are considered in the objective function. Typically, values between 150 and 200 rays have been used, and good results could be achieved.

6. LIGHT SOURCE CALIBRATION

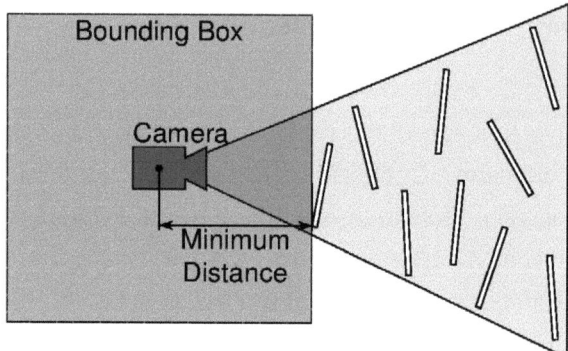

Figure 6.5: The bounding box used for the optimizer: The extent in all three spatial directions is the same, and just big enough to reach the closest point of any calibration rectangle seen by the camera.

6.3 Modelling Constant Intensity Disturbances

The theory developed above assumes that the image measurements behave exactly according to our assumptions, which is normally not the case. Most importantly, we were assuming that there is no other source of light in the scene, which means that we neglect any indirect, scattered light affecting the images. Such indirect lighting, however, is nearly impossible to suppress, and constitutes a major source of calibration error.

We propose to address this issue by incorporating a constant "ambient" brightness term in our optimization. This is motivated as follows: The objects in a calibration setting that cause this undesired scattered light are usually objects that themselves exhibit diffuse reflection properties: White walls, floor carpets, chairs etc. This means that the reflected light typically is also very diffuse. Such diffuse light often shows very little variation in light strength. The same effect of reflecting light from diffuse surfaces is used by photographers to produce a homogeneous, soft light.

For each calibration rectangle, this term is assumed to be con-

6.3 Modelling Constant Intensity Disturbances

stant, such that the original law (6.3) turns into

$$\mathcal{I}_i(\pi(\mathbf{K} \cdot \mathbf{y}_{i,j})) = \mathrm{d}_{i,j} \cdot \frac{c_{i,j}}{r_{i,j}^2} + \mathbf{a}_i. \tag{6.7}$$

where $\mathbf{a}_i$ is the constant ambient light term for frame i. We can solve for a per-ray intensity value $\widetilde{\mathrm{d}}_j$ along with ambient light values $\mathbf{a}_i$ in a least-squares sense, minimizing the following objective:

$$\sum_{i=1}^{M} v_{i,j} \cdot \left(\mathcal{I}_i(\pi(\mathbf{K} \cdot \mathbf{y}_{i,j})) - \widetilde{\mathrm{d}}_j \cdot \frac{c_{i,j}}{r_{i,j}^2} + \mathbf{a}_i \right)^2. \tag{6.8}$$

Assuring that the points $\mathbf{x}_j$ lie on the calibration rectangles is no longer enough to guarantee solvability of the resulting least-squares system. However, we can compute a valid solution in all cases by performing an eigen decomposition of the system, which will yield a valid solution even in degenerate cases.

The objective function is then also adapted to the ambient light estimation:

$$o(\mathbf{l}_\mathrm{t}) = \frac{\sum_{j=1}^{N} \sum_{i=1}^{M} v_{i,j} \cdot \left(\widetilde{\mathrm{d}}_j \cdot \frac{c_{i,j}}{r_{i,j}^2} + \mathbf{a}_i - \mathcal{I}_i(\pi(\mathbf{K} \cdot \mathbf{y}_{i,j})) \right)}{\sum_{j=1}^{N} \sum_{i=1}^{M} v_{i,j}}. \tag{6.9}$$

This modification turned out to be very useful. Figure 6.6 shows calibration results using the plain algorithm described earlier, and the algorithm with additional estimation of ambient light values. It is evident that the results are better when ambient light is estimated as well: In the left image, the crossover edges between calibration patterns are still visible. The lower half of the intensity profile is darker than the upper half, and there is a visible crossover line just above the lower text line. The right image is much smoother overall.

6. LIGHT SOURCE CALIBRATION

Figure 6.6: Calibration results for intensity profile of a projector. Left: without estimating ambient light, Right: with ambient light estimation.

6.4 Determining the Intensity Profile

After the projection center has been found, the next step is determining the full intensity profile of the light source. We proceed as follows:

1. Determine the rotation $\mathbf{l}_r$ such that the light source "camera" faces the calibration patterns. Each calibration pattern can be associated with a number of pixels, and each of these pixels corresponds to a 3D point. All calibration images $\mathcal{I}_i$ thus define point clouds, and we choose the rotation such that the z axis associated with the light source points towards the centroid of the point cloud made up of all pixels belonging to calibration patterns in all images.

2. Compute an intrinsic camera matrix such that the point cloud of calibration rectangles just fits completely into one light intensity image $_L\mathcal{I}$ that has the same resolution as the camera images $\mathcal{I}_i$.

3. Each pixel of the intensity profile can be identified with a ray from the light source through the scene, possibly hitting one or more calibration patterns. Thus, by shooting rays through

6.4 Determining the Intensity Profile

each pixel of the intensity profile, we may calculate intersection points with the calibration rectangles and determine the intensity value $\widetilde{d}_j$ associated with that light ray.

The last step of calculating the per-ray intensities could theoretically be solved by calculating the least-squares solution to (6.9), as we have done before. However, this is infeasible in practice, due to the size of the resulting system of equations. If the intensity profile has a resolution of 640×480, the system matrix will exceed a size of $(640 \cdot 480) \times (640 \cdot 480)$ for one-channel gray-scale images. Storing such a matrix would already be a big problem, since the memory required to do so exceeds 700 GB. Additionally, we would need to calculate an eigen decomposition of that matrix, which is completely out of the question for a matrix of this size.

Instead, we re-use the ambient light values that have been estimated when finding the light source projection center, and subtract those values from the image intensities. Afterwards, we can compute the ray intensity according to Equation (6.5) directly, without the need to resort to an eigen decomposition.

6. LIGHT SOURCE CALIBRATION

7. Experimental Results

We have tested all of our algorithms on a variety of synthetic data sets with known ground truth as well as on real camera images where the ground truth is not known. For the synthetic datasets, we are able to make precise statements about the performance of the algorithms. Furthermore, we can analyse the influence of system parameters on the reconstruction results.

The synthetic datasets have been generated using POV-RAY[1] in the extended MEGAPOV variant[2], augmented with the VLPOV[3] patch by A. Vedaldi. The patch allows generation of motion data and a ground truth depth map for a scene.

7.1 Ground Truth Comparison Method

When comparing results generated by POV-RAY with the reconstruction estimates, we would like to evaluate the quality of the estimated depth map, rotation, and translation. Defining meaningful similarity measures on these quantities is not at easy as it might seem on first sight. Monocular reconstruction is always only possible up to scale, so first of all, the scale of the estimated depth and translation will likely differ from the scale of the ground truth values.

The usual way to address such scaling problems is the application of scale-invariant similarity measures such as normalized

---

[1] http://www.povray.org/
[2] http://megapov.inetart.net/
[3] http://www.vlfeat.org/~vedaldi/code/vlpovy.html

7. EXPERIMENTAL RESULTS

cross-correlation (NCC). However, our experiments revealed that such a simple approach does not provide meaningful results on our problem. It is known that correlation measures are very sensitive to outliers [80], which explains our observation. Thus, instead of using NCC as similarity measure, we rely on a different method, first performing a registration of depth maps and subsequently determining the overlap between ground truth and estimated surface. This allows us to calculate an estimate of the ratio of the depth map that has been reconstructed correctly.

Before we start discussing our approach to depth map comparison, we will give some details on the normalized cross-correlation measure, and some examples where it performs sub-optimal. The normalized cross-correlation between two vectors $\mathbf{x}, \mathbf{y}$ is typically defined as

$$\left(\frac{\mathbf{x} - \mathbf{1}_n \cdot \overline{\mathbf{x}}}{|\mathbf{x}|}\right)^\mathrm{T} \cdot \left(\frac{\mathbf{y} - \mathbf{1}_n \cdot \overline{\mathbf{y}}}{|\mathbf{y}|}\right), \quad (7.1)$$

where $\overline{\mathbf{x}}, \overline{\mathbf{y}}$ denotes the mean value of vectors $\mathbf{x}, \mathbf{y}$, respectively. The range of normalized cross correlation is typically between -1 and 1, where the value of 1 signifies maximum agreement between the vectors, and -1 indicates that values are directly opposed to each other.

In our case, we skip the step of subtracting the mean, since only the scale of the reconstruction and the ground truth might differ, but there can be no additive offset between both. Thus, we define the depth map correlation function as

$$\mathcal{C}_\mathrm{D}(\mathbf{x}, \mathbf{y}) = \left(\frac{\mathbf{x}}{|\mathbf{x}|}\right)^\mathrm{T} \cdot \left(\frac{\mathbf{y}}{|\mathbf{y}|}\right). \quad (7.2)$$

We skip the step of subtracting the mean before computing the dot product between vectors, but we still normalize their scales. Note that since the depth values cannot become negative, the range of

7.1 Ground Truth Comparison Method

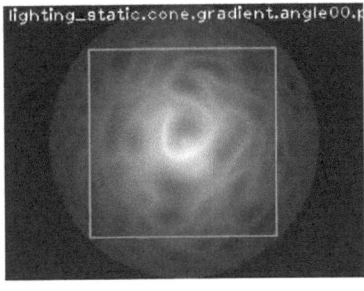
(a) Template image and ROI.

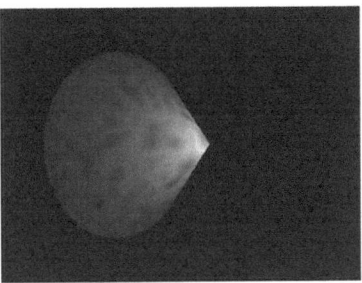
(b) Final image of sequence.

Figure 7.1: Left: The template image used for reconstruction, with ROI marked in green. Right: The last image of the sequence. Notice the significant self-occlusion of the cone.

similarity measures is between 0 and 1 for depth maps, where the value 1 is reached in maximum agreement, when both vectors are equal up to scale.

Now we are ready to give an example of a situation where the NCC similarity behaves in an undesired way. One of our synthetic testing cases is a sequence of images of a cone, with the camera orbiting around the tip of the cone. As soon as the camera reaches a certain angle, a part of the cone's surface becomes occluded. Figure 7.1 visualizes the situation. The last four frames of the sequence are affected by this occlusion. When using our reconstruction algorithm without the sliding-window technique, it is very sensitive to such occlusions, generating significantly corrupted depth maps. One example for this can be seen in Figure 7.2.

The NCC values for the reconstructed depth maps behave in a quite inconsistent way on these results. From visual inspection of the reconstructed 3D model, it appears that the depth map corruption present in the last four frames of the sequence is roughly the same. It seems that slightly more than half of the surface is still reconstructed successfully, while the rest is significantly distorted.

7. EXPERIMENTAL RESULTS

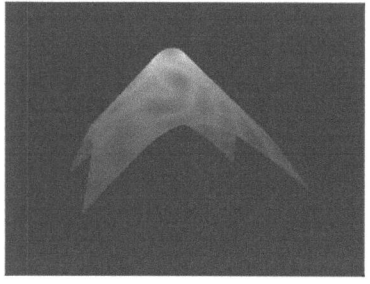 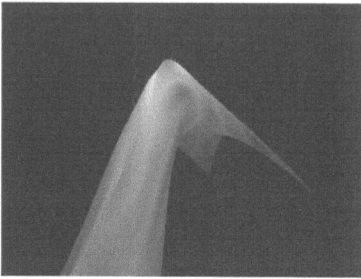

(a) Successful reconstruction.　　　(b) Corrupted reconstruction.

Figure 7.2: The left picture shows a successful reconstruction result, and the right image shows a corrupted result due to self-occlusion.

Since the occlusion becomes slightly larger during these four frames due to the increasing angle, we would expect the reconstruction quality to reduce slightly for these frames.

However, the NCC values show quite the contrary behaviour: In the frame just before the occlusion happens, the NCC value is at 0.999996, which indicates virtually perfect alignment. For the following frames, the values are 0.83, 0.87, 0.91 and 0.93, so the NCC values are increasing, which would normally indicate an improvement of the depth map. Our registration-based similarity measure gives an estimate of the percentage of the surface that could not be reconstructed, and it produces the values 39.0%, 41.5%, 41.6%, 45% for said four frames, which agrees with our reasoning that the reconstruction quality should decrease. Figure 7.3 shows the error of the depth map for the last frame of the sequence.

Furthermore, as we are using splines as an inverse depth model, it is not possible to model sharp peaks such as the tip of the cone. However, in the case of non-occlusion, the NCC value still indicates a nearly perfect match of the whole depth map, which seems inadequate. Our proposed similarity measure, however, correctly recognizes this discrepancy between ground truth and the estimate, and

7.1 Ground Truth Comparison Method

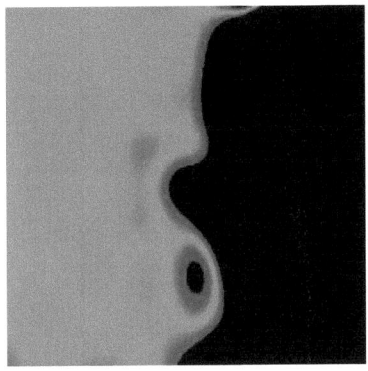
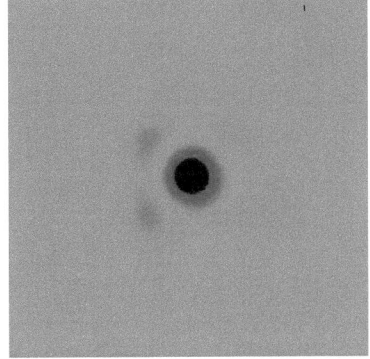

(a) Similarity values for distorted cone.   (b) Similarity values for good cone result.

Figure 7.3: Example similarity measurement results, where red indicates high error, green low error, and black areas indicate outlier values that are classified as unsuccessfully reconstructed. The left image is based on a reconstruction using the last image of the cone sequence with heavy occlusion, the right image is based on the non-occluded case.

estimates that 0.8% have not been reconstructed accurately. Figure 7.3 shows the per-pixel error assigned by our method. You can see there that the tip of the cone is correctly recognized as outlier.

When analysing this observation, we quickly find that the problem is the normalization of the depth map values involved in computing the NCC ratio. Figure 7.4 shows a schematic example of the problem that the normalization causes. Since the depth map is corrupted, the normalization is not able to bring the depth maps in significant overlap. Rather, the depth maps overlap at parts that do not constitute a valid reconstruction result at all, which explains the unexpected behaviour.

7.1.1 Depth Map Registration Approach

In the following, let $\mathbf{d} \in \mathbb{R}^n, \mathbf{d}^* \in \mathbb{R}^n$ denote the estimated and ground truth depth maps in a vectorized format, such that all n depth values are stacked on top of each other. Furthermore, let $\varepsilon \in \mathbb{R}$ with

7. EXPERIMENTAL RESULTS

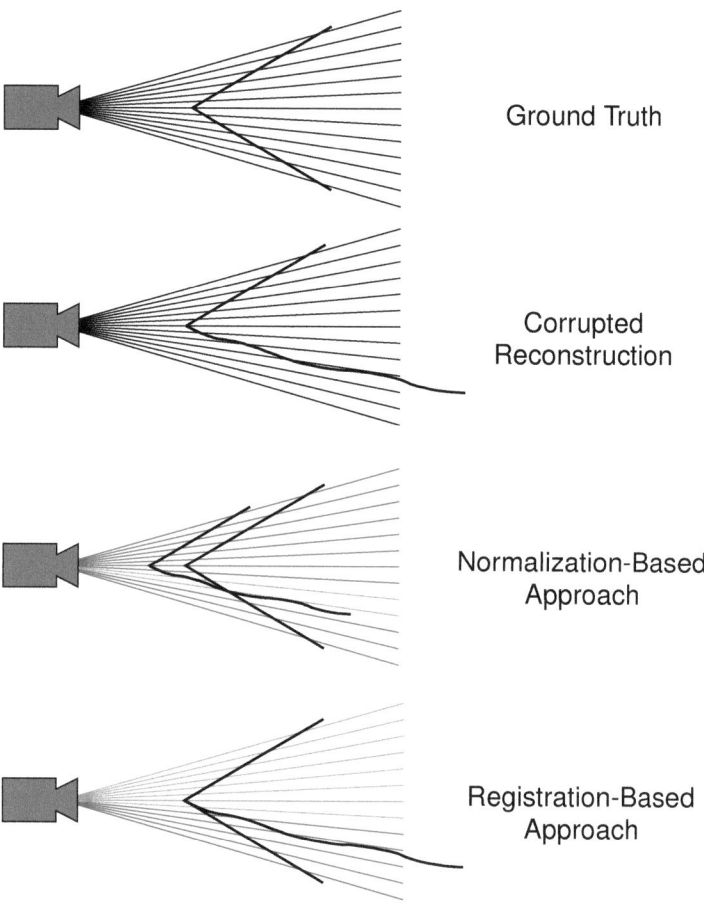

Figure 7.4: An intuitive explanation for the bad performance of NCC: The normalization of both depth map and estimate does not lead to a maximal overlap of both, in contrast to the registration-based approach. The green lines indicate overlap, while the red lines indicate disagreement.

7.1 Ground Truth Comparison Method

$\varepsilon > 1$ denote a threshold tolerance parameter. For some scaling value $s \in \mathbb{R}$, we would then consider the values $s \cdot \mathbf{d}_i$ and $\mathbf{d}_i^*$ to be in overlap if they are "similar enough", which we define mathematically as

$$\mathcal{M}_\mathrm{T}(\mathbf{d}_i, \mathbf{d}_i^*, s) = \begin{cases} 1 & \text{if } \frac{\mathbf{d}_i^*}{\varepsilon} < s \cdot \mathbf{d}_i < \mathbf{d}_i^* \cdot \varepsilon, \\ 0 & \text{otherwise.} \end{cases} \qquad (7.3)$$

It is important to use a multiplicative threshold here, since the notion of matching depth values must be independent of the scale of the ground truth depth map d. To see this, let us look at the case of an additive threshold, where the matching function would be defined as

$$\mathcal{M}_\mathrm{A}(\mathbf{d}_i, \mathbf{d}_i^*, s) = \begin{cases} 1 & \text{if } |s \cdot \mathbf{d}_i - \mathbf{d}_i^*| < \varepsilon, \\ 0 & \text{otherwise.} \end{cases} \qquad (7.4)$$

If the scale of d* is changed, the inlier/outlier classification of the values of d may change, which is undesirable. This is not the case for our function $\mathcal{M}_\mathrm{T}$, where intuitively, larger discrepancies are allowed for larger ground truth depth values. Furthermore, using a multiplicative threshold takes into account that large depth values are more difficult to reconstruct accurately, and thus larger error values should be allowed for them.

The matching function $\mathcal{M}_\mathrm{T}$ can be reformulated into an equivalent form as follows:

$$\mathcal{M}_\mathrm{LT}(\mathbf{d}_i, \mathbf{d}_i^*, s) = \begin{cases} 1 & \text{if } |\log(s) - \log\left(\frac{\mathbf{d}_i^*}{\mathbf{d}_i}\right)| < \log(\varepsilon), \\ 0 & \text{otherwise.} \end{cases} \qquad (7.5)$$

To find a value s that leads to a maximal agreement of depth map functions under the similarity indicator function $\mathcal{M}_\mathrm{LT}$, we minimize

7. EXPERIMENTAL RESULTS

the objective function

$$^{\text{LT}}O(s) = -\sum_{i=1}^{n} \mathcal{M}_{\text{LT}}(\mathbf{d}_i, \mathbf{d}_i^*, s), \qquad (7.6)$$

which is simply the number of inliers generated by the scaling value s. To perform this minimization, we use the approach proposed by Papazov and Burschka [79], which has been applied with great success to the much more complicated problem of 3D point set registration. The method also copes very well with our optimization objective.

However, as mentioned in the article by Papazov and Burschka, even better registration results can be achieved by replacing the simple thresholding mechanism with a continuous approximation. They propose to use the function $(\alpha + \beta \cdot \delta^2)^{-1}$ as a smooth matching indicator, where δ is the difference between the values to be matched. Applied to our threshold-based matching function, this leads to the definition of a soft matching function as follows:

$$\mathcal{M}_{\text{LS}}(\mathbf{d}_i, \mathbf{d}_i^*, s) = \left[\alpha + \beta \cdot \left(\log(s) - \log\left(\frac{\mathbf{d}_i^*}{\mathbf{d}_i}\right)\right)^2\right]^{-1}. \qquad (7.7)$$

Replacing the matching function in the optimization objective above with this smooth function generally leads to a higher quality of fit with a smaller residual error on the matched parts, so we prefer this matching function over the simple threshold function. Some guidelines for choosing the values α and β are given in the article by Papazov and Burschka. For our registration method, we use the values $\varepsilon = 1.02$, $\beta = \frac{20-1}{\log(\varepsilon)^2}$, and $\alpha = 1$.

Once the scale has been retrieved through optimization, we are able to compute the ratio of outlier depth values to total depth values, which finally yields one scalar similarity measure for depth

7.1 Ground Truth Comparison Method

maps. For this computation, we use the threshold-based matching function, because interpretation of the soft matching values in such a sense is difficult.

Another interesting question is the quality of the reconstruction in those parts of the surface that could be reconstructed at all. Again, we should use a scale-invariant measure here, and thus associate the errors on a logarithmic scale, such that the error value calculated for some entry d_i of the estimated depth map would be $|\log(s) - \log\left(\frac{d_i^*}{d_i}\right)|$.

We have already shown two examples for error images created using these values in Figure 7.3, where green color signifies a low error value, red color signifies high error value, and black areas denote estimation outliers, so the images aim to show both the reconstructed area of a depth map and the reconstruction quality in that area. For computing a scalar measure of reconstruction quality for the reconstructed parts only, we will compute the root mean squared error of the values $|\log(s) - \log\left(\frac{d_i^*}{d_i}\right)|$ for all i.

7.1.2 Rotation and Translation Similarity Measures

For comparing two rotations, there are several known similarity measures. The article by Huynh [81] gives a good overview of the most commonly used ones, and also provides an analysis of each of those rotation metrics. Among the six comparison measures analysed, there is also one that operates on rotation quaternions, which is very convenient for us since our implementation also works with rotation quaternions. Let q, q^* denote the rotation estimate and the ground truth rotation, respectively. Then, we adapt the metric described as Φ_3 in the article by Huynh, and define our rotation simi-

7. EXPERIMENTAL RESULTS

larity measure as

$$\mathcal{C}_R(\mathbf{q},\mathbf{q}^*) = \arccos(|\mathbf{q}^T \cdot \mathbf{q}^*|) \cdot \frac{2}{\pi}. \tag{7.8}$$

This similarity measure yields values in the range $[0,1]$, where 0 indicates maximum agreement.

For comparing translations, we have to deal with the same scale ambiguity as in the case of the depth maps. The correct scale s, however, is determined through the depth map registration process. Denoting with $\mathbf{t}$ our translational motion estimate and with $\mathbf{t}^*$ the ground truth motion, we can calculate an error relative to the average of the depth map as

$$\mathcal{C}_T(\mathbf{t},\mathbf{t}^*) = \frac{s \cdot \mathbf{t} - \mathbf{t}^*}{\overline{\mathbf{d}}^*}, \tag{7.9}$$

where $\overline{\mathbf{d}}^*$ denotes the average of the ground truth depth values. The values of the translation comparison function will be greater or equal to 0, with 0 indicating minimal error.

7.2 Synthetic Datasets Used for our Evaluation

For evaluating our algorithms, we have set up an automated testing environment that generates testing data and evaluates the reconstruction results for a set of combinations of scenes, camera motion paths, textures, and lighting conditions. We have used five different synthetic scenes:

- The surface of a sphere. This has turned out to be a quite easy scenario for our algorithms, mainly because a sphere surface can be easily approximated by a spline surface.

- A slanted plane. Again, this is can be modelled quite well

7.2 Synthetic Datasets Used for our Evaluation

using a spline surface.

- A cone that is viewed from above. The tip of the cone presents some difficulty to the algorithms, since its first order derivative would be non-continuous, which is something that cannot be modelled well using a spline.

- A plane with 4 bumps on its surface. The bumps are modelled as half-spheres. This scenario is more difficult than the cone scenario, since the depth surface has a non-continuous second-order derivative along the joining line between the half-spheres and the plane.

- Finally, we emulate a setting similar to video-endoscopy with a scene containing a tube that the camera is viewing downwards. This has turned out to be the most difficult scenario for the algorithm, due to the large variations in depth and presence of a discontinuity.

Snapshots of all the above scenes are shown in Figure 7.5.

As for camera motion, we have tried a number of different paths for the camera to follow:

- Linear motion in x-direction, with the camera looking at a fixed point close to the object to be reconstructed.

- Spiralling motion in the $x-y$ plane, with the camera looking at a fixed point.

- Linear zoom-out motion, where the camera moves backwards along z direction.

- A linear motion parallel to the viewing plane in $x-y$ direction.

7. EXPERIMENTAL RESULTS

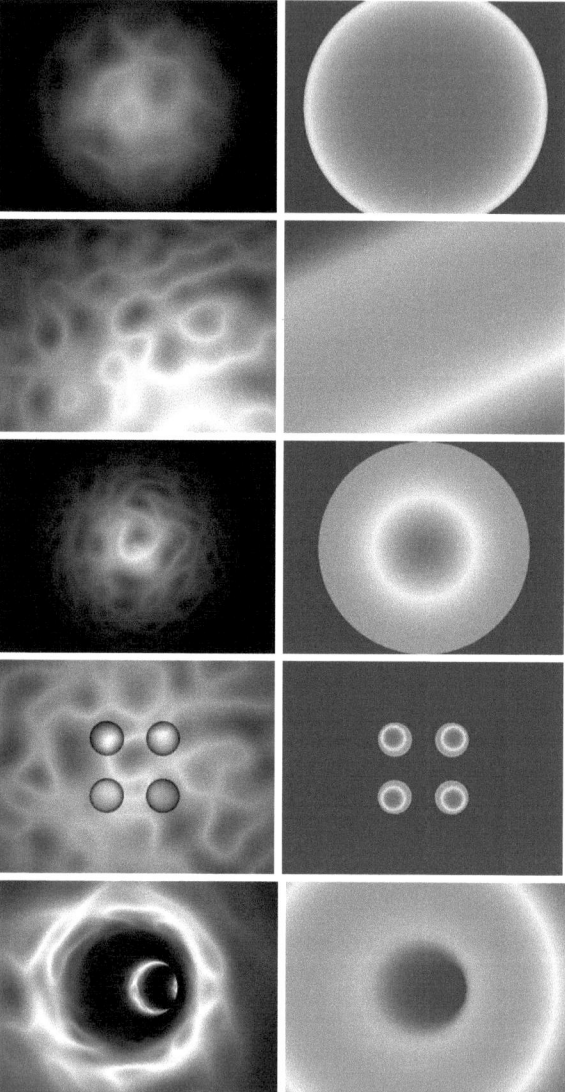

Figure 7.5: An overview of our rendered scenes, along with associated inverse depth maps. From top to bottom: A sphere, a slanted plane, a cone viewed from above such that its tip is in the image center, a plane with four half spheres attached, and a tube.

7.2 Synthetic Datasets Used for our Evaluation

- As a special case for the tube scenario, there is a motion path that moves backward along the tube. The motion is backwards to assure that as much of the reference image as possible remains visible in the subsequent images.

Schematic views of all those motion paths are shown in Figure 7.6.

Finally, we have also tested the influence of the texturedness of the surfaces. To this end, we have run tests with two different textures exhibiting medium and low texturedness. The textures are shown in Figure 7.7.

Not all combinations of scenes and motion paths lead to meaningful scenarios. When combining, e.g., the tube scenario with the spiralling motion path, the camera moves through the boundary wall of the tube, such that a reconstruction becomes completely impossible at that point. Thus, we only use the specialized tube following motion path in conjunction with the tube scenario, and all other motion paths in combination with all other scenarios. Not counting the tube scene, we have then 4 scenes to combine with 4 paths and 2 textures, which makes all in all 32 scenarios. The tube scene is only combined with the two different texture choices, yielding another 2 testing scenarios.

The data is evaluated as follows: We have defined several sets of parameter values in order to systematically determine the influence of system parameters on reconstruction results. The reconstruction algorithm is then run on all possible combinations of scenes, motion paths, textures, and parameters, which generates a lot of data. We calculate the similarity of the estimated quantities with the ground truth, using the comparison functions defined above. If nothing else is mentioned, we use an empirically determined baseline set of parameters which worked well in most cases. Those parameters are:

- The spline order is 2 in both directions, so we are using a bi-

7. EXPERIMENTAL RESULTS

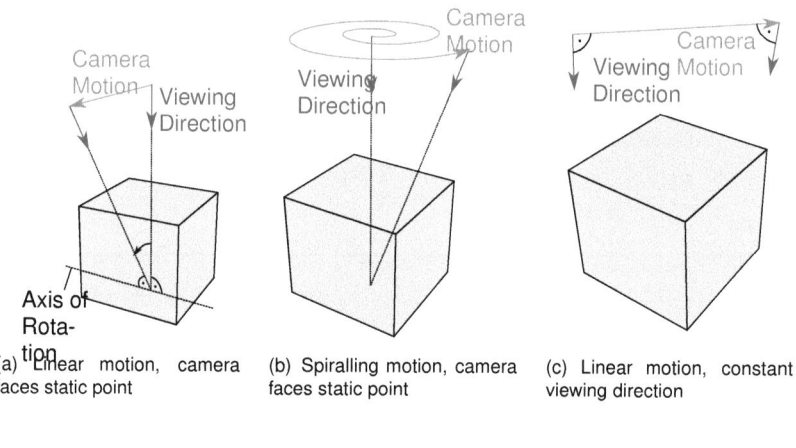

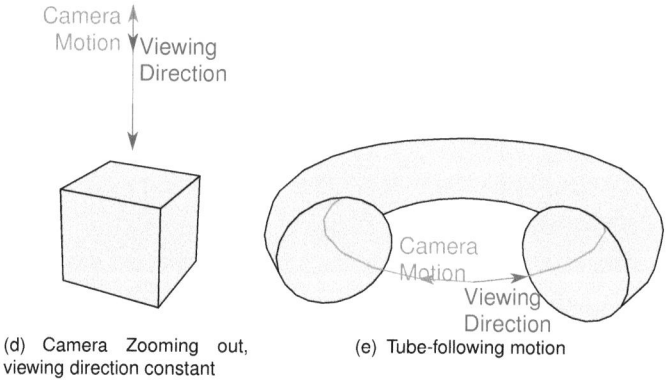

Figure 7.6: Schematic overview of different motion paths used in our evaluation. Note that these plots are not accurate, but are only intended to illustrate the different motion types.

7.2 Synthetic Datasets Used for our Evaluation

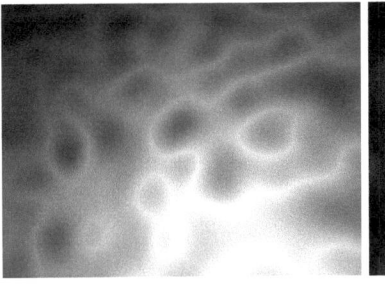 

Figure 7.7: The two different types of textures used in our experiments: A soft, diffuse cloud-like pattern, and a more structured, granite-like one.

quadratic spline.

- The number of control points is 8 in both directions.

- The sliding window buffer size is 3.

- The regularization multiplier is 0.01.

We have tested the behaviour of the system under the following changes of the baseline parameter set:

- Different window sizes: No sliding window, and window sizes 2 up to 4.

- Regularization multiplier: The influence of different regularization weights was tested for values 0, 0.001, 0.01, 0.1, 0.2, 0.5, and 1.

- Spline resolution: The number of control points used in the spline surface model affects the level of detail that can be achieved using that model. We have tested 6, 7, 8, 9, 10, and 11 control points.

All in all, this amounts to testing $4 + 7 + 6 = 17$ parameter sets in combination with the 34 different scenarios we have described

7. EXPERIMENTAL RESULTS

above, amounting to 578 test scenario runs all in all. There have been additional, separate evaluation runs for empirically analysing the sensitivity of the algorithm to different amounts of motion.

We want to analyse the expected behaviour of the algorithms under certain settings, and to do this, we proceed as follows:

1. For the parameter we are interested in, say a certain setting of the regularization multiplier, we evaluate the performance of the algorithm for each of the 34 test scenarios. We determine the associated average performance values that have been achieved for depth map similarity, motion similarity, and rotation similarity each. If the parameter settings can be ordered in a sequential manner, we can analyse the behaviour of the algorithm by plotting said evaluation results sequentially.

2. Sometimes, it is more informative to look at the progression of the reconstruction performance values over time. This is the case, e.g., when examining the performance of the algorithm on different scenes, because there is no clear ordering on the scenes, as opposed to, e.g., the regularization multiplier or the spline resolution. To obtain information about the expected behaviour, we group the values per frame, so that we can calculate the average performance of the system per frame for a specific setting.

The graphs display the depth map, rotation, and angular comparison values as defined above, and we use the colors red, green, and blue, respectively. An example for the first kind described above can be seen in Figure 7.24, which shows the overall reconstruction performance for different regularization settings. An example for the second kind of plot can be seen in Figures 7.20 to 7.23. These plots show the development of the estimates over time, where we distin-

7.3 Static Lighting Conditions

guish between worst case and median performance values for each frame of the specified sequence.

7.3 Static Lighting Conditions

We will start our evaluation with the most simple case, which is the case of static lighting. Our evaluation will discuss several different aspects that influence the reconstruction and motion estimation quality. Furthermore, we have run some experiments on a publicly available benchmarking data set, and we will show the results here. Finally, we will also present some reconstruction results on real data whose quality can be evaluated only through visual inspection.

7.3.1 Importance of Adequate Initialization

Intuitively, we would expect the system to be a lot more robust against large motions once it has been initialized properly. This is because the distance between the parameter sets that explain measurements for successive images are much smaller if the surface parameters have already been computed correctly, and it is easier for the optimization algorithm to find a way from one parameter set to the other. We have verified this conjecture using a specialized data set that uses a motion path that uses two different movement speeds. This allows us to choose the movement speed for the initialization frames and the other frames independently.

For this experiment, we have again used the cone scene. The movement path was a special movement path where the camera moves along a Lissajous curve with $x = 2 \cdot \sin(2 \cdot t), y = \sin(3 \cdot t)$. Figure 7.8 visualizes the camera motion. The speed of camera motion for the initialization frames was varied from very small to very high. The speed for the other frames was chosen constant, but high

7. EXPERIMENTAL RESULTS

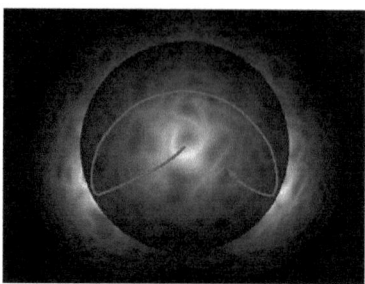

Figure 7.8: The motion path used for our test of the importance of proper initialization. The red line denotes the motion curve of the tip of the cone.

enough that the system would not be able to initialize from these images. To quantify the amount of camera motion, we specify the ratio $\frac{|t|}{d^*_{\max}}$ of the translation baseline magnitude in relation to the maximum value $d^*_{\max}$ of the vectorized depth map d^*. We will call this measure the *normalized baseline*.

The algorithm has shown the following behaviour: For smaller initial motion, it was able to initialize properly, as well as track the subsequent images exhibiting very fast object movement. For a larger amount of initial camera motion, the system was not able to initialize properly from the first few frames, and the fast movement after the initialization frames prevented the system from recovering from the bad initial reconstruction. Figure 7.9 shows the average performance of the algorithm against the average normalized baseline for the initialization frames.

The plots show that while an increase in the baseline leads to a better average performance at first, having a baseline that is too large leads to unrecoverable problems. As seen in the best case plot, which shows the best reconstruction similarity values achieved during the whole 20 frame sequence, the performance is really bad as soon as the average baseline exceeds a certain value. This is caused by the inability of the algorithm to initialize properly from the

7.3 Static Lighting Conditions

first few images, and it is subsequently not able to recover due to the quick motion of the camera.

7.3.2 Sensitivity of the Initialization to Motion

One of the most important steps in our system is the initialization of the depth map. We have seen in the previous section that without a proper initialization, the algorithm can get lost in a local minimum easily and it might not be able to recover. In this section, we will try to answer the question of which motion paths and motion speeds are likely to lead to a good initialization. To quantify the amount of motion in a scale-independent way, we again use the normalized baseline as introduced above.

For this test, we consider the slanted plane, sphere, cone, and plane with bumps scenarios, in combination with the paths (a)-(d) shown in Figure 7.6. The tube scenario is left out because it is an especially difficult case that shall be discussed separately.

We have evaluated the initialization performance achieved when using the mentioned paths at different speeds, computing our similarity measures for the first three images of the sequence after the initialization. Our first will be on focused on the performance of the different motion paths using different motion speeds. Figures 7.10 to 7.17 show plots of the average reconstruction accuracy against the normalized baseline.

There are several things that we want to show with this experiment:

- Certain types of motion are more suitable for initialization than others.

- The normalized baseline between frames must neither be too small nor too large.

7. EXPERIMENTAL RESULTS

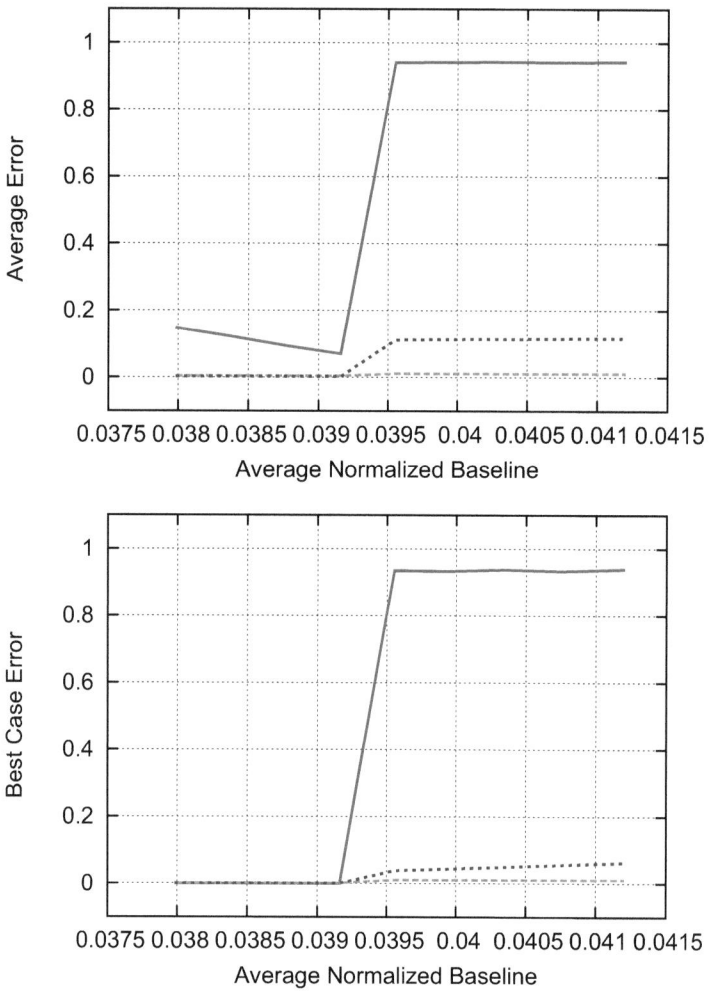

Figure 7.9: Evaluation results for different average normalized baseline values. The left plot shows the average performance of the reconstruction algorithm for the 20-image sequence against the ground truth average normalized baseline in the first three frames, the right plot shows the best case similarity obtained.

7.3 Static Lighting Conditions

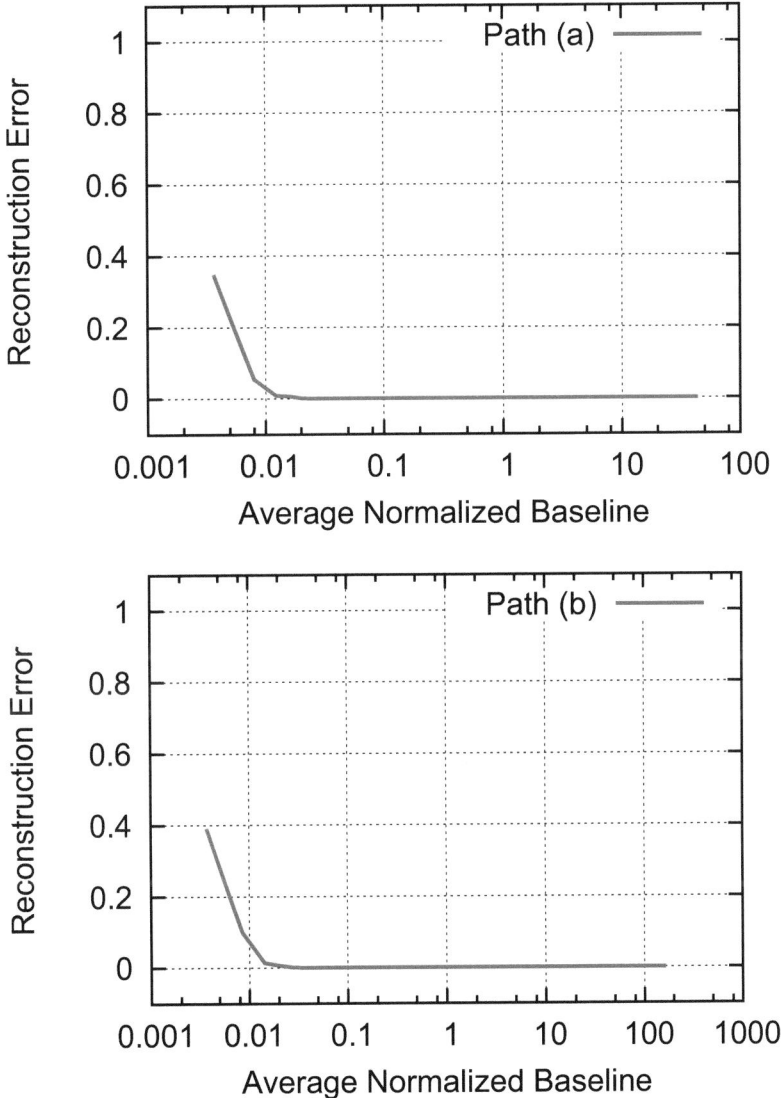

Figure 7.10: Initialization results for paths a and b on the slanted plane scenario, where different motion speeds have been used. All plots show the average reconstruction accuracy against the average normalized baseline during the first 5 frames on a logarithmic scale.

7. EXPERIMENTAL RESULTS

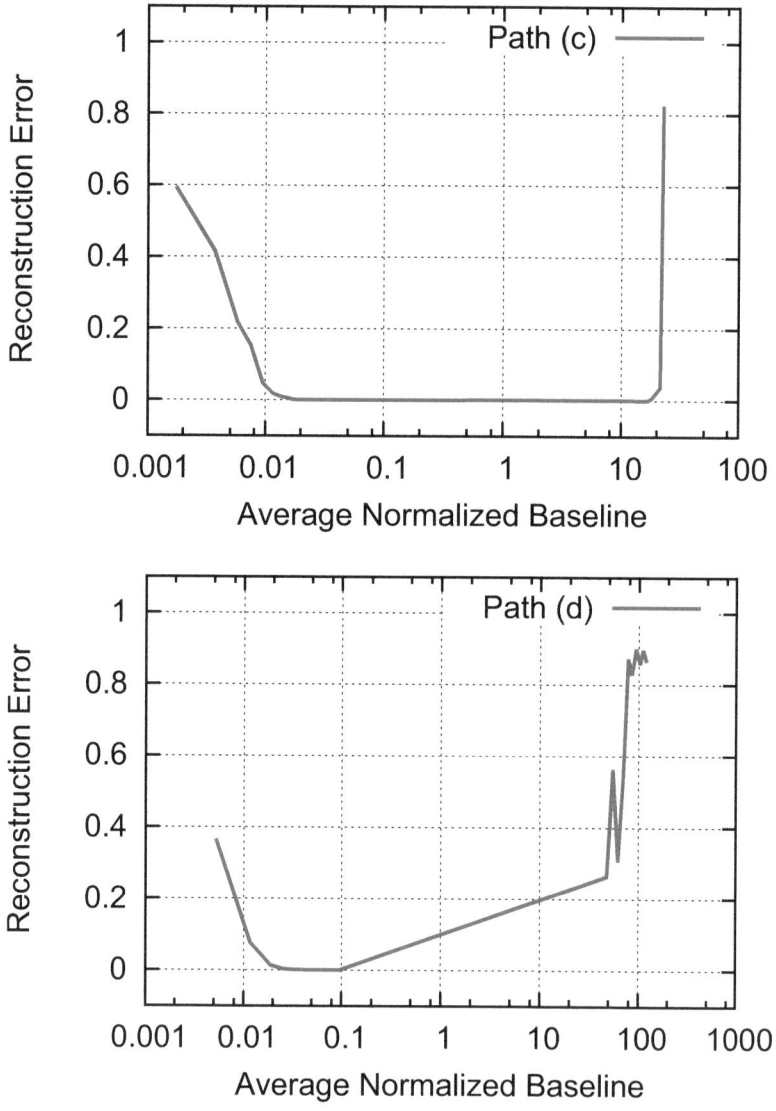

Figure 7.11: Initialization results for paths c and d on the slanted plane scenario, where different motion speeds have been used.

7.3 Static Lighting Conditions

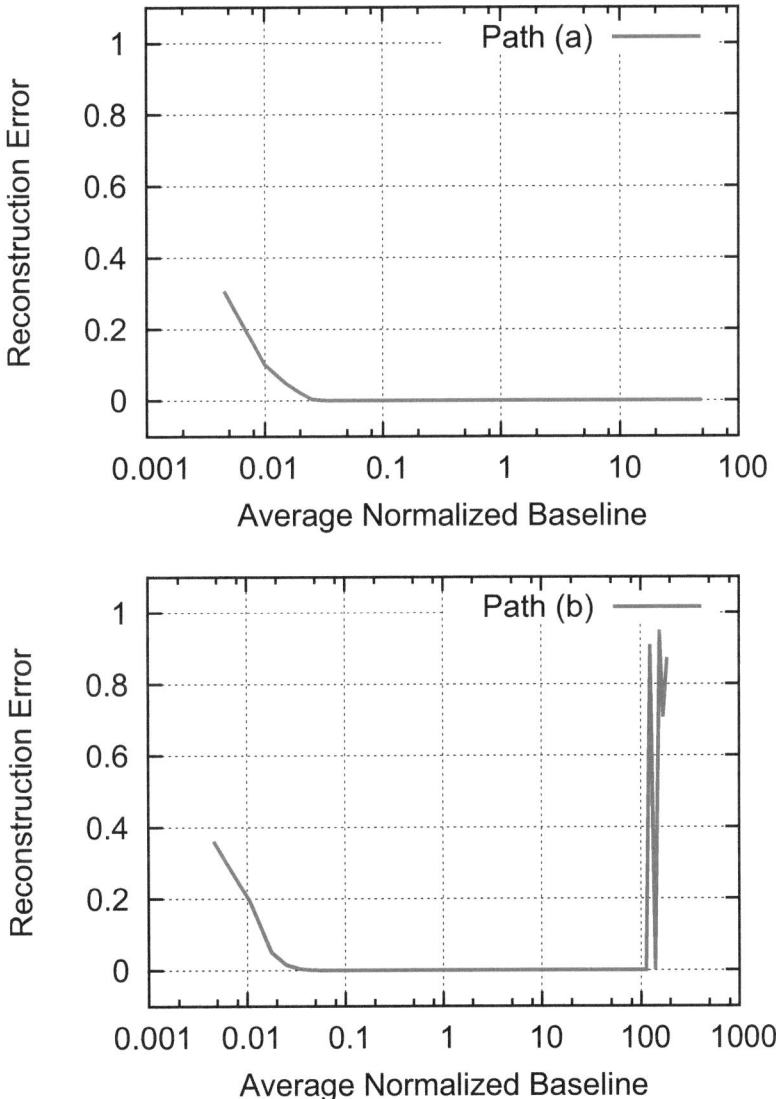

Figure 7.12: Initialization results for paths a and b on the sphere scenario, where different motion speeds have been used.

7. EXPERIMENTAL RESULTS

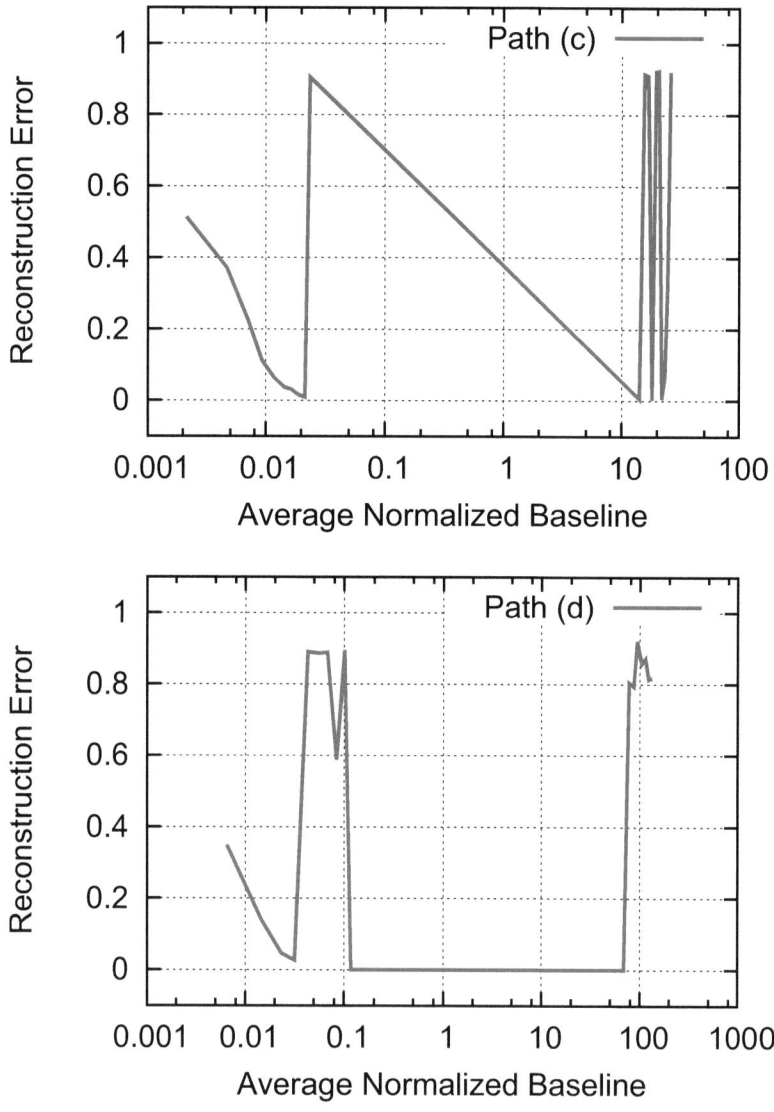

Figure 7.13: Initialization results for paths c and d on the sphere scenario, where different motion speeds have been used.

7.3 Static Lighting Conditions

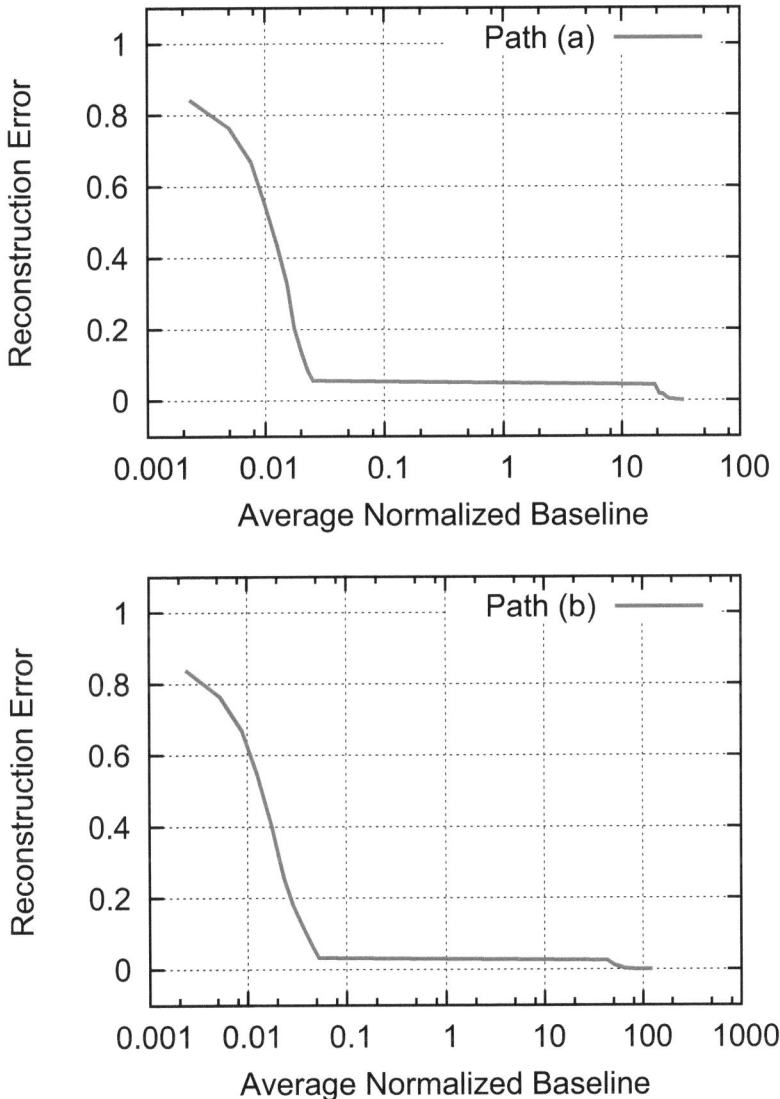

Figure 7.14: Initialization results for paths a and b on the cone scenario, where different motion speeds have been used.

7. EXPERIMENTAL RESULTS

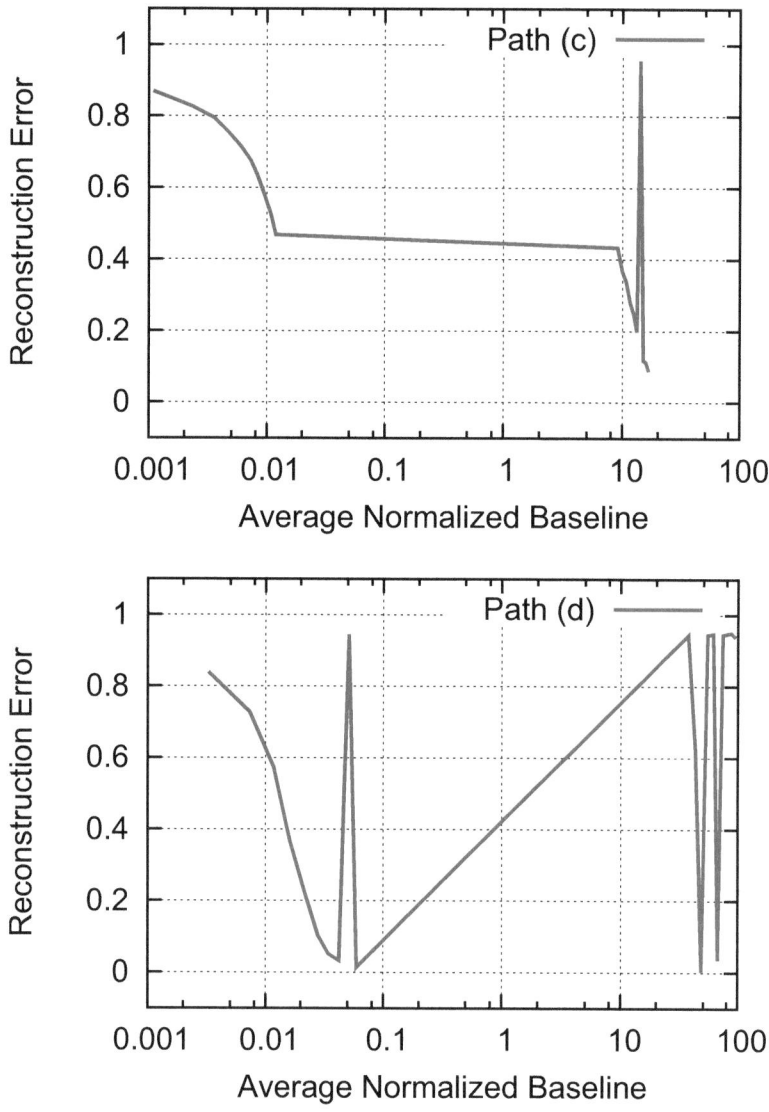

Figure 7.15: Initialization results for paths c and d on the cone scenario, where different motion speeds have been used.

7.3 Static Lighting Conditions

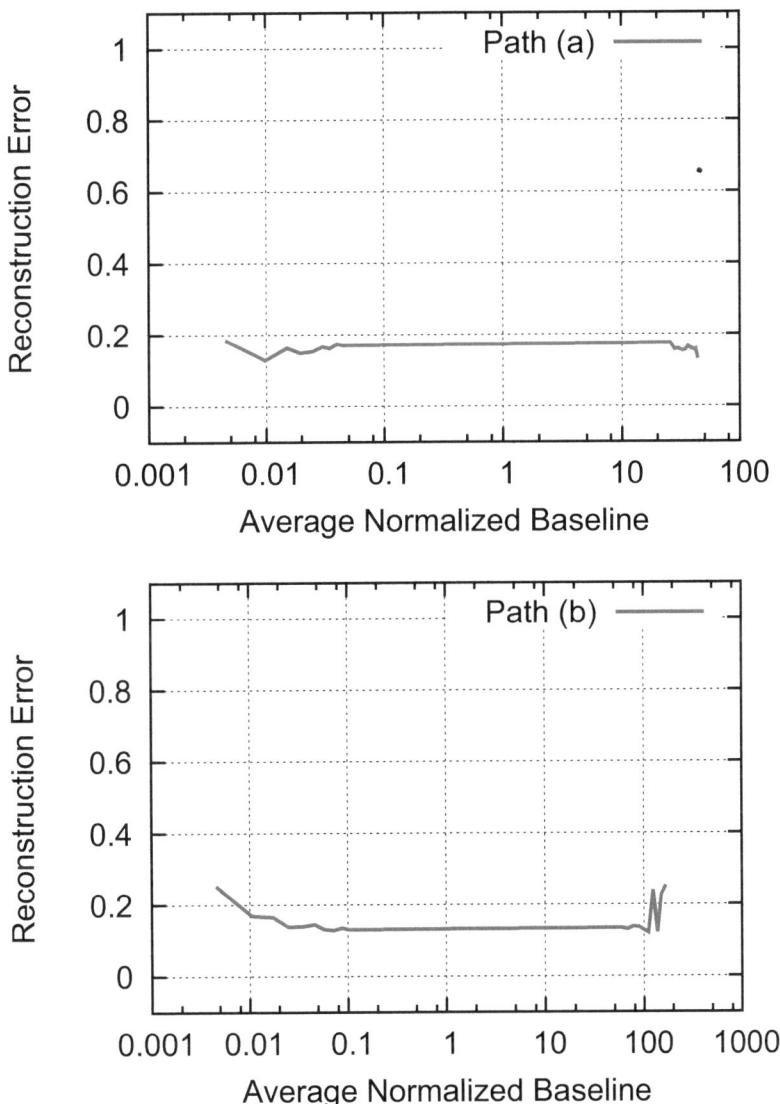

Figure 7.16: Initialization results for paths a and b on the plane-with-bumps scenario, where different motion speeds have been used.

7. EXPERIMENTAL RESULTS

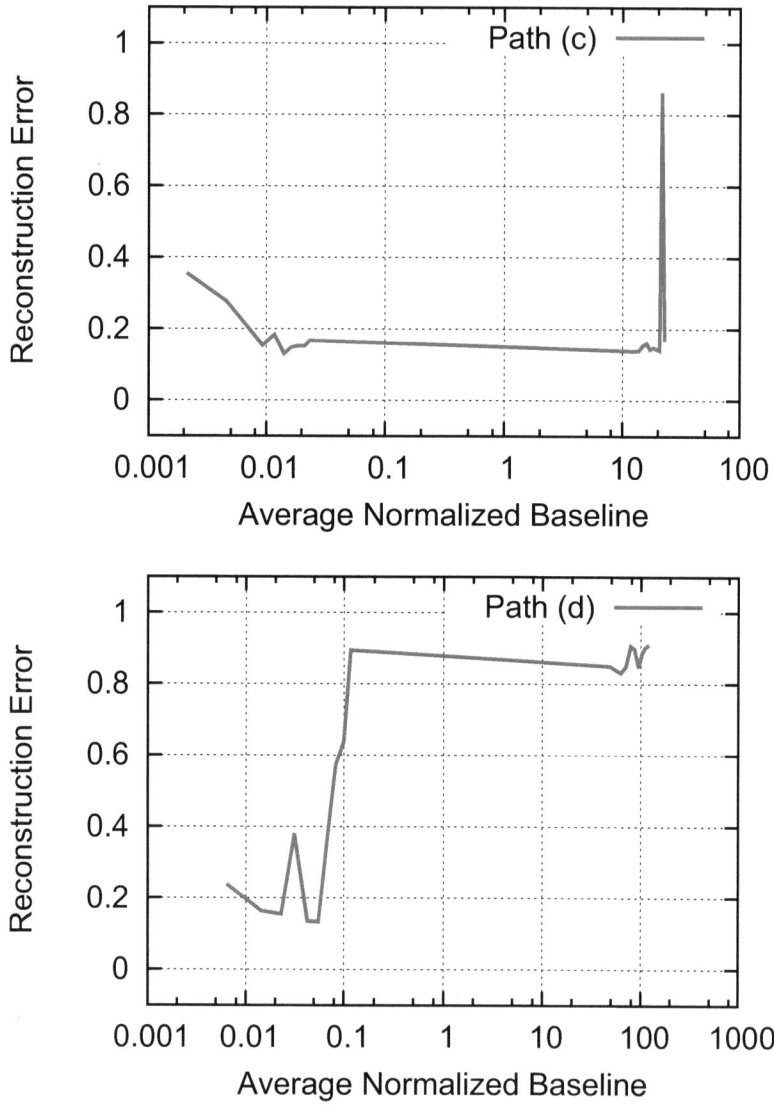

Figure 7.17: Initialization results for paths c and d on the plane-with-bumps scenario, where different motion speeds have been used.

7.3 Static Lighting Conditions

- Initialization is "easier" when the initial surface model is close to the actual model.

As for the most suitable type of motion, the plots clearly indicate that the two paths (a) and (b), which combine translational and rotational motion, perform best, while paths (c) and (d) that consist of purely translational motion consistently perform worse. This observation can be explained by noting that the camera facing a constant point in the scene leads to a bigger overlap of surface regions in consecutive images, while at the same time allowing a large baseline without the ROI leaving the image region. The initial overlap helps the algorithm to correctly align the rest of the image, while the comparatively large baseline makes the determination of depths easier. The bad performance of the zoom-out motion can be explained by observing that the camera moves away from the surface, which has the effect that the depth resolution quickly gets worse.

Finally, we can see that the initialization of the system performs better when the initial surface model, which is a plane parallel to the camera plane, is close to the ground truth model. The initial model is a plane at distance 1, which means that the initial model does not need to be modified much for the slanted plane and plane with bumps scenarios. For the slanted plane scenario, it is only necessary to rotate the initially estimated plane slightly, and in the plane with bumps scenario, the initial guess is already perfect except for the bumps. The plots show that the error values are very good already for a small normalized baseline. For the sphere and cone scenarios, this is not the case, and larger motion is required to achieve an accurate reconstruction.

7. EXPERIMENTAL RESULTS

7.3.2.1 Ambiguous Configurations

During our experiments, we have found another class of motions that lead to undesirable behaviour. This is the class of motions that perform pure rotations and no additional translations. We have tested variants of both paths (a) and (b) that were pure rotations about the look-at point. The performance of the algorithm under this class of motion was highly unstable, sometimes leading to a good reconstruction, but almost equally often leading to a surface model that resembles a stretched mirror image of the actual depth map. Figure 7.18 shows an example for this phenomenon on our synthetic data.

We are not sure about the reason for these singularities. It is known that there exist some configurations [82] that are critical for euclidean multi-view reconstruction, and do not admit a unique solution. However, considering the appearance of these reversed reconstructions, it seems unlikely that our testing cases belong to this class. A different class of ambiguities for euclidean structure-from-motion problems has been described by Oliensis [83]. The author describes the reconstructions as resembling inverse perspective images, which seems to fit our observations well. This makes it seem quite likely that this is the ambiguity that our algorithm encounters. However, a thorough analysis of this situation has yet to be done.

The described problem of reversed depth maps is encountered very rarely on real camera images. One example is shown in Figure 7.19, showing the result of a face reconstruction from two sequences with different camera motion. The surfaces shown in the top two images are viewed from different camera positions, in order to better highlight the distortion of the model. The bottom images show what the inverted model would look like under small translation from the camera's reference position. Note that the camera motion

7.3 Static Lighting Conditions

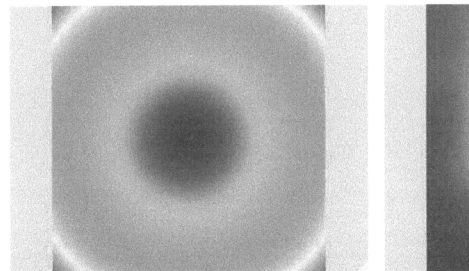
(a) Ground truth ROI depth map for cone scenario.

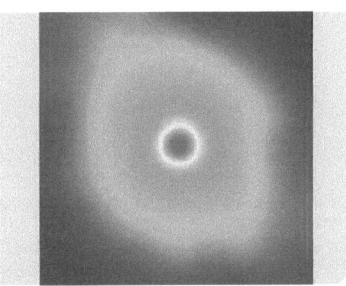
(b) Reconstructed depth map.

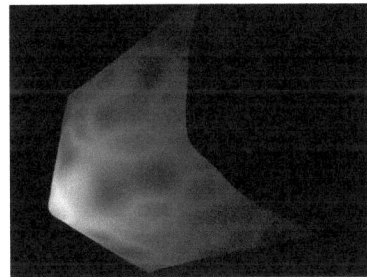
(c) Successful cone reconstruction.

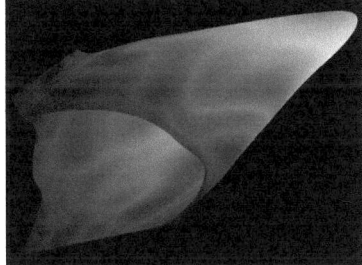
(d) Reverse reconstruction.

Figure 7.18: Some reconstruction results showing the reverse depth map phenomenon for the synthetic cone dataset. Note that the reconstructed surfaces are shown from approximately the same camera position.

7. EXPERIMENTAL RESULTS

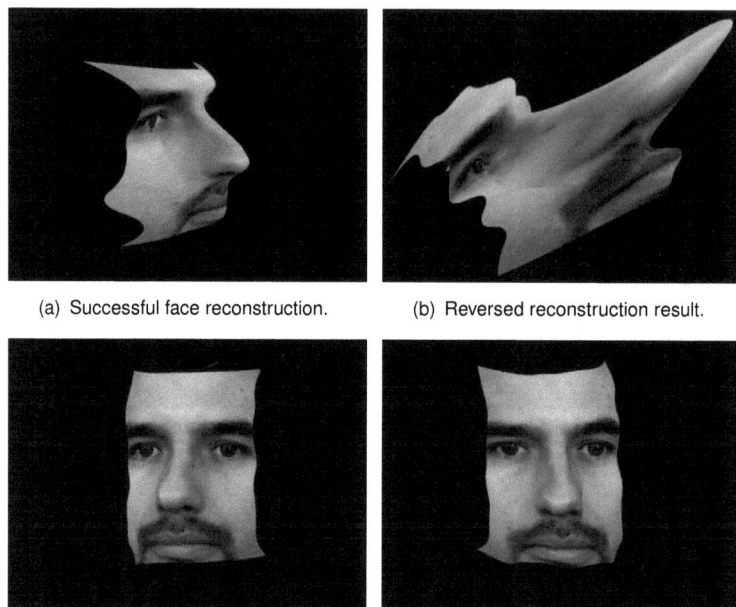

(a) Successful face reconstruction.

(b) Reversed reconstruction result.

(c) Reversed reconstruction, front view, camera moved slightly to the left.

(d) Reversed reconstruction, front view, camera moved slightly to the right.

Figure 7.19: Face reconstruction results, showing a comparison between successful and reversed reconstructions.

is exactly the inverse of what one would expect. These images show that the reverse depth map is actually a good approximation to the actual images for small camera displacements.

7.3.3 Importance of Window Size

One of the main contributions of this work is the transferral of the sliding-window technique to the domain of intensity-based algorithms. Thus, this benchmark is of special importance to us. The results are shown in Figures 7.20 to 7.23 for the window sizes 1 up to 4, respectively. From looking at the plots, it is apparent that the reconstruction results are consistently better for increasing window sizes, both in

7.3 Static Lighting Conditions

the worst case and on average.

Note that the algorithm tends to diverge towards the end of some sequences, as seen in the upper left plot and the one below. This phenomenon is due to partial self-occlusion in the cone and sphere scenarios when paths (a) and (b) are used. The disastrous effect that such a self-occlusion can have on the reconstruction has already been shown in Figures 7.2 and 7.3. For window sizes 3 and 4, however, the robustness of the algorithm against this occlusion is improved significantly. The corresponding plots show almost no increase of the reconstruction error for the last couple of frames.

Furthermore, it is apparent that the overall reconstruction quality is also improved by using a bigger window size. Very good results are achieved for window sizes 3 and 4. The difference in quality between window sizes 3 and 4 is marginal, which is why we have settled for a window size of 3 as baseline for our tests due to its lower computational complexity.

7.3.4 Influence of Regularization

The usage of spline surfaces in our algorithm already provides some inherent regularization for surface points that are close to each other. If there are large homogeneous regions in the image, this local regularization will not suffice, and additional regularization can be helpful. We have described our implementation of a regularization term in Section 5.8, and now we want to determine the multiplier that should be used for the regularization term.

We have run all of our test cases for the regularization multipliers $0, 0.001, 0.01, 0.1, 0.2, 0.5, 1$, and the results are shown in Figure 7.24. We show both the failure rates and the average reconstruction accuracy achieved. A reconstruction run is classified as failure if the best reconstruction quality achieved is below 50%, or if the initialization

7. EXPERIMENTAL RESULTS

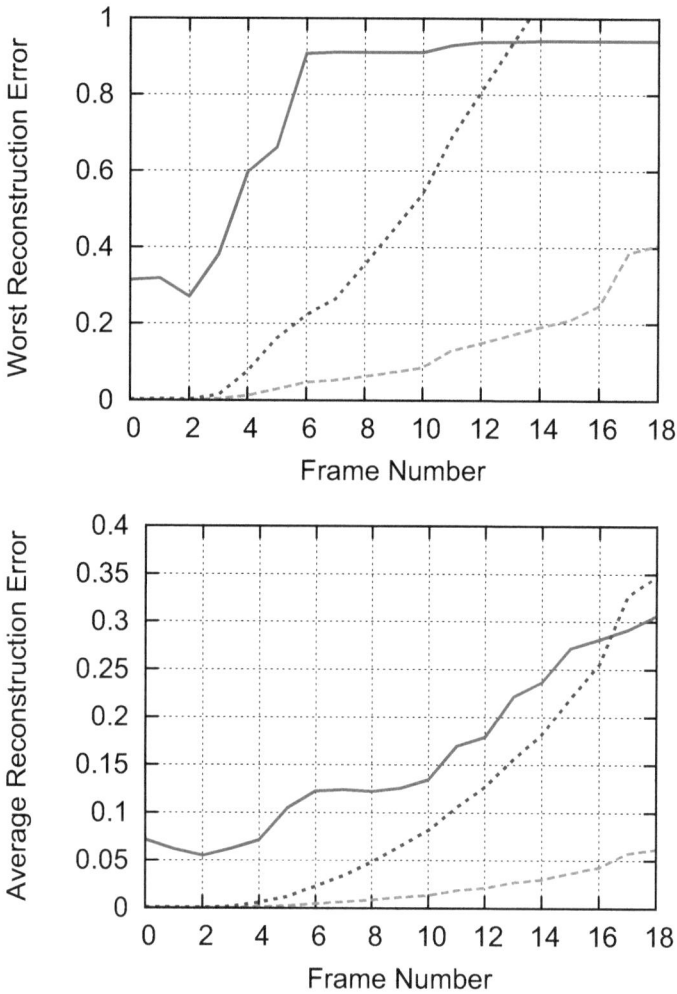

Figure 7.20: Evaluation results for sliding window size 1. The plots on the top and bottom show the worst and average performance values over time, respectively.

7.3 Static Lighting Conditions

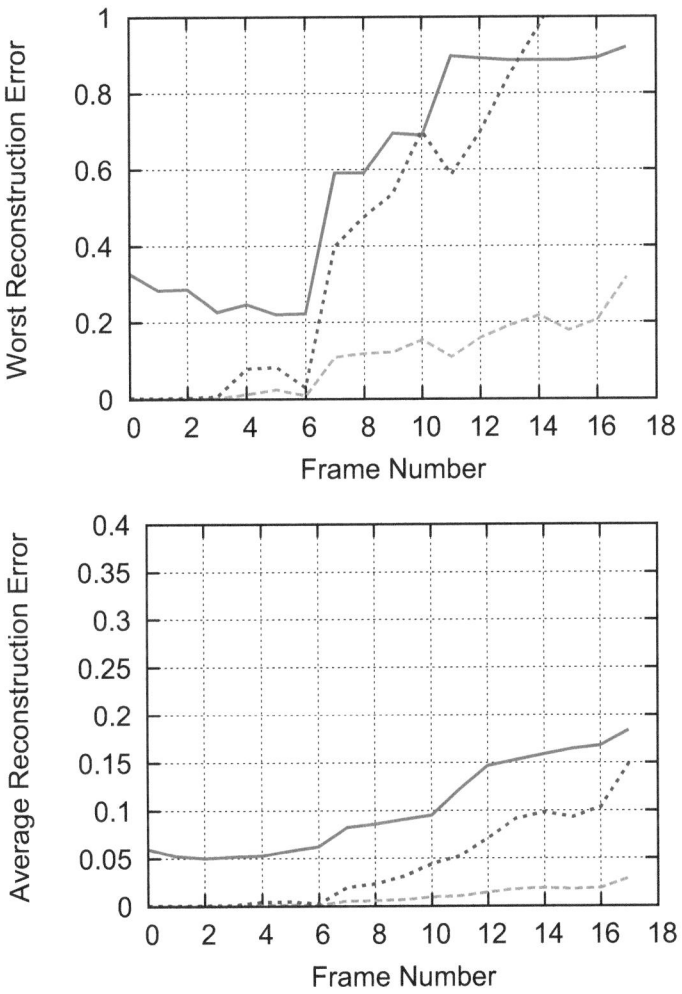

Figure 7.21: Evaluation results for sliding window size 2. The plots on the top and bottom show the worst and average performance values over time, respectively.

7. EXPERIMENTAL RESULTS

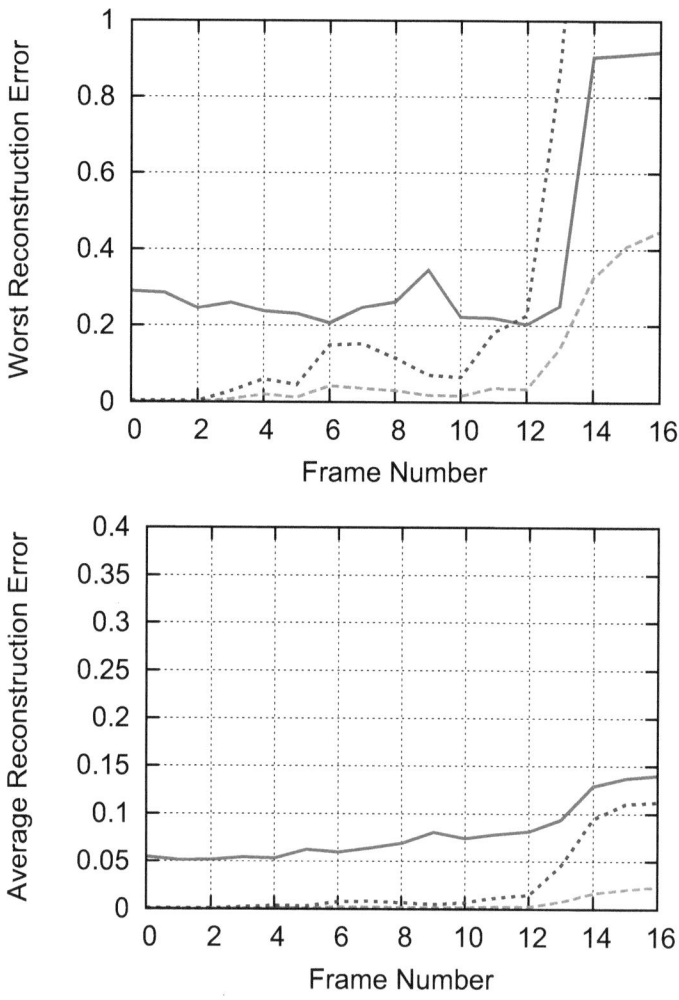

Figure 7.22: Evaluation results for sliding window size 3. The plots on the top and bottom show the worst and average performance values over time, respectively.

7.3 Static Lighting Conditions

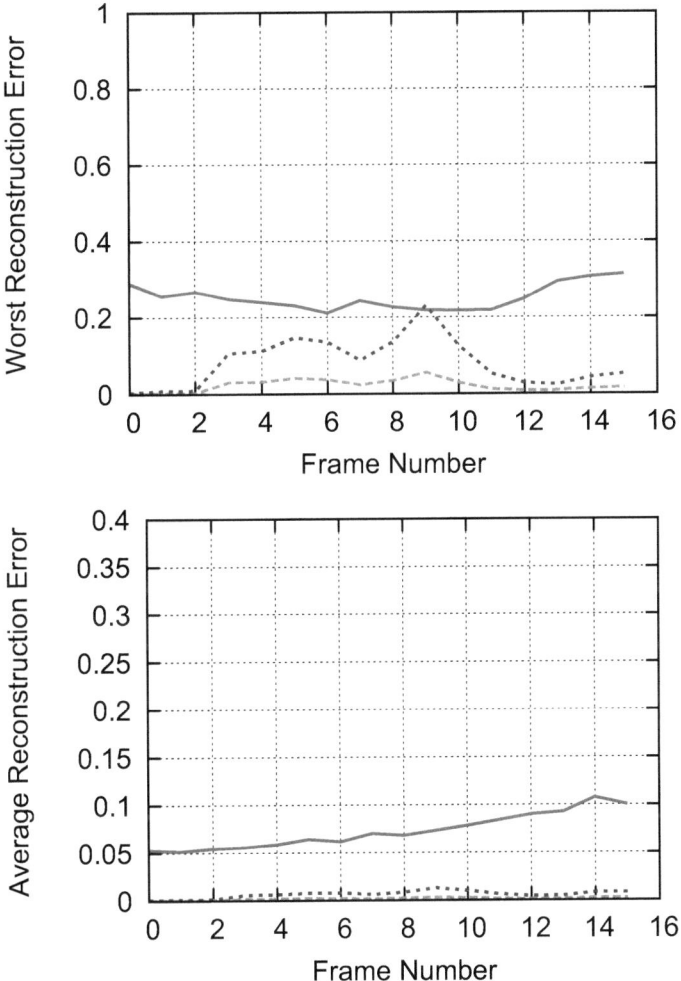

Figure 7.23: Evaluation results for sliding window size 4. The plots on the top and bottom show the worst and average performance values over time, respectively.

7. EXPERIMENTAL RESULTS

completely fails. To assure comparability of the results used in the reconstruction quality evaluation, we consider only scenarios that have not been classified as failure for any regularization parameter setting.

The plots show that the failure rates are lowest for the multiplier values between 0 and 0.2, while they rise significantly for higher multiplier values. The quality plot, on the other hand, reveals that the reconstruction quality reaches the best value for the third parameter setting, which corresponds to a multiplier of 0.1. Overall, it seems that a regularization multiplier of 0.1 performs best with respect to the achieved quality as well as failure rates.

7.3.5 Effect of Spline Resolution

Another parameter of our system is the number of control points used to determine the shape of the reconstructed surface. With an increasing number of spline control points, we are able to model the surfaces at higher detail. On the other hand, the additional degrees of freedom make the parameter estimation problem more difficult. The behaviour we would expect from the system is as follows:

- For a small number of control points, the reconstruction accuracy should be worse, because small details cannot be modelled well. On the other hand, when data is ambiguous due to large homogeneous regions, lowering the number of control points can help to retrieve better reconstructions, because this increases the effect of the regularization inherent to spline surfaces.

- When increasing the number of control points, the reconstruction quality should increase. However, a higher number of control points also means that the surface has more degrees of

7.3 Static Lighting Conditions

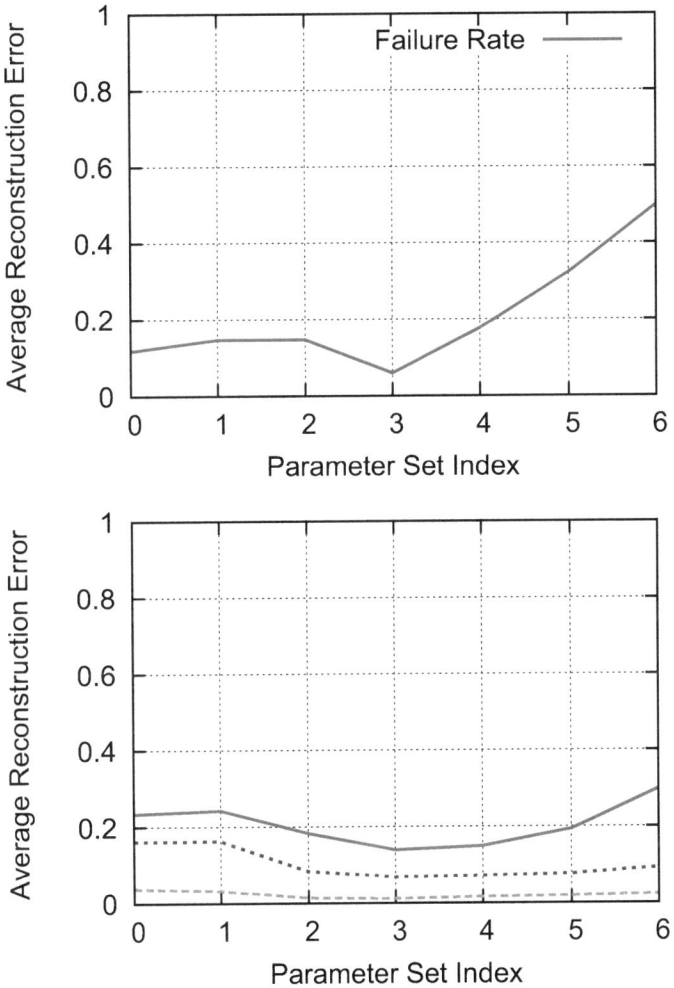

Figure 7.24: Evaluation results for different regularization multipliers. The top plot shows the failure rates associated with different regularization multipliers. The bottom plot shows the average reconstruction error achieved by different parameter settings. The x axis represents different parameter settings $0 - 6$, which correspond to the regularization multipliers $0, 0.001, 0.01, 0.1, 0.2, 0.5, 1$.

7. EXPERIMENTAL RESULTS

freedom for deformation, and this can lead to undesired overfitting.

We have tested our synthetic data sets with spline resolution parameters 6 up to 11, and the results are shown in Figures 7.25 to 7.27. We can see that the influence of the spline resolution is surprisingly small. Looking closely at the plots, it seems that spline resolutions 9×9 and 11×11 yielded the best results, even though the improvement is not substantial.

This is most likely the result of the scenes that have been used for this evaluation. Most of them can already be modelled well with a low spline resolution. The only scene that has some smaller details is the plane with bumps scene, and here, the differences between reconstruction results are also most pronounced. Also, the tube scenario did benefit slightly from an increased spline resolution. See Figures 7.28 and 7.29 for reconstruction results under different spline resolutions.

The reconstruction results for the plane with bumps scenario shows that for a very low spline resolution 6×6, the surface is reconstructed as an almost perfect plane. This is visible from the error map, which shows that the bumps are completely ignored by the algorithm for this spline resolution, but the plane is reconstructed well. For the higher 11×11 resolution, the reconstructed surface now contains the bumps, but there are also artefacts at their borders.

These artefacts are due to the inability of splines to model surfaces with discontinuities in their first derivative. Thus, we see that the increased detail level accounts only for a slight improvement in quality. Our similarity measure gave an error measure of 9.1% for the 6×6 resolution result, and 5.9% error for the 11×11 result, which is a rather minor improvement.

7.3 Static Lighting Conditions

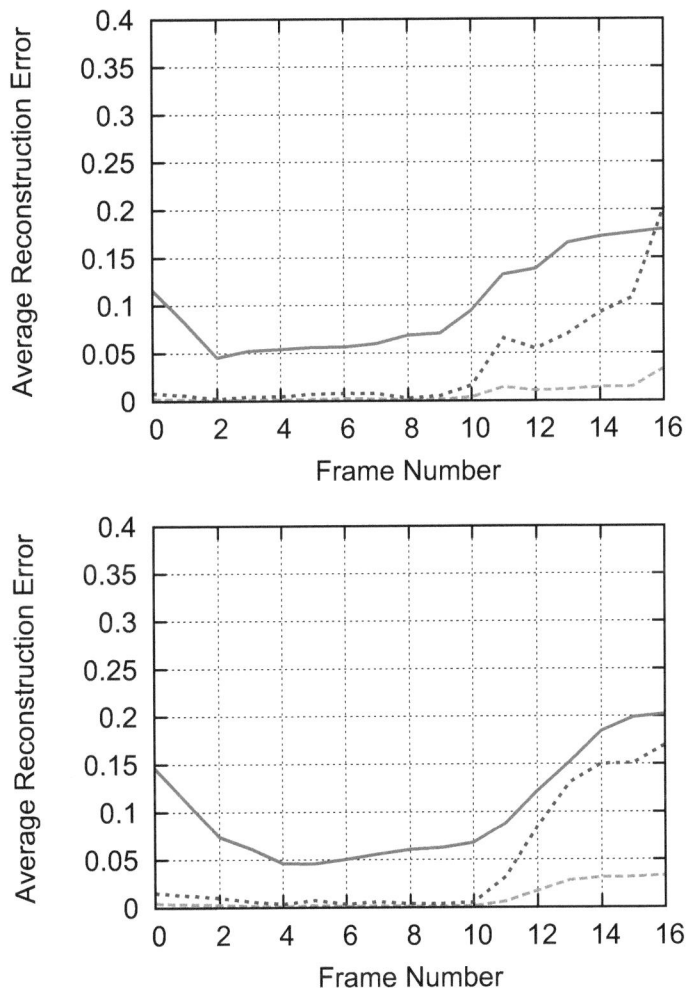

Figure 7.25: Evaluation results for different spline resolutions 6×6 and 7×7.

7. EXPERIMENTAL RESULTS

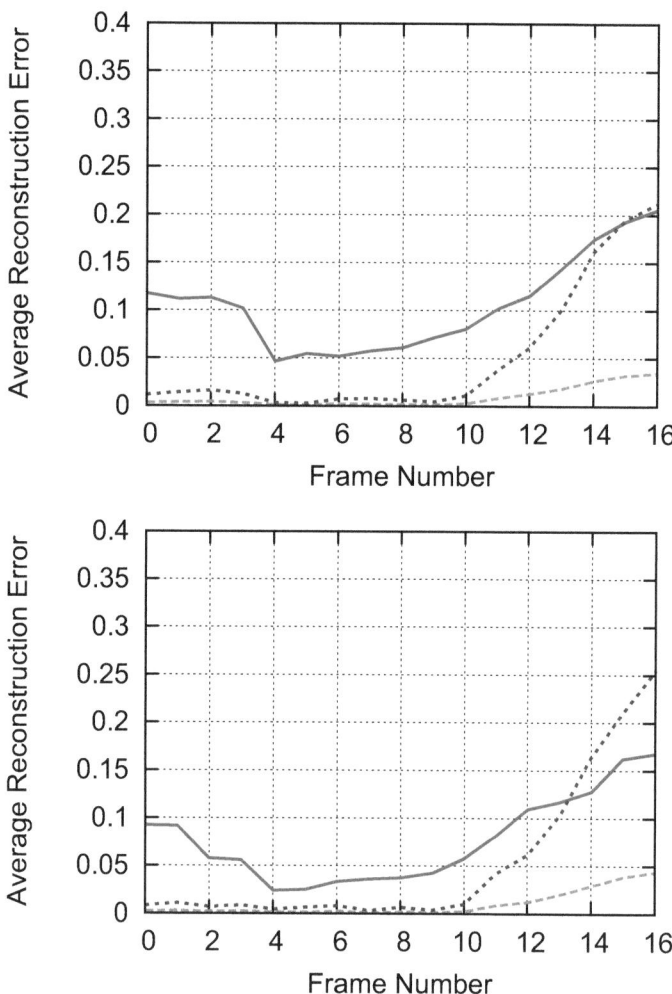

Figure 7.26: Evaluation results for different spline resolutions 8×8 and 9×9.

7.3 Static Lighting Conditions

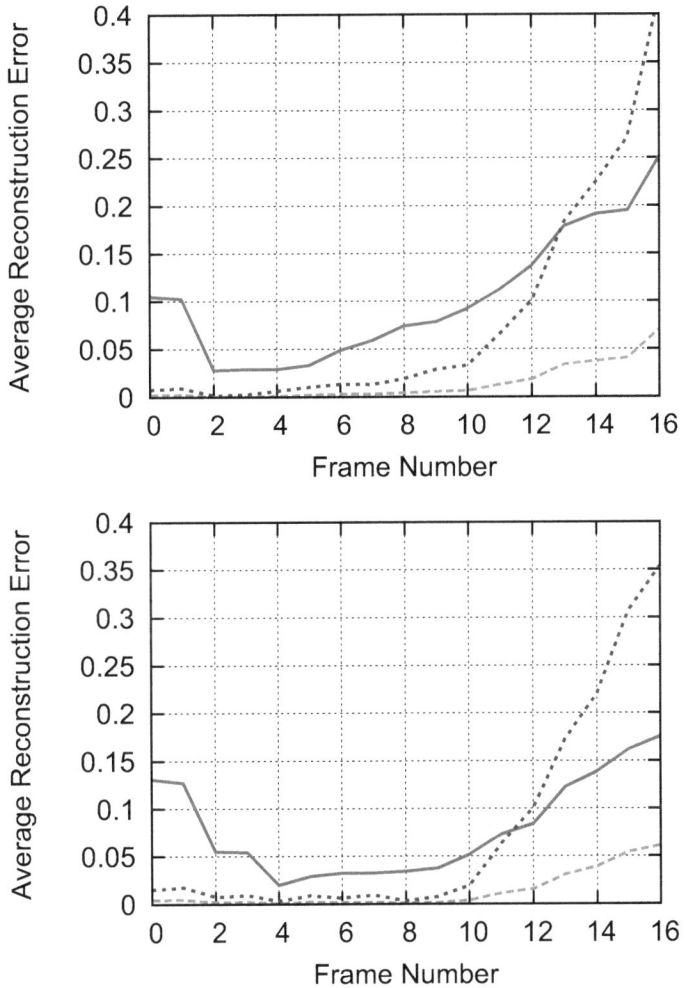

Figure 7.27: Evaluation results for different spline resolutions 10×10 and 11×11.

7. EXPERIMENTAL RESULTS

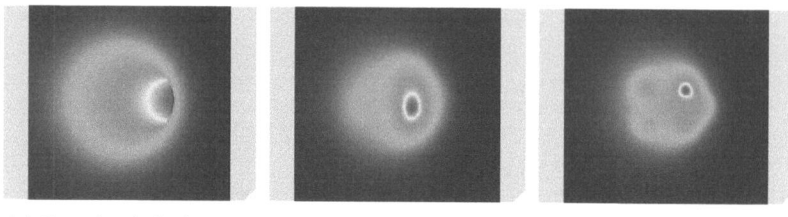

(a) Ground truth depth map.   (b) Reconstructed depth map, resolution 8×8.   (c) Reconstructed depth map, resolution 11×11.

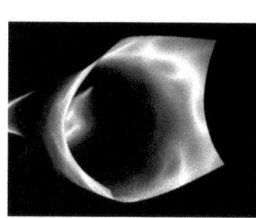 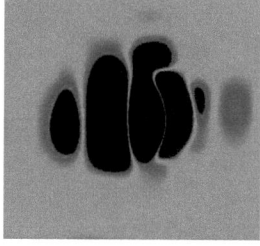 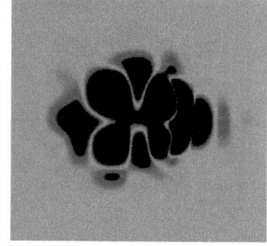

(d) Reconstructed surface for 11×11 resolution.   (e) Error map, resolution 8×8.   (f) Error map, resolution 11×11.

Figure 7.28: Tube reconstruction results for different spline resolutions.

For the tube sequence, the improvement at a higher spline resolution is even smaller. For a resolution of 11×11, the tube was reconstructed with an error of 16.7%, while the result for a resolution of 8×8 was 19.1%. From inspecting the reconstructed surface, it is apparent that the algorithm did a good job for reconstructing the tube walls close to the camera, but was not successful in determining the depths for the parts of the tube that are further away.

7.3.6 Behaviour for Medium and Weak Textures

Even though our algorithm can deal quite well with weakly textures surfaces, a higher degree of texturedness does improve the reconstruction results slightly. We have already shown the textures that are used in our evaluation in Figure 7.7. The cloud-like texture does provide considerably less structure than the granite-like one, so we

7.3 Static Lighting Conditions

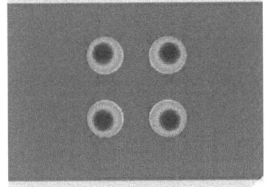 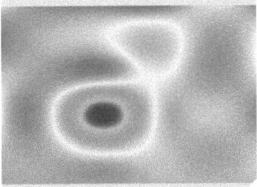 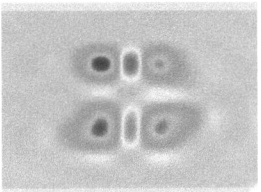

(a) Ground truth depth map.   (b) Reconstructed depth map, resolution 6×6.   (c) Reconstructed depth map, resolution 11×11.

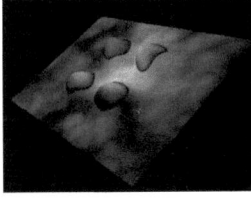 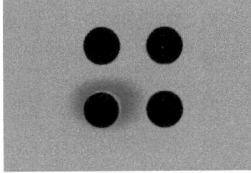 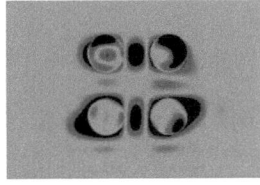

(d) Reconstructed surface for 11×11 resolution.   (e) Error map, resolution 6×6.   (f) Error map, resolution 11×11.

Figure 7.29: Plane with bumps reconstruction results for different spline resolutions.

would expect better results when using the granite texture.

Figure 7.30 shows the average reconstruction errors for both texture types. And indeed, the system behaves according to our expectation: The reconstruction results are consistently better for the granite texture, even though not by a large margin. This shows that while the system can cope well with weakly textured surfaces, stronger texturedness does help.

7.3.7 The Tube Scenario

As we have mentioned earlier, the tube scenario is an especially difficult scenario to reconstruct. This can be explained as follows:

- As we have seen, B-splines already have trouble modelling surfaces whose first-order derivative is non-continuous, leading to such artefacts as shown in Figure 7.29. The tube sce-

7. EXPERIMENTAL RESULTS

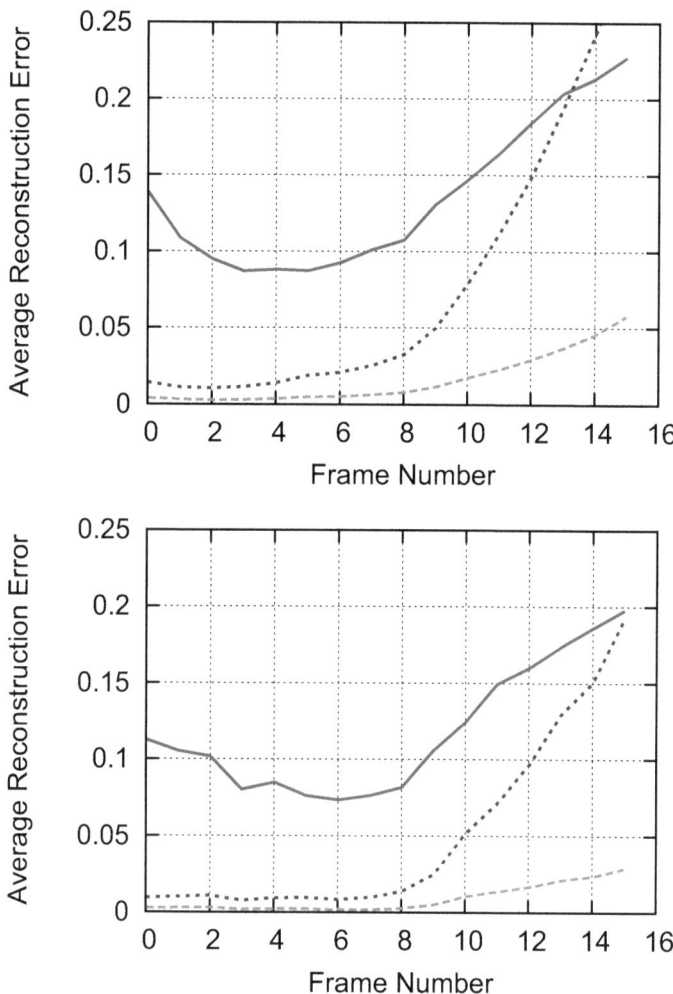

Figure 7.30: Evaluation results for different texture types. The top and bottom plots show the average reconstruction performance when using the cloud-like texture and the granite-like texture, respectively.

7.3 Static Lighting Conditions

nario, however, is even more difficult, because its depth map is itself already non-continuous.

- As we have mentioned, the initial surface model is a plane that is parallel to the camera plane. This surface shape, however, is very far away from that describing a tube in parameter space. This makes it especially difficult for the optimization algorithm to converge towards a usable approximation to the tube shape.

Despite these difficulties, we were able to successfully reconstruct the tube, but the success rate was only about 50% across all different parameter settings. Furthermore, we experimented a long time with different camera motions, and we found the tube-following motion moving backwards through the tube to performed quite well. This is a bit surprising, given that this kind of motion is very similar to the zoom-out camera motion which has been shown to perform rather suboptimal for the other scenarios.

Some reconstruction results have already been shown in the discussion on spline resolution in Section 7.3.5, see Figure 7.28. Figure 7.31 shows the best and worst reconstruction results that can be expected from our algorithm.

It can be seen that the algorithm is able to reconstruct the parts that are close to the reference camera quite accurately, but has trouble retrieving the correct depths for parts of the tube that are far away. From visual inspection, the difference between both reconstructions is quite difficult to see. However, the error map shows that the main difference is the reconstruction quality in the vicinity of the reference camera.

These observations show that reconstruction of tube-like structures is indeed possible using our system, even though such reconstructions are difficult and have some accuracy problems for parts

7. EXPERIMENTAL RESULTS

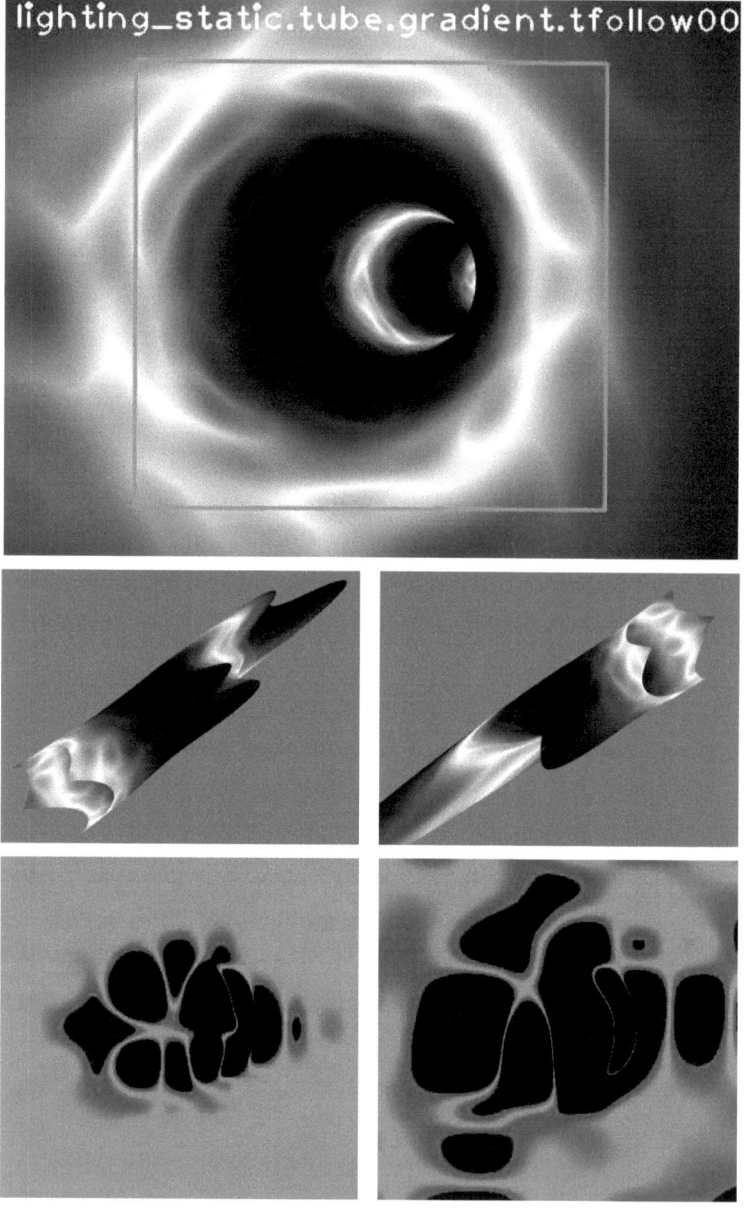

Figure 7.31: Tube scenario reconstruction results.

7.3 Static Lighting Conditions

of the depth map that are far away. It would probably be possible to drastically improve the performance of the algorithm by initializing the system properly. Furthermore, there are probably other depth map models than B-spline surfaces that could be better suited for representing tube-like structures. Exploring such improvements is one of our topics for future work.

7.3.8 Results on Independent Benchmarks

To our knowledge, there are no proper benchmarks for such direct structure-from-motion algorithms as proposed in this work. However, there is a benchmark for evaluating planar tracking algorithms by Lieberknecht et al. [84]. We have run our constant-light reconstruction algorithm on two of their data sets, making only one minor change to our reconstruction algorithm, namely the usage of a purely planar surface model.

The datasets we have used for this evaluation are the "bump sign" and "stop sign" sequences, which are classified as weakly textured scenarios in the benchmark. We have also restricted our tests to the "angle" sequences in both cases, because these are the only sequences where the tracking target stays within the image. We have not yet taken measures to make the algorithm robust against parts of the ROI leaving the image, so our algorithm is at an disadvantage here. This is the main reason why we have only verified our algorithm with the two mentioned datasets.

The benchmark expects as input the 2D pixel coordinates of four reference pixels that should be tracked by the algorithm, and it evaluates the accuracy of the tracking result by computing the root mean squared error for the coordinates of these four pixels. Frames where this mean squared error is below 10 pixels are counted as successfully tracked, and another RMS value is computed based only on

7. EXPERIMENTAL RESULTS

these successfully tracked images. The evaluation results for both mentioned datasets are shown in Figure 7.32.

The results show that, with tracking success rates of 80.4% and 99.8% and average pixel RMS errors of 3.13 and 3.0, our algorithm performs better than any of the feature-based tracking methods evaluated by Lieberknecht et al. in their original paper. Three feature-based tracking methods have been tested, using the FERNS [85], SURF [11] and SIFT [10] feature detection and matching methods, and the performance of all these algorithms is consistently below 50%, supporting our conjecture that intensity-based methods are better suited for tracking and reconstructing sparsely textured scenes.

The only algorithm that performs better than ours is the ESM [86] algorithm, which is also a direct method. This is, however, not very surprising, since the ESM algorithm specializes in tracking of pre-specified planar targets. In other words, the ESM algorithm already knows what the planar tracking template looks like, and merely has to find it in the image.

Our method, on the other hand, performs a simultaneous reconstruction while tracking the ROI, which is more difficult. It does not know what the planar template looks like at the beginning, but it determines the template on the fly while tracking. All in all, the benchmark results show that our algorithm is well capable of tracking and reconstructing real-world planar scenes that exhibit only low texturedness.

7.3.9 Non-Verified Reconstruction Results

Finally, we would like to present some results of reconstruction on real-world images where we do not have any ground truth to compare to. The only way to verify these results is by visual inspection.

7.3 Static Lighting Conditions

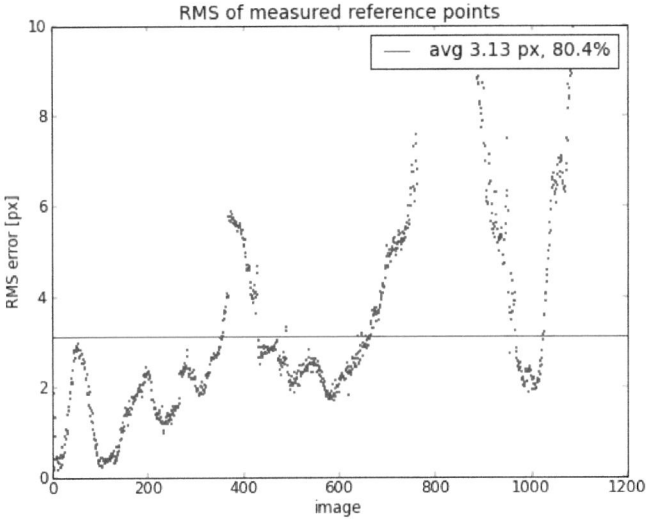

(a) Benchmark results for bump sequence.

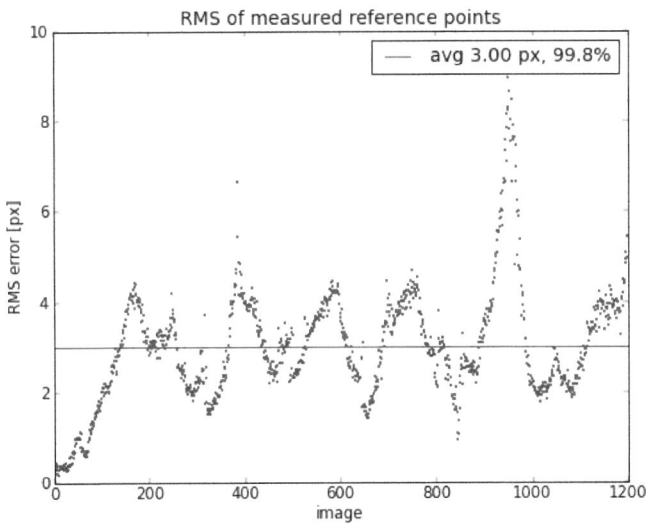

(b) Benchmark results for stop sign sequence.

Figure 7.32: Tracking results for the planar tracking benchmark.

7. EXPERIMENTAL RESULTS

Figure 7.33 shows the reconstruction results for a cup that has been covered by a piece of white cloth. As can be seen from the images, the scene exhibits very little texture. Still, the reconstruction seems to be accurate, since the shape of the cup under the cloth is clearly recognizable.

Furthermore, we present two more face reconstruction results in Figure 7.35. These reconstructions have been performed using 11×11 spline control points, and a sliding window size of 4. The results are quite good, but especially from the profile views it is apparent that the spline surfaces offer only limited modelling accuracy. However, generating high-detail models of the environment is not the main focus of our algorithm, our intent is instead to facilitate reconstruction under difficult situations.

7.4 Camera-Centered Light Source

For evaluating the illumination-modelling reconstruction algorithm that assumes a light source at the camera position, we are again relying mainly on synthetic data sets, where ground truth is available. We are using the same scenarios as in the case of constant light. Generally, we have found the light-modelling algorithm's performance to be very similar to that of the constant-light algorithm. There were, however, also some differences:

- We have claimed that the changing illumination actually helps to improve the reconstruction results of our algorithm, since the changing pixel intensities actually contribute additional information about the shape that is being observed. This is reflected in the reconstruction accuracy.

- However, initialization is more difficult than with the constant-light algorithm. This can be explained by observing that the

7.4 Camera-Centered Light Source

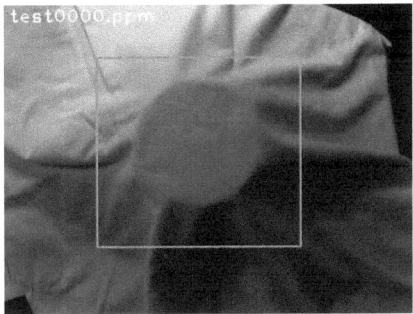

(a) Cup under cloth template image.

(b) Reconstruction result.

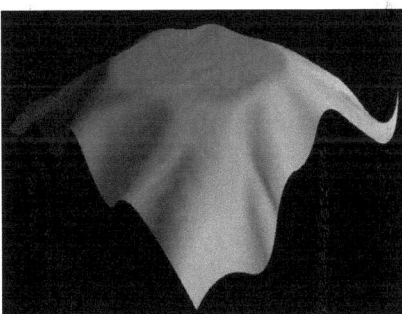

(c) Different view of result.

Figure 7.33: Reconstruction results for a cup that has been placed under a white piece of cloth.

7. EXPERIMENTAL RESULTS

(a) Template image.

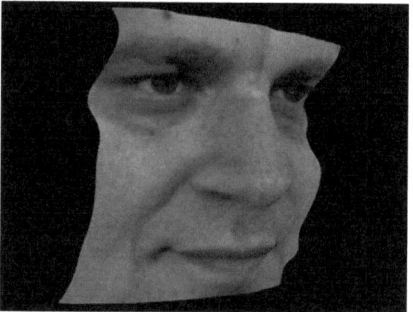

(b) Reconstruction at $\sim 45°$ angle.

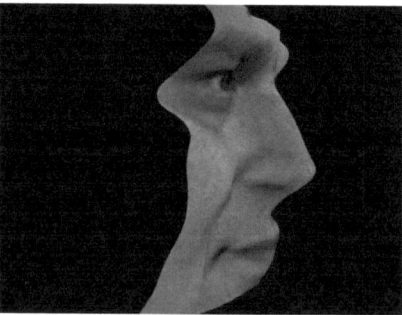

(c) Profile view of reconstruction.

Figure 7.34: Face reconstruction example.

7.4 Camera-Centered Light Source

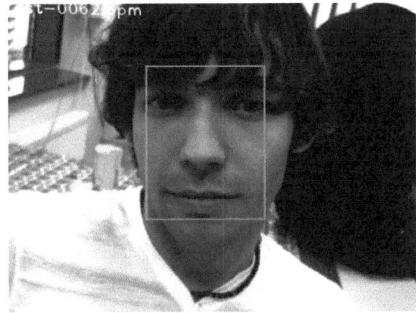

(a) Template image.

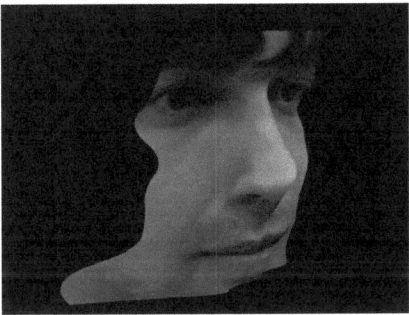

(b) Reconstruction at $\sim 45°$ angle.

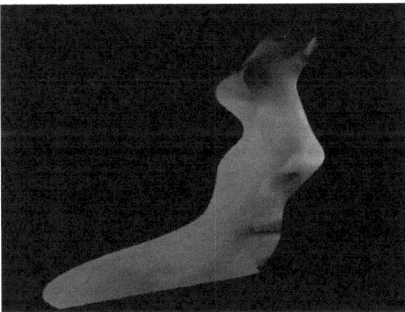

(c) Profile view of reconstruction.

Figure 7.35: Another face reconstruction example. Note that there is an outlier that is caused by a depth discontinuity in the ROI.

7. EXPERIMENTAL RESULTS

intensity-warping function used to explain the intensity changes introduces even more non-linearity into the non-convex optimization problem, so it can be hard for the algorithm to find its way to a correct minimum.

The plots in Figure 7.36 show that the reconstruction quality of the light-modelling algorithm is indeed slightly better than that of the static-light algorithm for the major part of the frames. However, it can also be seen that the decline in quality over last couple of frames is higher than in the constant light case. It seems that the partial occlusions that appear at the end of some of the synthetic sequences are more problematic for the light-modelling algorithm than for the simple constant-light algorithm.

We have also performed the benchmark for suitable initialization motions and speeds that has been performed for the static light algorithm in Section 7.3.2. According to our expectation, the initialization of the illumination-modelling algorithm is much more difficult than that of the static-light algorithm. We have prepared some plots showing the relation between baseline and motion types and initialization accuracy in Figures 7.37 to 7.44. We can see that the algorithm is much more sensitive to the initial baseline. For example, the paths (a) and (b) produced very good results when using the static-light algorithm, but in this case, we can see that the initialization fails quickly if the baseline becomes too big. Also, the results for some of the other movement paths look drastically worse.

Furthermore, for the tube scenario, it was not possible to initialize the system at all unless the initialization described in Section 3.3, Equation (3.12) was used. This shows that, as expected, the initialization of the system is made considerably more difficult because of the additional non-linearity introduced through the intensity warping function.

7.4 Camera-Centered Light Source

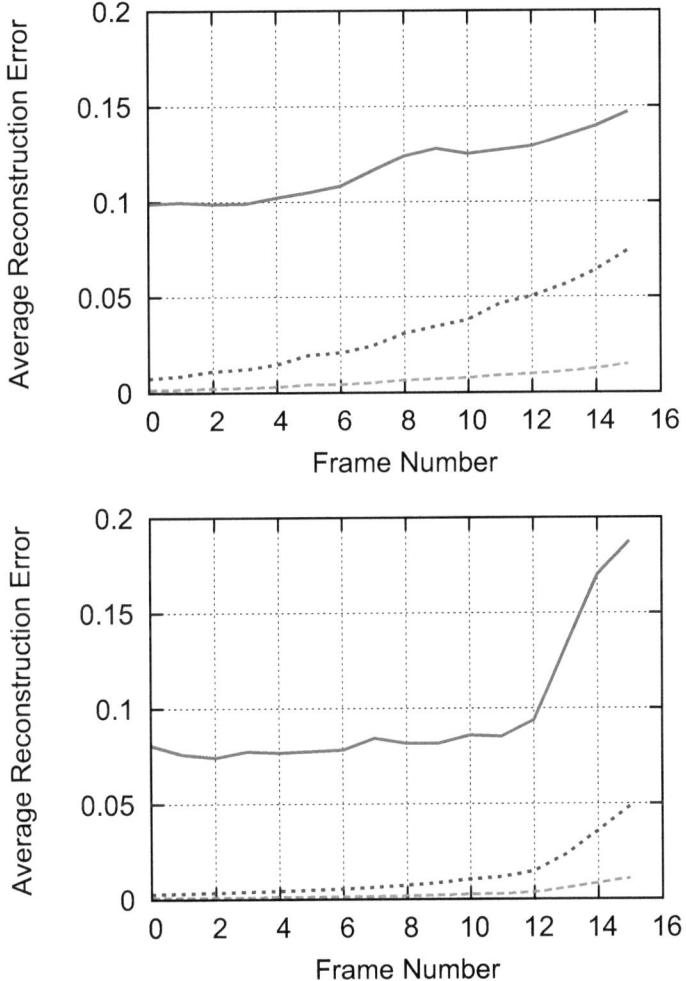

Figure 7.36: Per-frame average performance results for the static lighting case on the left and for the camera-centred lighting case on the right.

7. EXPERIMENTAL RESULTS

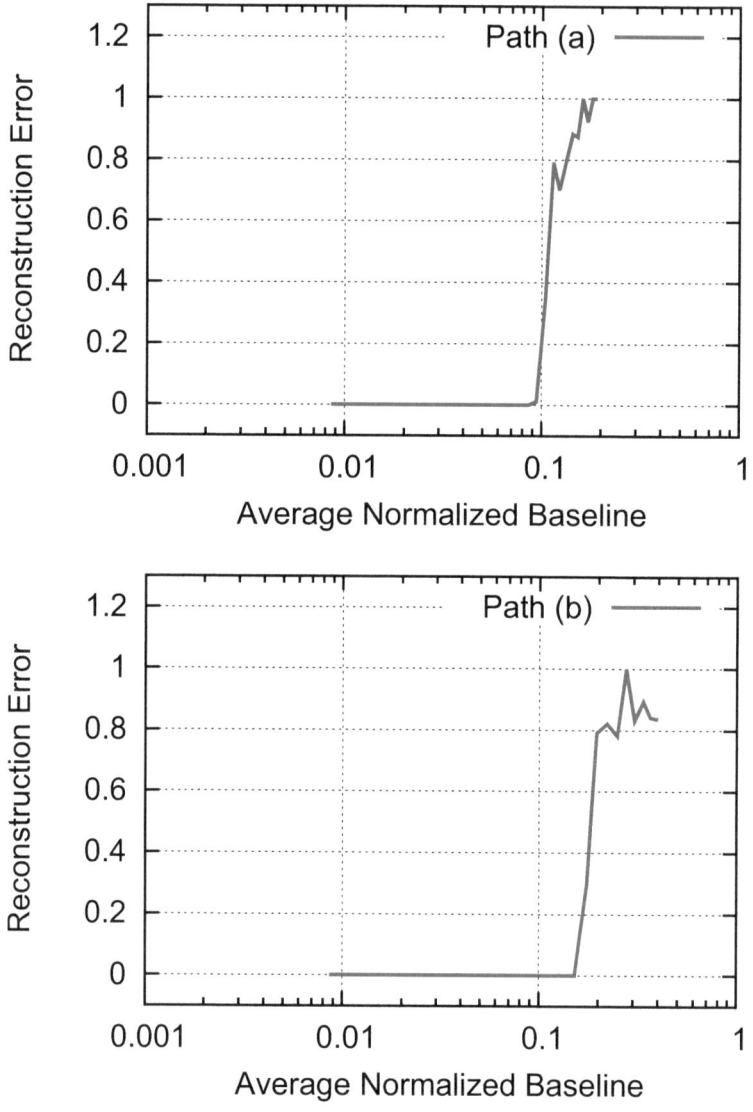

Figure 7.37: Initialization results for paths a and b on the slanted plane scenario, where different motion speeds have been used. All plots show the average reconstruction accuracy against the average normalized baseline during the first 5 frames on a logarithmic scale.

7.4 Camera-Centered Light Source

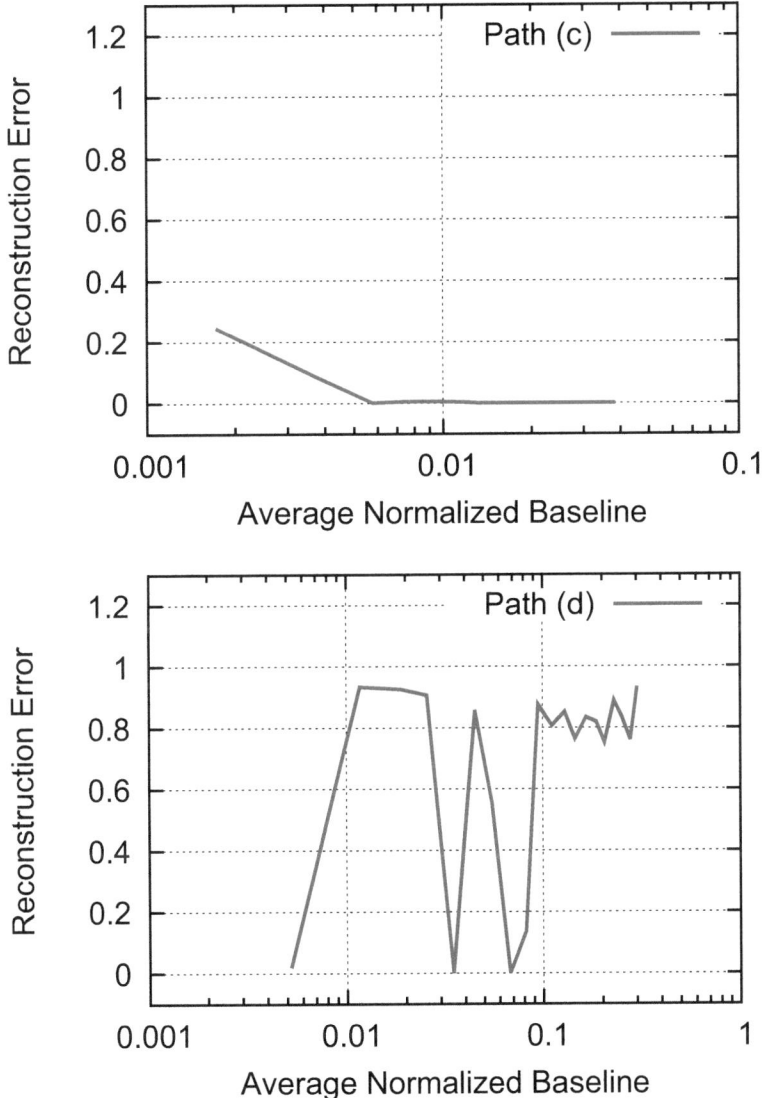

Figure 7.38: Initialization results for paths c and d on the slanted plane scenario, where different motion speeds have been used.

7. EXPERIMENTAL RESULTS

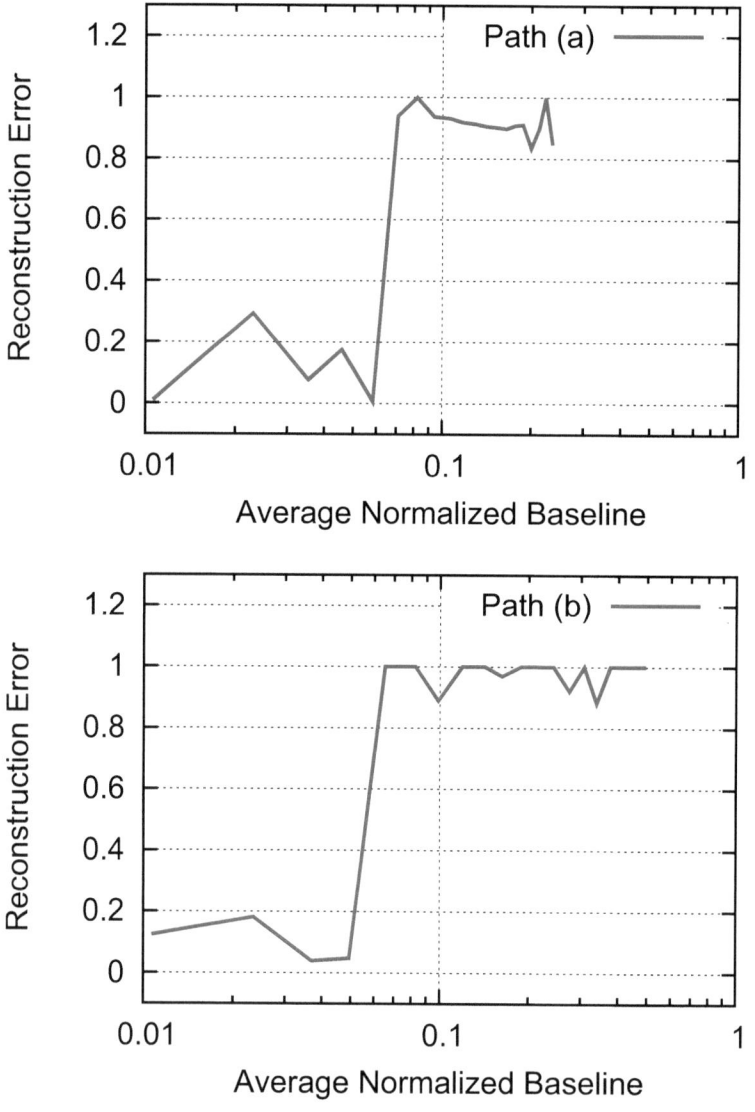

Figure 7.39: Initialization results for paths a and b on the sphere scenario, where different motion speeds have been used.

7.4 Camera-Centered Light Source

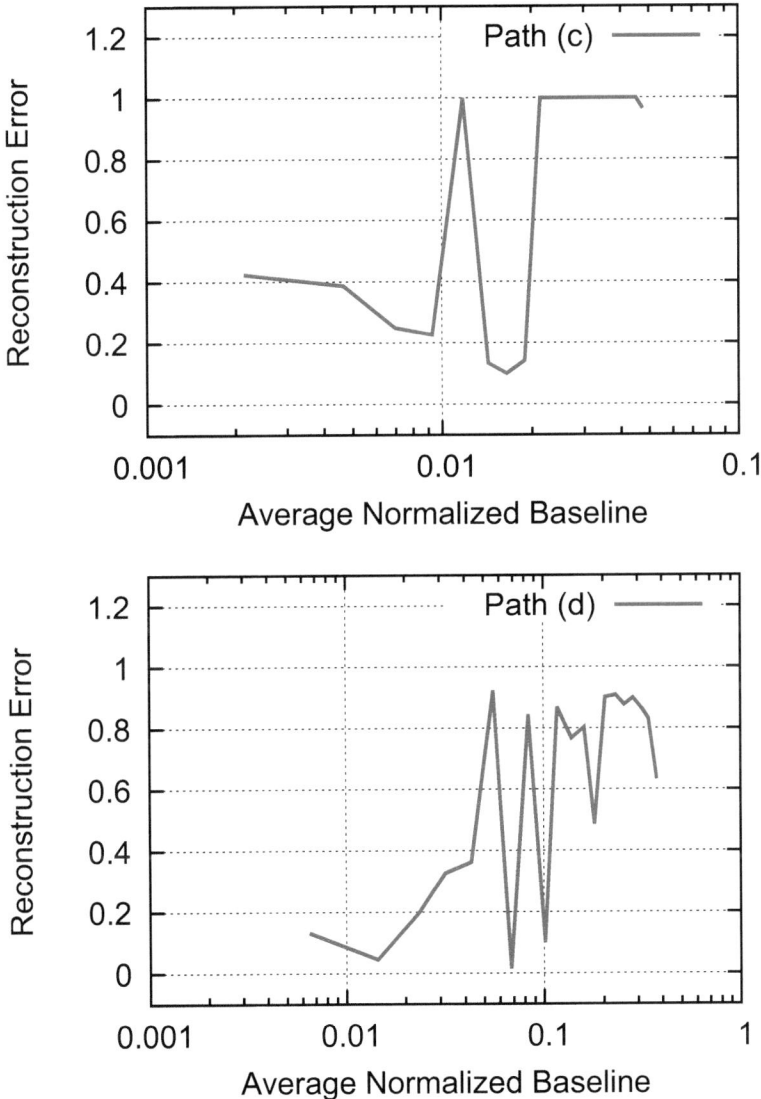

Figure 7.40: Initialization results for paths c and d on the sphere scenario, where different motion speeds have been used.

7. EXPERIMENTAL RESULTS

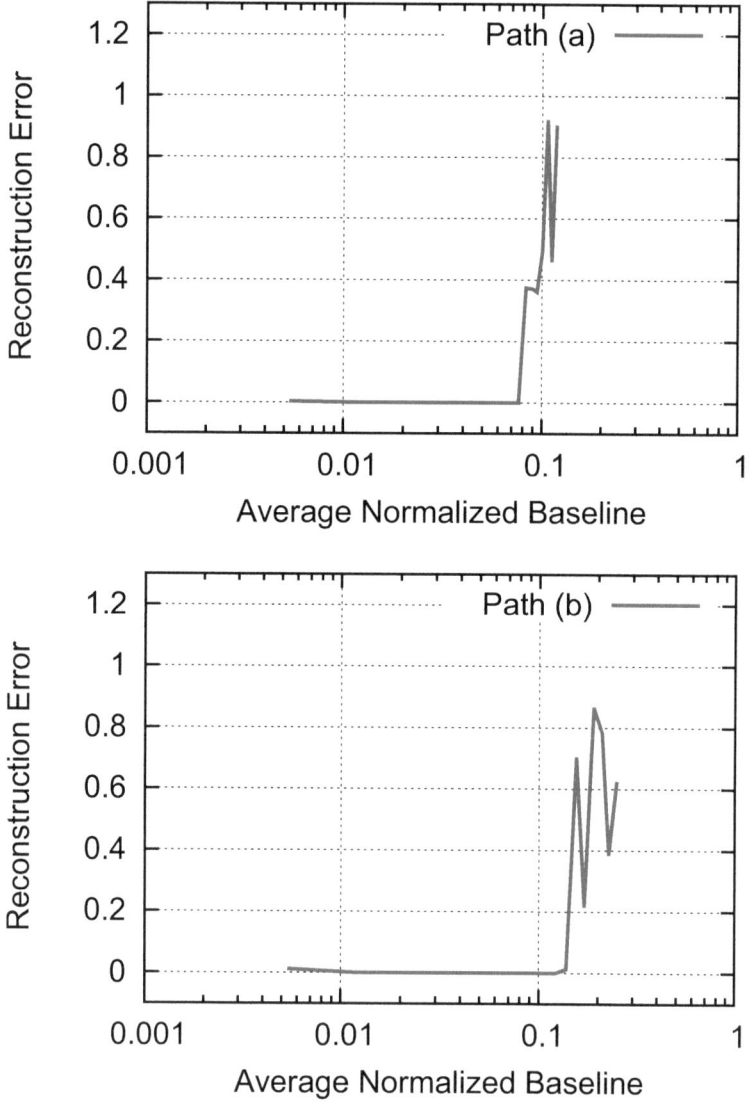

Figure 7.41: Initialization results for paths a and b on the cone scenario, where different motion speeds have been used.

7.4 Camera-Centered Light Source

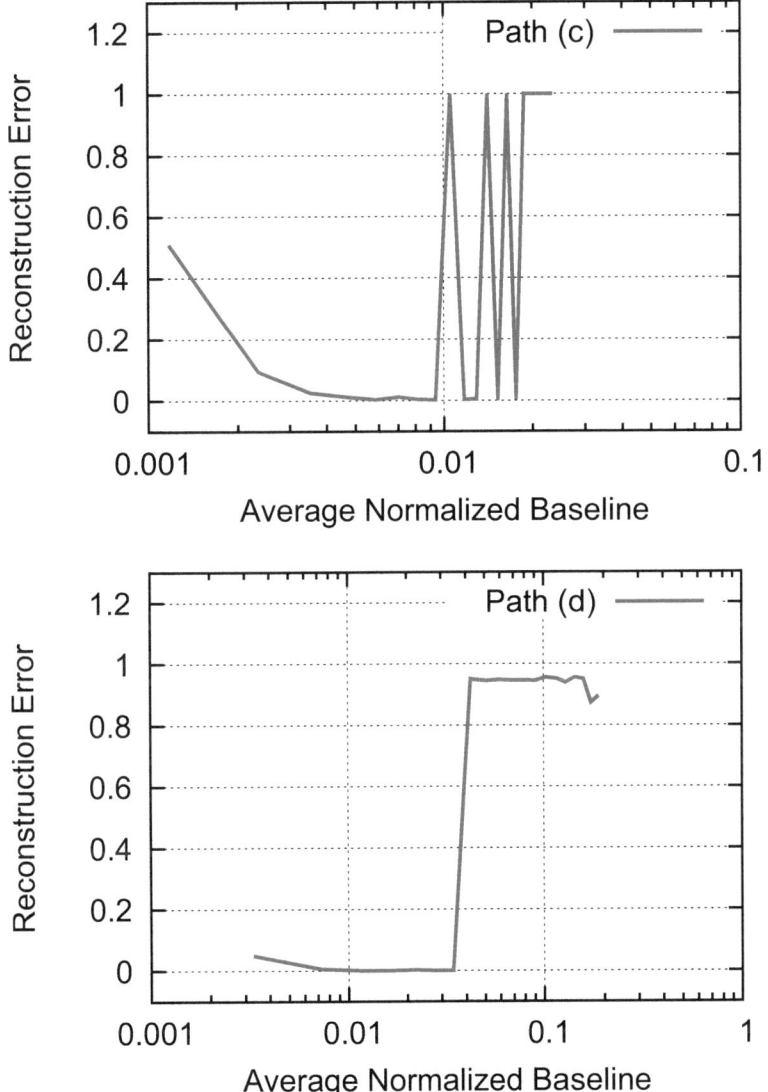

Figure 7.42: Initialization results for paths c and d on the cone scenario, where different motion speeds have been used.

7. EXPERIMENTAL RESULTS

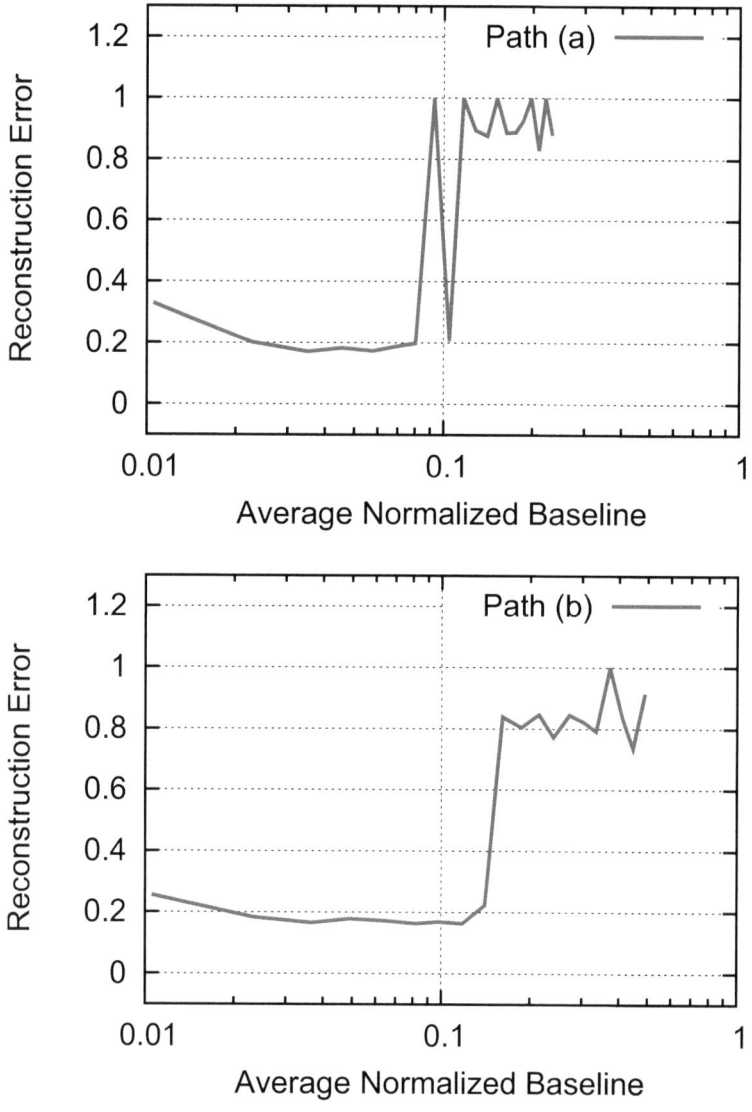

Figure 7.43: Initialization results for paths a and b on the plane-with-bumps scenario, where different motion speeds have been used.

7.4 Camera-Centered Light Source

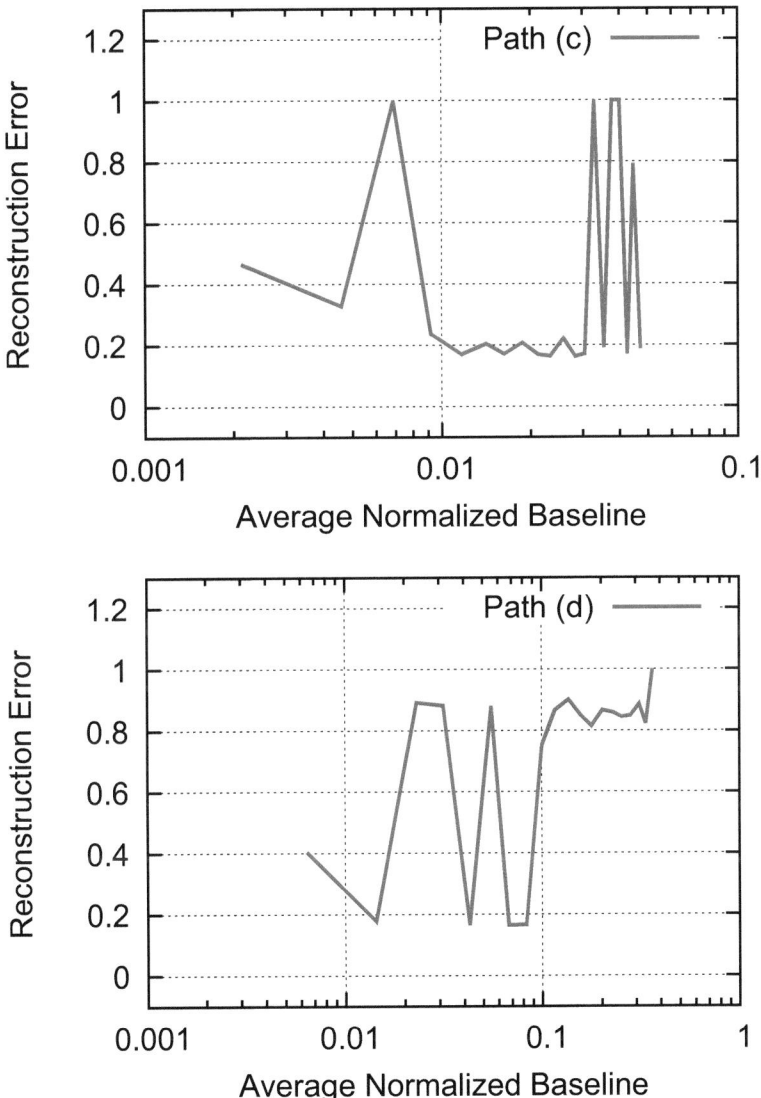

Figure 7.44: Initialization results for paths c and d on the plane-with-bumps scenario, where different motion speeds have been used.

7. EXPERIMENTAL RESULTS

However, it is also striking that the initialization results for small baselines, where successful, are very good, and mostly better than the corresponding results in the constant-light case. This is another observation that supports our claim that the changing image intensity values can contribute additional information to the system, leading to a better overall reconstruction quality.

7.4.1 Non-Verified Reconstruction Results

The reconstruction of real-world images using the illumination modelling approach has turned out to be much more difficult than for constant-light images. The main reason is that our algorithm is quite sensitive to sub-optimal photometric characteristics of the employed system. We have only had the chance to work with images that were not photometrically rectified, so that vignetting and a non-linear camera response could not be removed from the images. Furthermore, as we have described above, reconstruction results may be affected considerably by a non-zero displacement between the camera and the light source.

Nevertheless, we present here two reconstruction results obtained from video-endoscopic images, shown in Figure 7.45. The first result is a reconstruction of a rolled-up newspaper, and the other image shows a reconstruction of an airway. For comparison, we also show the reconstruction of a nearly "perfect" circular tube from synthetic data, which has been evaluated as showing an error of $\sim 24\%$ by our comparison method. The reconstruction is accurate for the opening area of the tube, and is only inaccurate for the part of the tube that is far away.

It is apparent that the reconstruction quality is not quite optimal for the real-world images, however the newspaper reconstruction came out lot better than the airway reconstruction. The rolled-up

7.4 Camera-Centered Light Source

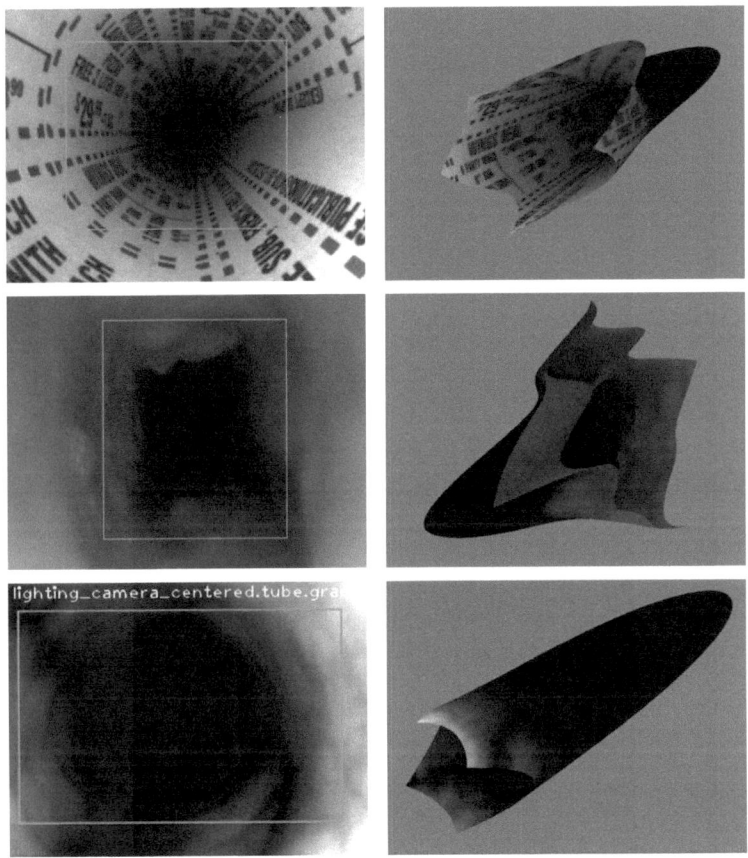

Figure 7.45: Reconstruction results on two real-world sequences (top two rows) and one synthetic sequence for comparison (bottom row).

7. EXPERIMENTAL RESULTS

newspaper result shows one large outlier corresponding to one corner of the ROI. Apart from that, the reconstruction seems quite close to the reconstruction of the synthetic tube.

For the airway result, we can only say that the shape of the tube has been reconstructed very roughly. The border of the ROI has been reconstructed with unsatisfactory accuracy, showing several outliers. We attribute these difficulties to four factors:

- The photometric response curve of the employed camera system is not known.

- The vignetting profile is also unknown.

- Even though the light source is very close to the camera, there still is a notable displacement between the light source and the camera center.

- Assuming a point light source is unrealistic, and it would be better to approximate the light source as a point light with non-uniform spatial intensity distribution.

The last two points have been discussed, e.g., by Wu et al.[24], who have shown that these two problems can be dealt with through proper calibration. Overall, it is hard to say which of these four sources of error is most problematic for our method. Exploring possible measures to alleviate these problems is a subject of future work.

7.4.2 A Short Evaluation of Mutual Information

To support our claim that illumination modelling is necessary to achieve satisfying reconstruction results, we have compared our approach to the method of mutual information (MI) [59], which has a reputation of being resistant against many types of lighting changes.

7.4 Camera-Centered Light Source

We were, however, able to show that mutual information performs considerably worse than our proposed algorithm in the specific case of a light source at the camera center.

This can be explained by realizing that mutual information can deal well with uniform changes of intensities that affect the whole image, but not with local changes, where one part of the image becomes brighter and another part darker due to the moving light source. By maximizing the mutual information between two sample sets, we are essentially aligning the histograms associated with those sets. The mutual information similarity measure rewards situations where the joint histogram between both sample sets is sparse, and penalizes dispersed joint histograms. However, a non-uniform change in intensities provokes a non-uniform change in histograms as well, and mutual information cannot align such histograms.

To support this claim, we have equipped our algorithm in the static-light variant with the mutual information similarity measure, and compared the results with those from our illumination-modelling algorithm. The results can be seen in Figure 7.46. It is apparent that while the reconstruction using MI does not fail completely, it generates a lot of artificial bumps and other outliers in the reconstructed result, and thus performs significantly worse than our proposed algorithm on both real-world and synthetic datasets. For generating these reconstructions, we have tried a lot of different parameter settings, and we show the best results we could achieve.

The cone reconstruction results are especially bad and the surface reconstructions are basically unusable, since they hardly resemble a cone any more. The images show the results of two different reconstruction runs with different parameters. While the tube reconstruction result looks OK when viewed from the outside, a close look from inside the tube through the opening reveals that the bor-

7. EXPERIMENTAL RESULTS

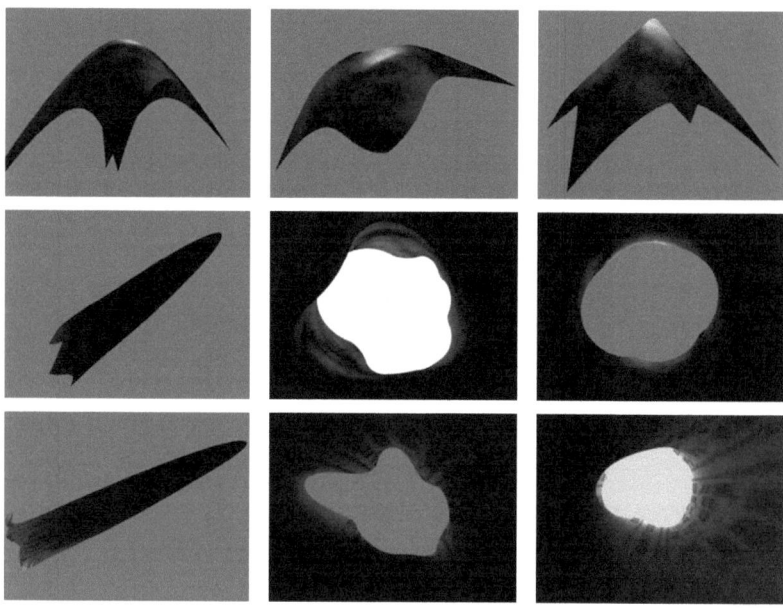

Figure 7.46: Some reconstruction results generated by using the mutual information similarity measure (left two columns), and reconstruction results produced by our proposed algorithm for comparison (right column).

7.4 Camera-Centered Light Source

der is strongly distorted, which is not the case for the reconstruction that has been retrieved using our algorithm. The result using our algorithm has been verified to be accurate in the region around the opening, which proves that the quality of the MI reconstruction is sub-optimal. Note that there are four small, but visible corners in our reconstruction result. These are no errors, but are caused by the corners of the ROI in the template image.

Even for real-world images, the mutual-information based reconstruction is inferior to the one produced by our algorithm. The reconstruction results from our algorithm are not flawless, but clearly better than that of the MI-based algorithm. We do not know the ground truth for the rolled-up newspaper images, but it seems reasonable to assume that the surface should look very similar to the cone reconstruction. We conclude that using a robust similarity measure such as mutual information is by no means enough to perform surface recovery under moving light conditions, and explicit illumination modelling, as performed by our algorithm, produces much better results.

7.4.3 Effect of Camera-Light Source Displacement

For real-world images, it is physically impossible to have the light source coincide with the camera position. This will always only be approximately the case, and it has already been shown that the position of the light source relative to the camera has a substantial influence on reconstruction accuracy in the case of shape-from-shading methods [24]. Having a non-zero displacement between the camera and the light source violates our assumption of having a light source at the camera center, and in this section, we examine the exact effects of this violation on our reconstruction results.

For this test, we have used the scenarios as in Section 7.3.2

7. EXPERIMENTAL RESULTS

in combination with the same camera motion paths. However, instead of varying the speed of the camera motion, we vary the displacement of the light source against the camera, such that the light source is moved in positive x direction, to the right of the camera.

Our results show that already for very small displacements, the reconstruction quality is reduced drastically. Figures 7.47 and 7.48 shows the plots of average reconstruction qualities for different normalized light displacement values. The normalization is performed by dividing the light displacement vector through the maximum depth value of the ground truth depths, so these values are analogous to the normalized baseline values introduced earlier. It is evident that the light displacement severely disturbs the reconstruction algorithm, and the error values rise consistently with the displacement.

Figures 7.49 and 7.50 show some reconstruction results that visualize the typical distortions that can be expected when camera and light are not coincident. From visual inspection, we can see that the reconstructed surfaces do still resemble the true surfaces, but are distorted. The surfaces show a specific distortion where the surface seems to deform towards one direction. In addition to that, the blurry texture of the surface leads to the algorithm shifting towards false matches, which produces artificial bumps on the surfaces. This can be seen especially well in the plane reconstruction results.

All in all, we have shown that the algorithm is rather sensitive to violations of its essential assumption that the light source is located at the camera center, which in turn reinforces our claim that proper calibration is necessary to further improve reconstruction results.

7.4 Camera-Centered Light Source

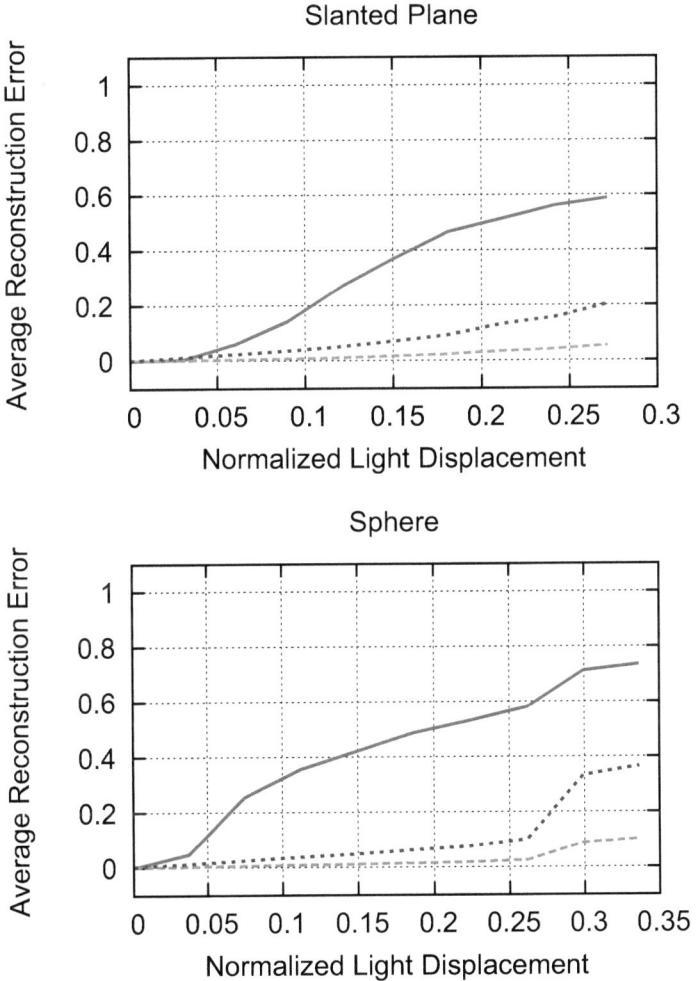

Figure 7.47: Evaluation results for different amounts of light displacement. The plots show the average error for all 20 frames per normalized light displacement.

7. EXPERIMENTAL RESULTS

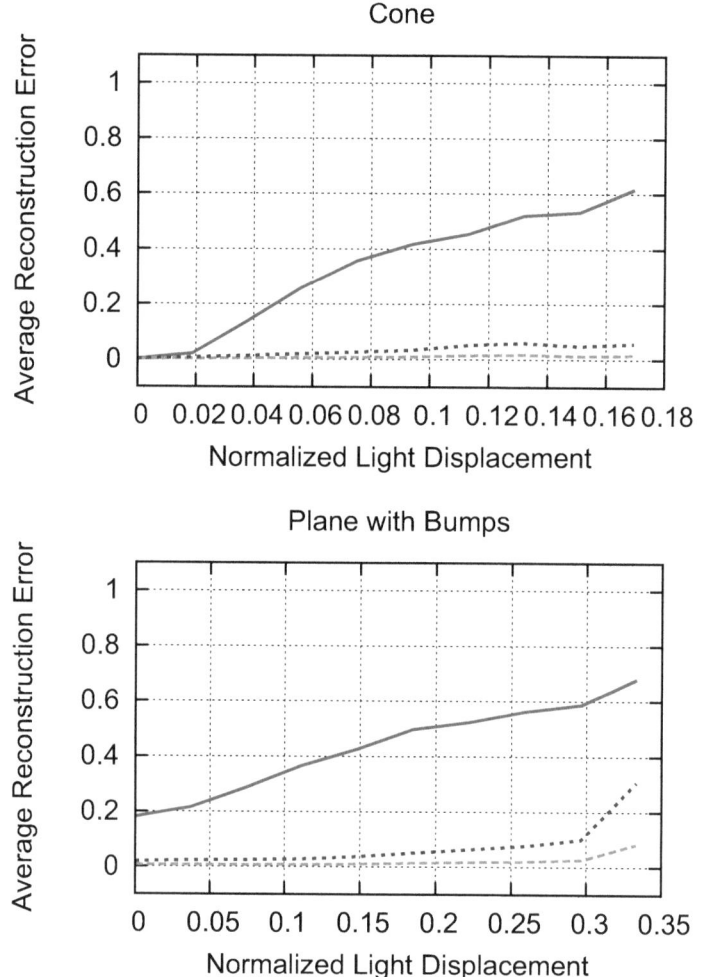

Figure 7.48: Evaluation results for different amounts of light displacement for the cone and plane with bumps scenarios.

7.4 Camera-Centered Light Source

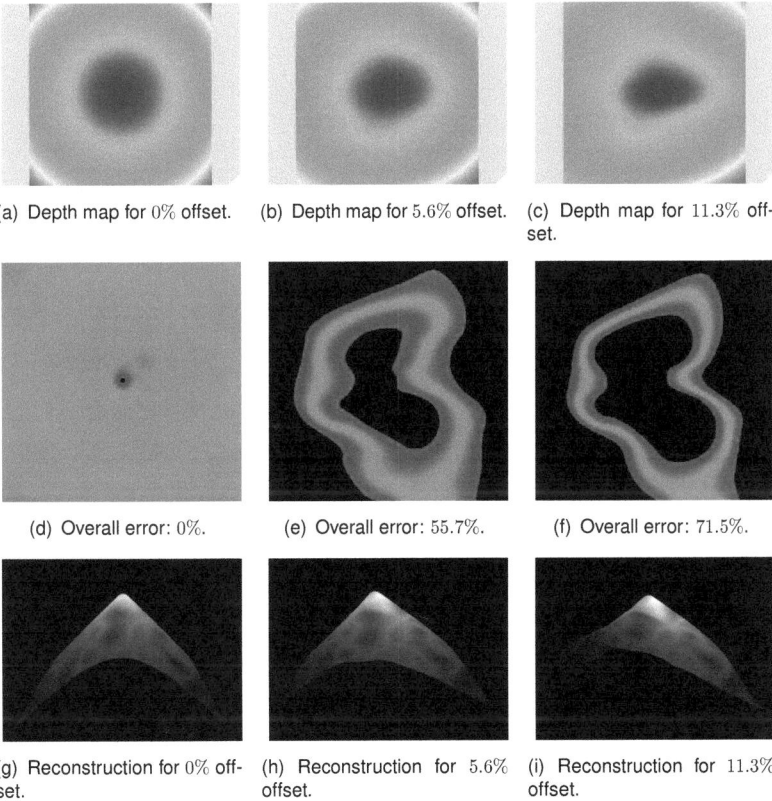

(a) Depth map for 0% offset. (b) Depth map for 5.6% offset. (c) Depth map for 11.3% offset.

(d) Overall error: 0%. (e) Overall error: 55.7%. (f) Overall error: 71.5%.

(g) Reconstruction for 0% offset. (h) Reconstruction for 5.6% offset. (i) Reconstruction for 11.3% offset.

Figure 7.49: Reconstruction results for the cone scenario under increasing light displacement.

7. EXPERIMENTAL RESULTS

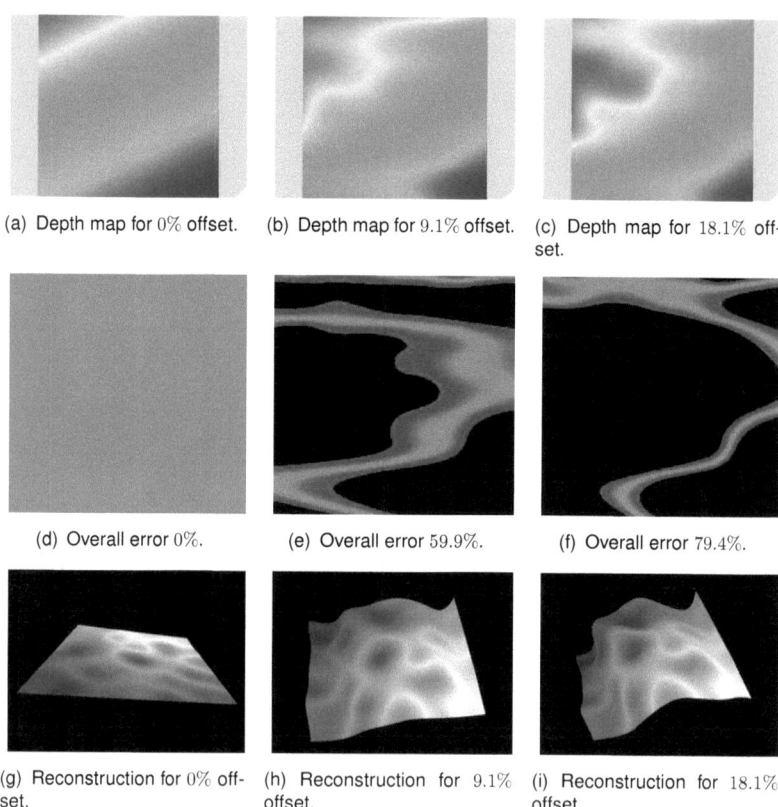

(a) Depth map for 0% offset. (b) Depth map for 9.1% offset. (c) Depth map for 18.1% offset.

(d) Overall error 0%. (e) Overall error 59.9%. (f) Overall error 79.4%.

(g) Reconstruction for 0% offset. (h) Reconstruction for 9.1% offset. (i) Reconstruction for 18.1% offset.

Figure 7.50: Reconstruction results for the slanted plane scenario under increasing light displacement.

7.5 Light Source Calibration Results

Before we move on to our reconstruction results when using a calibrated light source, we first show some example calibration results on synthetic data. Two results of the light source calibration method on some real-world images have already been shown in the corresponding Chapter 6, see Figures 6.2 and 6.6.

There is no way to specify an intensity profile for a light source in POV-RAY. Rather, one has to create semi-transparent objects that affect the color of the light passing through it. This makes it rather difficult to obtain the ground truth profile, so we rely on visual inspection instead. We have created three test cases that can be verified quite easily that way. The calibration results for these cases are shown in Figure 7.51.

We have used a calibration pattern size of 640×480 for all three test cases. For the first example, we have used a plain white light source. We would expect the intensity profile to be completely white as well, and the algorithm indeed computes such a uniform intensity profile. The light projection center has been determined as $(100.51, -302.28, -102.31)^\mathrm{T}$, where $(100, -300, -100)^\mathrm{T}$ would be the true values. The error is thus very low relative to the size of the calibration pattern.

In the second example, we have added some semi-translucent spheres between the light source and the calibration patterns, which results in the projection of coloured circles onto the calibration planes. The intensity profile can be seen to be very accurate, since the circles are reproduced as nearly perfect ellipses in the intensity profile. The projection center of the light source has been computed as $(400.97, 296.97, -1.17)^\mathrm{T}$, and the ground truth is $(400, 300, 0)^\mathrm{T}$, again a very low error in relation to the observed objects.

Finally, for the third example, we have created a translucent tex-

7. EXPERIMENTAL RESULTS

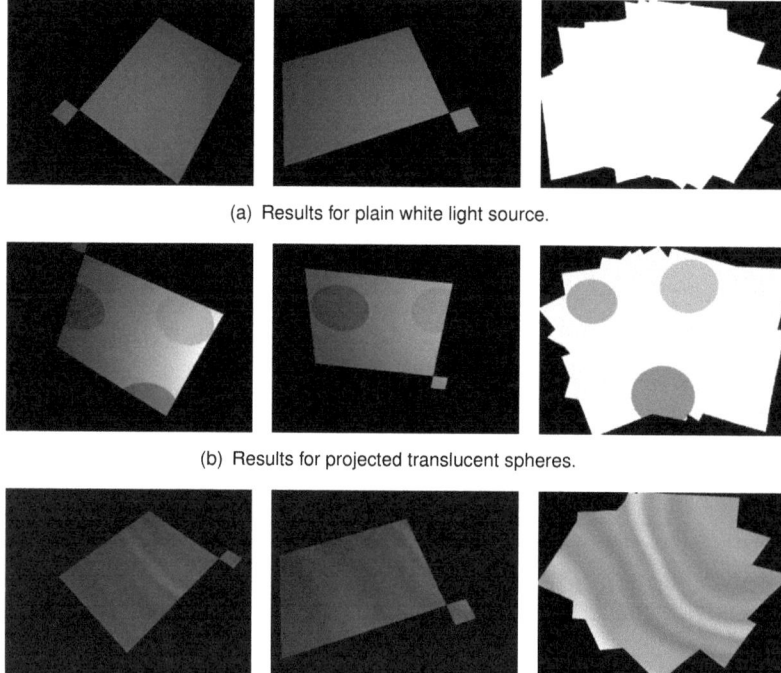

(a) Results for plain white light source.

(b) Results for projected translucent spheres.

(c) Results for complex structured light.

Figure 7.51: Light calibration results on synthetic data. The left two images in each row show rendered images used for the calibration. The rightmost image shows the calibrated intensity profile.

7.6 Tracking with a Calibrated Light Source

tured sphere with a complex pattern around the light source. In addition to that, we have made the images brighter, to show that our algorithm can cope well with the problem of uniform, diffuse ambient light. Indeed, we can see that the calibrated intensity profile reproduces the projected pattern quite well. The light source position has been determined as $(398.11, -403.19, 3.11)^\mathrm{T}$, where $(300, -400, 0)^\mathrm{T}$ is the ground truth position.

7.6 Tracking with a Calibrated Light Source

The case of using a calibrated light source is rather difficult when compared to the other two cases of reconstruction scenarios. This is mainly because the reconstruction is now no longer up to scale, due to the baseline between camera and light source. However, this also means that we cannot initialize the scene estimate with arbitrary scale, but we need a good initial estimate of the actual depth.

This turned out to be a considerable problem in our experiments. We were not able to find an efficient method for computing a useful initialization state for the system. However, it was at least possible to show that the system is able to track the object under consideration after the system parameters had been initialized adequately.

We show here the data obtained for one run of the cone sequence, using motion path (a) and the granite texture. For determining the light calibration parameters, we have used our light calibration method. The system has been initialized with an approximate model of the cone and also the translational part of the camera motion has been specified. The initialization is not perfect, however, as can be seen from the error image shown in Figure 7.52. The initial surface has been evaluated to have an error of 7%. The initial motion was evaluated with error values of 0.03 for the translational

7. EXPERIMENTAL RESULTS

error and 0.014 for the rotational error.

The surface reconstruction error is already low to begin with, but it improves considerably after the first optimization run during initialization, and stays low throughout the 20-frame sequence. This shows that the method is at least capable of tracking and refining a 3D surface under calibrated lighting.

All in all, the results look promising, but without a way to properly initialize the system, the method can not be used for anything else than tracking at present. Finding a solution to the initialization problem is one of the topics for future work.

7.7 Performance Considerations

While we have taken some efforts in order to improve performance of our algorithms, the efficiency of our methods was never the main concern of our work. Through our optimization framework, we have sought a compromise between flexibility and performance. Consequently, none of our algorithms are currently real-time capable. Depending on the type of algorithm that is used, and also on some parameters such as sliding window size, number of control points, etc., the processing speed for typical reconstruction problems lies between roughly 5 and 0.2 frames per second.

However, there is much potential for performance improvement. First of all, we use a generic sparse Cholesky decomposition to solve the SQP equation system, which is sub-optimal. For feature-based bundle adjustment, it is well-known that the special structure of the bundle-adjustment equations can be exploited very well [47, 87]. It seems quite likely that this would be possible for our algorithms as well, leading to a faster, but more specialized algorithm.

Furthermore, many modern structure-from-motion algorithms exploit the computation power of GPUs [41, 68] to achieve real-time

7.7 Performance Considerations

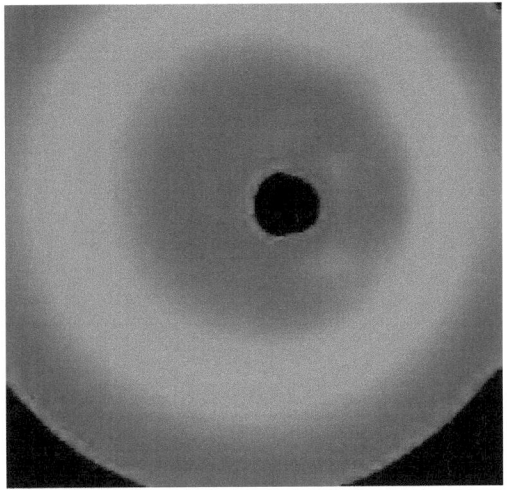

(a) Error image for initial model.

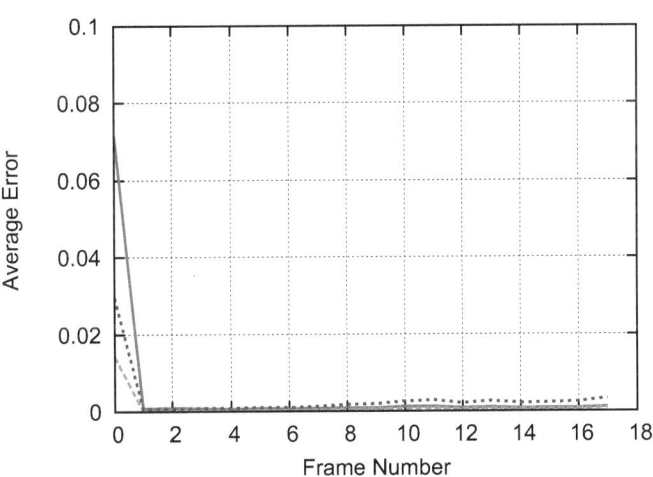

(b) Per-frame tracking accuracy.

Figure 7.52: Evaluation results for calibrated-light reconstruction and tracking. The plots show the average error per frame, and the first entry shows the accuracy of the initialization.

7. EXPERIMENTAL RESULTS

performance. We are quite confident that our algorithms would also benefit greatly from a GPU-based implementation, and would probably be able to achieve real-time performance then.

8. Conclusion

In this thesis, we presented three different algorithms for recovering structure and motion from monocular images based purely on image intensities under different lighting assumptions, and we described an optimization framework that allows implementation of these algorithms in a uniform, consistent and modular way. Furthermore, we have described a method for calibration of a camera-light pair, in which the light source is modelled as an inverse camera.

For our surface and motion recovery algorithms, the constant-light variant has shown the best overall performance, even though there are some minor problems with ambiguous solutions. The algorithm performs well for both synthetic and real camera images, and it can be easily initialized even from images with a very small baseline. For the algorithm using a camera-centered point light model, we have observed very good results on synthetic datasets, but there are some problems on real camera data. We have discussed possible causes for these problems, which are photometric inconsistencies that can probably be dealt with using calibration methods. Furthermore, we have seen that the camera-centred light algorithm is more difficult to initialize than the constant-light variant. The last type of algorithm, which uses an illumination model based on a calibrated light source, is currently only fit for tracking tasks, and only after the system has been initialized properly. The performance on synthetic data was satisfactory, but due to the initialization problems, we were not able to gather any results from real camera images.

8. CONCLUSION

Thus, as it is now, this algorithm is more of theoretical interest.

The optimization framework proposed in this work is powerful enough to implement the described algorithms in an efficient and uniform way, facilitating re-usability of components. It is specialized for implementing equality-constrained SQP-type optimization problems for compositional objective functions, where the involved derivatives are sparse and exhibit a static sparsity structure. The framework is the core technology used in our implementations.

Our proposed light calibration method has been shown to work well both on synthetic data and on real image data. It is also capable of dealing with constant additive disturbances to the image data, effectively cancelling out brightness shifts and minor scattered light effects.

8.1 Future Work

The topic of surface and camera motion recovery directly from image intensities is a very complex one, and within this thesis, we were only able to explore a limited set of aspects of this problem. Consequently, there are a number of possible improvements that we would like to investigate in the future. Roughly ordered in descending order by importance, these would be:

- As we have mentioned, the reconstruction algorithm for the case of using a calibrated light source is very difficult to initialize. Finding a way to solve this initialization problem is very important to improve the usability of the algorithm. Possible approaches to address the problem are as follows:

  - If the light source is close to the camera, we could generate an initial, scale-free estimate assuming that the light is located at the camera center, determine a preliminary

8.1 Future Work

scale for the estimate through a separate optimization, and finally use the generated estimate for initialization.

- We could perform some kind of well-defined motion at the beginning of a sequence such that at least the camera parameters can be initialized roughly.

• The centred-light algorithm seems to suffer from photometric inconsistencies that could be removed through proper photometric calibration. A thorough evaluation should be done, examining the potential of this method for video-endoscopy applications.

• The static-light algorithm has been shown to suffer from an ambiguity where "inverse perspective" reconstructions are generated. These solutions correspond to local minima. It should be possible to devise methods to detect these ambiguous configurations and subsequently avoid the erroneous reconstruction.

• All of our algorithms could probably benefit from an extended convergence radius by using a better approximation to the Hessian in our optimization. A potential candidate technology is the ESM method proposed by Malis [50], in the generalized variant described by Brooks and Arbel [61].

• The simple regularization that we have implemented has been shown to be useful, but we suspect that more sophisticated regularization schemes could further improve the performance of our algorithm. The anisotropic regularization scheme described by Werlberger et al. [88] would be a candidate for exploring the possible benefits of better regularization.

8. CONCLUSION

- We assume that the observed surfaces exhibit Lambertian reflectance, which is not the case for many surfaces. Using a more sophisticated surface reflectance model, such as Phong shading [89] or the Oren-Nayar reflectance model [90], would probably increase the reconstruction accuracy and make the algorithms more robust.

- Our algorithms are not real-time capable until now. However, real-time performance could probably be achieved easily if time-intensive computational parts are ported to the GPU, using CUDA[1] or OPENCL[2]. Furthermore, the sparsity structure of the intensity-based bundle adjustment problem could probably be exploited more efficiently [47, 87].

The most important improvements are the first two, because we expect them to have significant impact on our algorithm's performance on real video-endoscopic images, while they seem relatively easy to implement. Supporting different surface reflectance models also seems promising, but we would expect this to be more difficult to implement. Additional parameters might be needed to capture the reflectivity behaviour of surfaces, which means that the optimization formulation needs to be changed drastically. The other improvements are mainly of technical nature, and as such are "nice to have", but do not constitute essential improvements. All in all, we see that the framework we have created and the basic algorithms that have been implemented within it may well serve as a basis for future research projects.

---

[1] http://www.nvidia.com/object/cuda_home_new.html
[2] http://www.khronos.org/opencl/

A. Mathematical Notation

Symbol	Meaning
n	Scalar values are denoted by italic letters.
$f(x)$	This is a scalar function of the scalar variable x.
$\mathbf{v}$	Bold lower case letters are used to refer to vectors.
$\mathbf{v}(\mathbf{x})$	A multi-dimensional function $\mathbf{v}$ with vector-valued parameter $\mathbf{x}$.
$f \circ g, \mathbf{f} \circ \mathbf{g}$	If f resp. $\mathbf{f}$ and g resp. $\mathbf{g}$ are both functions, the $\circ$ operator denotes the composition of these functions.
$\mathrm{id}(x), \mathrm{id}(\mathbf{y})$	The identity function.
$\mathbf{T}(\mathbf{a}, \mathbf{b})$	A rigid transformation of the 3D coordinate vector $\mathbf{b}$ according to extrinsic parameters $\mathbf{a}$.
$\mathbf{R}(\mathbf{q})$	The rotation matrix associated with unit quaternion $\mathbf{q}$.
$\mathcal{C}(\mathbf{z}, \mathbf{y})$	A cost function that assigns a scalar penalty value to vectors $\mathbf{z}, \mathbf{y}$, where $\mathbf{z}$ is the prediction and $\mathbf{y}$ is the measurement.
$\boldsymbol{\pi}(\mathbf{v})$	The perspective divide function, performing a 3D-2D projection by dividing the first two elements of a vector $\mathbf{v} \in \mathbb{R}^3$ through the third component.
$\mathbf{v}_i$	Subscripts are used to refer to the elements of a vector, in this case the i-th element of $\mathbf{v}$.
	continued on next page

A. MATHEMATICAL NOTATION

continued from previous page	
$[\mathbf{a}+\mathbf{b}]_i$	Sometimes, we want to refer to a certain element of a vector-valued expression. To enhance readability, we use a subscript in conjunction with square brackets, such that the expression on the left would denote the i-th component of the sum of vectors $\mathbf{a}, \mathbf{b}$.
$\mathbf{M}$	Matrices are denoted by upper case bold letters.
$\mathbf{M}_{i,j}$	A specific element of a matrix is referred to by using two comma-separated subscripts. The element in row i and column j of $\mathbf{M}$ would be denoted as shown here.
$[\mathbf{A}+\mathbf{B}]_{i,j}$	If we want to refer to a certain element of a matrix-valued expression, we will use square brackets in conjunction with two comma-separated subscripts in order to enhance readability. The expression on the left would then denote the element in row i of column j of the sum of matrices $\mathbf{A}, \mathbf{B}$.
$[\mathbf{M}]_{i,*}$	This is the i-th row vector of the matrix $\mathbf{M}$.
$[\mathbf{M}]_{*,j}$	This is the j-th column vector of the matrix $\mathbf{M}$.
$\mathbf{I}_n$	The identity matrix of dimension $n \times n$.
$\mathbf{0}_{n,m}$	A matrix of zeros of dimension $n \times m$.
$\mathbf{0}_n$	A column vector of zeros of dimension n.
$\mathbf{1}_{n,m}$	A matrix of ones of dimension $n \times m$.
$\mathbf{1}_n$	A column vector of ones of dimension n.
$\mathbf{K}$	The camera projection matrix associated with a calibrated camera.
$\mathbf{K}_L$	The light projection matrix, containing the intrinsic parameters associated with a calibrated light source.
	continued on next page

	continued from previous page
$\mathbf{A} \cdot \mathbf{B}$	The dot denotes a regular matrix product. The inner product of vectors $\mathbf{a}, \mathbf{b}$ would be denoted as $\mathbf{a}^\mathrm{T} \cdot \mathbf{b}$.
$\mathbf{A} \otimes \mathbf{B}$	The symbol $\otimes$ denotes Kronecker matrix product.
$\mathbf{A} \circ \mathbf{B}$	The symbol $\circ$, when used with matrices, denotes the Hadamard matrix product, which is the component-wise product of matrices.
$\widehat{\mathbf{A}}$	The hat symbol is used to denote the Hadamard inverse of a matrix or vector, which is its component-wise inverse.
$\mathbf{A}^{\circ n}$	The superscript $\circ n$ denotes the Hadamard exponentiation of a matrix or vector, which calculated by raising all elements to the power of n. This means that $\mathbf{A}^{\circ(-1)} = \widehat{\mathbf{A}}$.
$\mathrm{vec}(\mathbf{A})$	The vectorization of the matrix $\mathbf{A}$, which is a column vector obtained by stacking all columns of $\mathbf{A}$ on top of each other, from left to right.
$\mathrm{diag}(\mathbf{v})$	A diagonal matrix with the vector $\mathbf{v}$ on its diagonal.
$\mathcal{S}(\mathbf{S})$	The $0-1$ matrix describing the sparsity structure of a sparse matrix $\mathbf{S}$.
$\mathrm{val}(\mathbf{S})$	Denotes the vector of values of the sparse matrix $\mathbf{S}$, obtained by stacking all non-zero values into one vector. The values are obtained in a column-major fashion, such that the values of columns are collected from left to right. Within a column, they are taken from top to bottom.
	continued on next page

A. MATHEMATICAL NOTATION

continued from previous page	
$\mathfrak{J}$	The image function. It can represent single-channel or multi-channel images. If n is the number of channels, then the function is of type $\mathbb{R}^2 \to \mathbb{R}^n$. When dealing with image sequences, a subscript is used to denote the number of that image within the sequence, such that $\mathfrak{J}_i$ denotes the i-th image.
$_L\mathfrak{J}$	The light intensity function. Represents the spatial light intensity from the light projection center in some direction.

Table A.1: Mathematical notation

B. Diagram Conventions

When displaying images of depth maps, error maps and similar entities, we are using the commonly adopted method of rainbow color maps. In such a map, the color blue represents the lowest value, while red color corresponds to the highest value. Intuitively, this can be understood as a "temperature" chart, with temperatures going from low to high. We usually use normalized plots, unless otherwise stated. Figure B.1 illustrates the usage of the colour map.

B. DIAGRAM CONVENTIONS

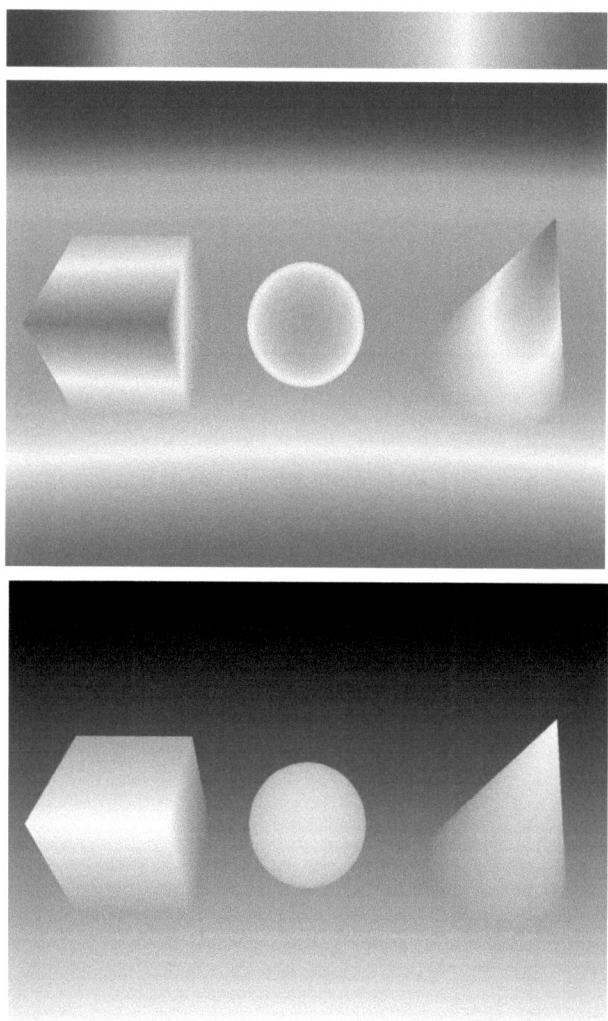

Figure B.1: Top: Colour-coding used for displaying magnitudes. The values are increasing from 0 on the left to 1 on the right. Middle: Colour-coded example depth map, bottom right: Corresponding gray-scale depth map.

Complete List of Author's Publications

[1] ELMAR MAIR, MICHAEL FLEPS, OLIVER RUEPP, MICHAEL SUPPA, AND DARIUS BURSCHKA. **Optimization Based IMU Camera Calibration**. In *Proceedings of the IEEE/RSJ International Conference on Intelligent Robots and Systems (IROS'11)*, September 2011.

[2] MARKUS HOLZER, ANDREAS KLEIN, MARTIN KUTRIB, AND OLIVER RUEPP. **Computational Complexity of NURIKABE**. *Fundamenta Informaticae*, **110**(1):159–174, Jan 2011.

[3] OLIVER RUEPP AND DARIUS BURSCHKA. **Fast Recovery of Weakly Textured Surfaces from Monocular Image Sequences**. In RON KIMMEL, REINHARD KLETTE, AND AKIHIRO SUGIMOTO, editors, *Computer Vision - ACCV 2010 - 10th Asian Conference on Computer Vision, Queenstown, New Zealand, November 8-12, 2010, Revised Selected Papers, Part IV*, **6495** of *Lecture Notes in Computer Science*, pages 474–485. Springer, 2010.

[4] OLIVER RUEPP, DARIUS BURSCHKA, AND ROBERT BAUERNSCHMITT. **Towards On-Line Intensity-Based Surface Recovery from Monocular Images**. In *Proceedings of the British Machine Vision Conference*, pages 77.1–77.11. BMVA Press, 2010. doi:10.5244/C.24.77.

COMPLETE LIST OF AUTHOR'S PUBLICATIONS

[5] OLIVER RUEPP AND MARKUS HOLZER. **The computational complexity of the KAKURO puzzle, revisited.** In *Proceedings of the 5th international conference on Fun with algorithms*, FUN'10, pages 319–330, Berlin, Heidelberg, 2010. Springer-Verlag.

[6] OLIVER RUEPP AND DARIUS BURSCHKA. **A Geometrically Inspired Approach to Active View Planning.** In *Proceedings of the Workshop on Vision in Action: Efficient strategies for cognitive agents in complex environments*. HAL - CCSD, 2008.

[7] DOMINIK STEINHAUSER, OLIVER RUEPP, AND DARIUS BURSCHKA. **Motion segmentation and scene classification from 3D LIDAR data.** *Intelligent Vehicles Symposium, 2008 IEEE*, pages 398–403, June 2008.

[8] HERMANN GRUBER, MARKUS HOLZER, AND OLIVER RUEPP. **Sorting the Slow Way: An Analysis of Perversely Awful Randomized Sorting Algorithms.** In PIERLUIGI CRESCENZI, GIUSEPPE PRENCIPE, AND GEPPINO PUCCI, editors, *FUN*, **4475** of *Lecture Notes in Computer Science*, pages 183–197. Springer, 2007.

[9] MARKUS HOLZER AND OLIVER RUEPP. **The Troubles of Interior Design-A Complexity Analysis of the Game Heyawake.** In PIERLUIGI CRESCENZI, GIUSEPPE PRENCIPE, AND GEPPINO PUCCI, editors, *FUN*, **4475** of *Lecture Notes in Computer Science*, pages 198–212. Springer, 2007.

References

[10] DAVID G. LOWE. **Object Recognition from Local Scale-Invariant Features**. In *ICCV*, pages 1150–1157, 1999. 1, 8, 222, 6, 143

[11] HERBERT BAY, ANDREAS ESS, TINNE TUYTELAARS, AND LUC VAN GOOL. **Speeded-Up Robust Features (SURF)**. *Comput. Vis. Image Underst.*, **110**:346–359, June 2008. 1, 8, 222, 6, 143

[12] STEFAN LEUTENEGGER, MARGARITA CHLI, AND ROLAND SIEGWART. **BRISK: Binary Robust invariant scalable keypoints**. In DIMITRIS N. METAXAS, LONG QUAN, ALBERTO SANFELIU, AND LUC J. VAN GOOL, editors, *ICCV*, pages 2548–2555. IEEE, 2011. 1

[13] ANDREW J. DAVISON, IAN D. REID, NICHOLAS D. MOLTON, AND OLIVIER STASSE. **MonoSLAM: Real-Time Single Camera SLAM**. *IEEE Transactions on Pattern Analysis and Machine Intelligence*, **26**(6):1052–1067, 2007. 1

[14] D. BURSCHKA AND G.D. HAGER. **V-GPS(SLAM): vision-based inertial system for mobile robots**. In *Robotics and Automation, 2004. Proceedings. ICRA '04. 2004 IEEE International Conference on*, **1**, pages 409 – 415 Vol.1, april-1 may 2004. 1

REFERENCES

[15] MOTILAL AGRAWAL AND KURT KONOLIGE. **FrameSLAM: From Bundle Adjustment to Real-Time Visual Mapping**. *IEEE Transactions on Robotics*, **24**(5), October 2008. 1, 7, 5

[16] GEORG KLEIN AND DAVID MURRAY. **Parallel Tracking and Mapping for Small AR Workspaces**. In *Proc. Sixth IEEE and ACM International Symposium on Mixed and Augmented Reality (ISMAR'07)*, Nara, Japan, November 2007. 1, 7, 16, 29, 5, 11, 19

[17] H. STRASDAT, J.M.M. MONTIEL, AND A.J. DAVISON. **Real-time monocular SLAM: Why filter?** In *Robotics and Automation (ICRA), 2010 IEEE International Conference on*, pages 2657 –2664, may 2010. 2, 1

[18] MICHAL IRANI AND P. ANANDAN. **About Direct Methods**. In Triggs et al. [91], pages 267–277. 3, 2

[19] S. BENHIMANE AND E. MALIS. **Real-time image-based tracking of planes using Efficient Second-order Minimization**. In *IEEE/RSJ International Conference on Intelligent Robots and Systems*, pages 943–948, 2004. 4, 2

[20] E. MALIS. **An efficient unified approach to direct visual tracking of rigid and deformable surfaces**. In *Intelligent Robots and Systems, 2007. IROS 2007. IEEE/RSJ International Conference on*, pages 2729 –2734, 29 2007-nov. 2 2007. 4, 2

[21] GERALDO SILVEIRA AND EZIO MALIS. **Unified Direct Visual Tracking of Rigid and Deformable Surfaces Under Generic Illumination Changes in Grayscale and Color Images**. *Int.*

REFERENCES

J. Comput. Vision, **89**:84–105, August 2010. 4, 7, 20, 101, 2, 5, 14, 69

[22] RUO ZHANG, PING-SING TSAI, JAMES EDWIN CRYER, AND MUBARAK SHAH. **Shape from Shading: A Survey**. *IEEE Trans. Pattern Anal. Mach. Intell.*, **21**:690–706, August 1999. 4, 2

[23] E. PRADOS AND O. FAUGERAS. **Shape from shading: a well-posed problem?** In *Computer Vision and Pattern Recognition, 2005. CVPR 2005. IEEE Computer Society Conference on*, **2**, pages 870 – 877 vol. 2, june 2005. 4, 30, 31, 2, 20

[24] CHENYU WU, SRINIVASA G NARASIMHAN, AND BRANISLAV JARAMAZ. **A Multi-Image Shape-from-Shading Framework for Near-Lighting Perspective Endoscopes**. *International Journal of Computer Vision*, February 2009. 4, 240, 243, 2, 149, 152

[25] GUO HUI WANG, JIU QIANG HAN, AND XIN MAN ZHANG. **Three-dimensional reconstruction of endoscope images by a fast shape from shading method**. *Measurement Science and Technology*, **20**(12):125801, 2009. 4, 2

[26] A W GRUEN. **Adaptive Least Squares Correlation: A Powerful Image Matching Technique**. *South African Journal of Photogrammetry, Remote Sensing and Cartography*, **14**:175–187, 1985. 7, 5

[27] F. ACKERMANN. **DIGITAL IMAGE CORRELATION: PERFORMANCE AND POTENTIAL APPLICATION IN PHOTOGRAMMETRY**. *The Photogrammetric Record*, **11**(64):429–439, 1984. 7, 5

REFERENCES

[28] M. OKUTOMI AND T. KANADE. **A multiple-baseline stereo**. In *Computer Vision and Pattern Recognition, 1991. Proceedings CVPR '91., IEEE Computer Society Conference on*, pages 63 –69, jun 1991. 7, 5

[29] OLIVER RUEPP, DARIUS BURSCHKA, AND ROBERT BAUERNSCHMITT. **Towards On-Line Intensity-Based Surface Recovery from Monocular Images**. In Labrosse et al. [92], pages 1–11. 7, 101, 5, 69

[30] OLIVER RUEPP AND DARIUS BURSCHKA. **Fast Recovery of Weakly Textured Surfaces from Monocular Image Sequences**. In RON KIMMEL, REINHARD KLETTE, AND AKIHIRO SUGIMOTO, editors, *ACCV (4)*, **6495** of *Lecture Notes in Computer Science*, pages 474–485. Springer, 2010. 7, 101, 5, 69

[31] BERTHOLD K.P. HORN AND BRIAN G. SCHUNCK. **Determining Optical Flow**. Technical report, Cambridge, MA, USA, 1980. 7, 5

[32] BRUCE D. LUCAS AND TAKEO KANADE. **An Iterative Image Registration Technique with an Application to Stereo Vision (IJCAI)**. In *Proceedings of the 7th International Joint Conference on Artificial Intelligence (IJCAI '81)*, pages 674–679, April 1981. 7, 5

[33] ZHENGYOU ZHANG AND YING SHAN. **Incremental Motion Estimation Through Local Bundle Adjustment**. Technical report, 2001. 7, 5

[34] R. I. HARTLEY AND A. ZISSERMAN. *Multiple View Geometry in Computer Vision*. Cambridge University Press, ISBN: 0521540518, second edition, 2004. 8, 9, 15, 74, 76, 77, 78, 95, 5, 6, 10, 49, 51, 52, 65

REFERENCES

[35] BILL TRIGGS, PHILIP F. MCLAUCHLAN, RICHARD I. HARTLEY, AND ANDREW W. FITZGIBBON. **Bundle Adjustment - A Modern Synthesis**. In Triggs et al. [91], pages 298–372. 8, 24, 5, 6, 16

[36] ZHENGYOU ZHANG. **Flexible Camera Calibration by Viewing a Plane from Unknown Orientations**. *Computer Vision, IEEE International Conference on*, 1:666, 1999. 9, 7

[37] H. C. LONGUET-HIGGINS. **A Computer Algorithm for Reconstructing a Scene from Two Projections**. In M. A. FISCHLER AND O. FIRSCHEIN, editors, *Readings in Computer Vision: Issues, Problems, Principles, and Paradigms*, pages 61–62. Kaufmann, Los Altos, CA., 1987. 15, 10

[38] FREDRIK KAHL. **Multiple View Geometry and the L_∞-norm**. In *ICCV*, pages 1002–1009. IEEE Computer Society, 2005. 15, 10

[39] K. LEVENBERG. **A method for the solution of certain nonlinear problems in least squares**. *Quarterly Journal of Applied Mathmatics*, II(2):164–168, 1944. 15, 40, 10, 27

[40] J. CIVERA, A.J. DAVISON, AND J. MONTIEL. **Inverse Depth Parametrization for Monocular SLAM**. *Robotics, IEEE Transactions on*, 24(5):932 –945, oct. 2008. 17, 11

[41] RICHARD A. NEWCOMBE AND ANDREW J. DAVISON. **Live dense reconstruction with a single moving camera**. In *Computer Vision and Pattern Recognition (CVPR), 2010 IEEE Conference on*, pages 1498–1505, 13-18 2010. 17, 146, 252, 11, 98, 158

REFERENCES

[42] DEQING SUN, STEFAN ROTH, AND MICHAEL J. BLACK. **Secrets of optical flow estimation and their principles**. In *CVPR*, pages 2432–2439. IEEE, 2010. 24, 136, 138, 147, 16, 91, 92, 98

[43] J. NOCEDAL AND S.J. WRIGHT. *Numerical optimization*. Springer series in operations research. Springer, 1999. 24, 39, 16, 27

[44] RUPERT BROOKS, TAL ARBEL, AND DOINA PRECUP. **Anytime similarity measures for faster alignment**. *Computer Vision and Image Understanding*, **110**(3):378–389, 2008. 28, 16

[45] N. SUNDERHAUF, K. KONOLIGE, S. LACROIX, AND P. PROTZEL. *Visual Odometry using Sparse Bundle Adjustment on an Autonomous Outdoor Vehicle*. Tagungsband Autonome Mobile Systeme. Springer Verlag, 2005. 29, 19

[46] GUO HUI WANG, JIU QIANG HAN, AND XIN MAN ZHANG. **Three-dimensional reconstruction of endoscope images by a fast shape from shading method**. *Measurement Science and Technology*, **20**(12):125801, 2009. 30, 20

[47] M.I. A. LOURAKIS AND A.A. ARGYROS. **SBA: A Software Package for Generic Sparse Bundle Adjustment**. *ACM Trans. Math. Software*, **36**(1):1–30, 2009. 40, 102, 252, 258, 27, 69

[48] DONALD W. MARQUARDT. **An Algorithm for Least-Squares Estimation of Nonlinear Parameters**. *SIAM Journal on Applied Mathematics*, **11**(2):431–441, 1963. 40, 27

REFERENCES

[49] M.I.A. LOURAKIS. **levmar: Levenberg-Marquardt nonlinear least squares algorithms in C/C++**. http://www.ics.forth.gr/~lourakis/levmar/, Jul. 2004. 40, 79, 27, 53

[50] EZIO MALIS. **Improving Vision-based Control using Efficient Second-order Minimization Techniques**. In *ICRA*, pages 1843–1848. IEEE, 2004. 45, 48, 257, 31, 33, 160

[51] BRIAN GUENTER. **Efficient symbolic differentiation for graphics applications**. In *ACM SIGGRAPH 2007 papers*, SIGGRAPH '07, New York, NY, USA, 2007. ACM. 50, 34

[52] ANDREAS GRIEWANK AND ANDREA WALTHER. *Evaluating Derivatives: Principles and Techniques of Algorithmic Differentiation*. Number 105 in Other Titles in Applied Mathematics. SIAM, Philadelphia, PA, 2nd edition, 2008. 51, 35

[53] UWE NAUMANN. **Optimal Jacobian accumulation is NP-complete**. *Math. Program.*, **112**(2):427–441, 2007. 53, 36

[54] ANDREAS ALEXANDER ALBRECHT, PETER GOTTSCHLING, AND UWE NAUMANN. **Markowitz-Type Heuristics for Computing Jacobian Matrices Efficiently**. In PETER M. A. SLOOT, DAVID ABRAMSON, ALEXANDER V. BOGDANOV, JACK DONGARRA, ALBERT Y. ZOMAYA, AND YURI E. GORBACHEV, editors, *Computational Science - ICCS 2003, International Conference, Melbourne, Australia and St. Petersburg, Russia, June 2-4, 2003. Proceedings, Part II*, **2658** of *Lecture Notes in Computer Science*, pages 575–584. Springer, 2003. 53, 36

[55] ERICH GAMMA, RICHARD HELM, RALPH JOHNSON, AND JOHN VLISSIDES. *Design patterns: elements of reusable object-oriented software*. Addison-Wesley Longman Publishing Co., Inc., Boston, MA, USA, 1995. 62, 43

REFERENCES

[56] THOMAS H. CORMEN, CHARLES E. LEISERSON, RONALD L. RIVEST, AND CLIFFORD STEIN. *Introduction to Algorithms, Second Edition.* The MIT Press and McGraw-Hill Book Company, 2001. 66, 67, 44, 45

[57] ANDREAS GRIEWANK AND UWE NAUMANN. **Accumulating Jacobians as chained sparse matrix products**. *Math. Program.*, **95**(3):555–571, 2003. 66, 45

[58] ANDREW BLAKE AND ANDREW ZISSERMAN. *Visual Reconstruction.* MIT Press, 1987. 76, 77, 51

[59] PAUL A. VIOLA AND WILLIAM M. WELLS III. **Alignment by Maximization of Mutual Information**. In *ICCV*, pages 16–23, 1995. 84, 85, 86, 240, 56, 57, 58, 149

[60] STANFORD UNIVERSITY. APPLIED MATHEMATICS, STATISTICS LABORATORY, E. PARZEN, AND UNITED STATES. OFFICE OF NAVAL RESEARCH. *On estimation of a probability density function and mode.* Defense Technical Information Center, 1961. 85, 57

[61] RUPERT BROOKS AND TAL ARBEL. **Generalizing Inverse Compositional and ESM Image Alignment**. *Int. J. Comput. Vision*, **87**:191–212, May 2010. 87, 138, 257, 58, 92, 160

[62] S BENHIMANE AND E MALIS. **Real-time image-based tracking of planes using efficient second-order minimization**. *2004 IEEERSJ International Conference on Intelligent Robots and Systems IROS IEEE Cat No04CH37566*, **1**(x):943–948, 2004. 101, 69

REFERENCES

[63] HARTMUT PRAUTZSCH, WOLFGANG BOEHM, AND MARCO PALUSZNY. *Bezier and B-Spline Techniques*. Springer-Verlag New York, Inc., Secaucus, NJ, USA, 2002. 103, 70

[64] ROBERT A. BEEZER. *A First Course in Linear Algebra*. Robert A. Beezer, 2009. http://linear.ups.edu. 118, 127, 80, 86

[65] JAN R. MAGNUS AND H. NEUDECKER. **The Commutation Matrix: Some Properties and Applications**. *The Annals of Statistics*, **7**(2):pp. 381–394, 1979. 125, 84

[66] CRISTIAN CONSTANTIN LALESCU. **Two hierarchies of spline interpolations. Practical algorithms for multivariate higher order splines**. *CoRR*, **abs/0905.3564**, 2009. 137, 91

[67] THOMAS POCK, DANIEL CREMERS, HORST BISCHOF, AND ANTONIN CHAMBOLLE. **Global Solutions of Variational Models with Convex Regularization**. *SIAM J. Imaging Sciences*, 3(4):1122–1145, 2010. 146, 98

[68] JAN STÜHMER, STEFAN GUMHOLD, AND DANIEL CREMERS. **Real-time dense geometry from a handheld camera**. In *Proceedings of the 32nd DAGM conference on Pattern recognition*, pages 11–20, Berlin, Heidelberg, 2010. Springer-Verlag. 146, 252, 98, 158

[69] THOMAS POCK, MARKUS UNGER, DANIEL CREMERS, AND HORST BISCHOF. **Fast and Exact Solution of Total Variation Models on the GPU**. In *CVPR Workshop on Visual Computer Vision on GPU's*, Anchorage, Alaska, USA, June 2008. 146, 98

[70] THOMAS POCK, DANIEL CREMERS, HORST BISCHOF, AND ANTONIN CHAMBOLLE. **Global Solutions of Variational Mod-**

REFERENCES

els with Convex Regularization. *SIAM J. Imaging Sciences*, 3(4):1122–1145, 2010. 149, 100

[71] W.H. PRESS. *Numerical recipes: the art of scientific computing*. Cambridge University Press, 2007. 149, 100

[72] GENE H. GOLUB AND CHARLES F. VAN LOAN. *Matrix computations (3. ed.)*. Johns Hopkins University Press, 1996. 154, 104

[73] JIARUI LIAO AND LILONG CAI. **A calibration method for uncoupling projector and camera of a structured light system**. In *Advanced Intelligent Mechatronics, 2008. AIM 2008. IEEE/ASME International Conference on*, pages 770 –774, july 2008. 159, 107

[74] SEON JOO KIM AND M. POLLEFEYS. **Robust Radiometric Calibration and Vignetting Correction**. *Pattern Analysis and Machine Intelligence, IEEE Transactions on*, 30(4):562 –576, april 2008. 162, 109

[75] DAN B GOLDMAN AND JIUN-HUNG CHEN. **Vignette and Exposure Calibration and Compensation**. In *The 10th IEEE International Conference on Computer Vision*, pages 899–906, Oct. 2005. 162, 109

[76] M.D. GROSSBERG AND S.K. NAYAR. **Modeling the Space of Camera Response Functions**. *IEEE Transactions on Pattern Analysis and Machine Intelligence*, 26(10):1272–1282, Oct 2004. 162, 109

[77] T. MITSUNAGA AND S.K. NAYAR. **Radiometric Self Calibration**. In *IEEE Conference on Computer Vision and Pattern Recognition (CVPR)*, 1, pages 374–380, Jun 1999. 162, 109

REFERENCES

[78] CHRISTOPHER C. SKIŚCIM AND BRUCE L. GOLDEN. **Optimization by simulated annealing: A preliminary computational study for the TSP**. In *Proceedings of the 15th conference on Winter Simulation - Volume 2*, WSC '83, pages 523–535, Piscataway, NJ, USA, 1983. IEEE Press. 167, 113

[79] CHAVDAR PAPAZOV AND DARIUS BURSCHKA. **Stochastic global optimization for robust point set registration**. *Comput. Vis. Image Underst.*, **115**:1598–1609, December 2011. 167, 180, 113, 122

[80] S J DEVLIN, R GNANADESIKAN, AND J R KETTENRING. **Robust estimation and outlier detection with correlation coefficients**. *Biometrika*, **62**(3):531–545, 1975. 174, 117

[81] DU Q. HUYNH. **Metrics for 3D Rotations: Comparison and Analysis**. *Journal of Mathematical Imaging and Vision*, **35**(2):155–164, 2009. 181, 123

[82] FREDRIK KAHL AND RICHARD I. HARTLEY. **Critical Curves and Surfaces for Euclidean Reconstruction**. In ANDERS HEYDEN, GUNNAR SPARR, MADS NIELSEN, AND PETER JOHANSEN, editors, *ECCV (2)*, **2351** of *Lecture Notes in Computer Science*, pages 447–462. Springer, 2002. 202, 133

[83] JOHN OLIENSIS. **A New Structure-from-Motion Ambiguity**. *IEEE Trans. Pattern Anal. Mach. Intell.*, **22**(7):685–700, 2000. 202, 133

[84] SEBASTIAN LIEBERKNECHT, SELIM BENHIMANE, PETER MEIER, AND NASSIR NAVAB. **Benchmarking Template-based Tracking Algorithms**. *to appear in IJVR*, 2011. 221, 141

REFERENCES

[85] Mustafa Özuysal, Pascal Fua, and Vincent Lepetit. **Fast Keypoint Recognition in Ten Lines of Code**. In *CVPR*. IEEE Computer Society, 2007. 222, 143

[86] S. Benhimane and E. Malis. **Homography-based 2D Visual Tracking and Servoing**. *Int. J. Rob. Res.*, **26**:661–676, July 2007. 222, 143

[87] Kurt Konolige. **Sparse Sparse Bundle Adjustment**. In Labrosse et al. [92], pages 1–11. 252, 258

[88] Manuel Werlberger, Werner Trobin, Thomas Pock, Andreas Wedel, Daniel Cremers, and Horst Bischof. **Anisotropic Huber-L1 Optical Flow**. In *Proceedings of the British Machine Vision Conference (BMVC)*, London, UK, September 2009. to appear. 257, 160

[89] Bui Tuong Phong. **Illumination for computer generated pictures**. *Commun. ACM*, **18**:311–317, June 1975. 258

[90] M. Oren and S.K. Nayar. **Generalization of Lambert's Reflectance Model**. In *ACM 21st Annual Conference on Computer Graphics and Interactive Techniques (SIGGRAPH)*, pages 239–246, Jul 1994. 258

[91] Bill Triggs, Andrew Zisserman, and Richard Szeliski, editors. *Vision Algorithms: Theory and Practice, International Workshop on Vision Algorithms, held during ICCV '99, Corfu, Greece, September 21-22, 1999, Proceedings*, **1883** of *Lecture Notes in Computer Science*. Springer, 2000. 268, 271, 167, 169

[92] Frédéric Labrosse, Reyer Zwiggelaar, Yonghuai Liu, and Bernie Tiddeman, editors. *British Machine Vision Con-*

REFERENCES

ference, BMVC 2010, Aberystwyth, UK, August 31 - September 3, 2010. Proceedings. British Machine Vision Association, 2010. 270, 278

i want morebooks!

Buy your books fast and straightforward online - at one of world's fastest growing online book stores! Environmentally sound due to Print-on-Demand technologies.

Buy your books online at
www.get-morebooks.com

Kaufen Sie Ihre Bücher schnell und unkompliziert online – auf einer der am schnellsten wachsenden Buchhandelsplattformen weltweit! Dank Print-On-Demand umwelt- und ressourcenschonend produziert.

Bücher schneller online kaufen
www.morebooks.de

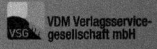 VDM Verlagsservicegesellschaft mbH
Heinrich-Böcking-Str. 6-8   Telefon: +49 681 3720 174   info@vdm-vsg.de
D - 66121 Saarbrücken   Telefax: +49 681 3720 1749   www.vdm-vsg.de

Printed by Books on Demand GmbH, Norderstedt / Germany